THE   ETHICS   OF   POSTMODERNITY

Northwestern University
Studies in Phenomenology
and
Existential Philosophy

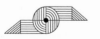

THE ETHICS OF POSTMODERNITY

Current Trends in Continental Thought

Edited by
Gary B. Madison and
Marty Fairbairn

Northwestern University Press
Evanston, Illinois

Northwestern University Press
625 Colfax Street
Evanston, Illinois 60208-4210

Printed in the United States of America

ISBN 0–8101-1375-9 (cloth)
ISBN 0–8101-1376-7 (paper)

Library of Congress Cataloging-in-Publication Data

The ethics of postmodernity : current trends in continental thought /
   edited by Gary B. Madison and Marty Fairbairn.
       p.   cm. — (Northwestern University studies in phenomenology &
   existential philosophy)
     Includes bibliographical references.
     ISBN 0-8101-1375-9 (alk. paper).—ISBN 0-8101-1376-7 (pbk. :
   alk. paper)
     1. Ethics, Modern—20th century. 2. Postmodernism.   I. Madison,
   Gary Brent.   II. Fairbairn, Marty.   III. Series.
   BJ319.E7854   1999
   170'.9'045—dc21   99-21665
                                                            CIP

Contents

Introduction

Gary B. Madison and Marty Fairbairn

A s anyone who has been following that ongoing conversation commonly referred to as "continental thought" will by now have distinctly noted, the "question of ethics" (to borrow an expression from Charles Scott) has in many ways become *the* question for scholars working in this particular field. The question of ethics has clearly displaced earlier, more traditional concerns over epistemological issues. The advent of postmodernity (vague and protean though that term may be) signals a shift of attention away from purely theoretical issues to the concerns of *practical philosophy* in the Aristotelean sense of the term, to, that is, an overriding concern for the realm of human *praxis*. For the first time since the advent of modern philosophy, ethics has become the dominant issue for philosophical reflection (for Descartes, as for moderns in general, the question of ethics was a subsidiary issue, almost an after-thought; witness Descartes' letter to Princess Elizabeth). In postmodernity, however, the question of the *good* has preempted that of the *true*. As William James, a veritable postmodern *avant la lettre*, ever insisted, "the true" is merely one species of "the good." What is good for living, James in effect maintained, takes precedence over, and in fact determines, what is true for thinking.

At the same time that ethics has become an issue of major concern, however, the very possibility of working out a philosophical ethics—one which, like all philosophical disciplines, could claim for itself universal scope and validity—has been widely called into question. As Paul Ricoeur recently observed, "ethics has become problematic as to its ultimate justification."[1]

Observers of the contemporary scene will no doubt also have noted that this cultural phenomenon is as much in evidence in analytic philosophy as it is in continental philosophy. Indeed, one of the more curious (and welcome) developments of recent years is the way in which the deep-seated animosity between these two camps has begun to erode, thanks to efforts by scholars and thinkers on both sides to erect bridges over what for so long had been though to be an unbridgeable chasm. Philosophers on both sides of the Great Divide are, as one contributor to this volume has remarked, beginning to work through the outworn and counterproductive dichotomy of "continental" and analytic philosophy.[2] If, as the interpretive economist Donald McCloskey has noted, "English-writing philosophers like Richard Rorty, Stephen Toulmin, and Alasdair MacIntyre [have attempted] to reintroduce the English readers of philosophy to the wider philosophical conversation, from which the English readers in their pride have absented themselves for the better part of a century,"[3] it is equally the case that "continentals" like Jacques Derrida, Jean-François Lyotard, Paul Ricoeur and others have attempted to engage "English-writing philosophers" in a common dialogue. That dialogue is now proceeding apace.

If there is a common thread running through this developing "intercontinental" and multi-textured dialogue, it is that of *the ethical* or, to be more precise, *the ethico-political*.[4] This should not be misconstrued to mean that what we are now witnessing is a revival of that traditional branch of philosophy known as "ethics." (In modern philosophy, ethics was always a somewhat flimsy branch of the philosophical tree, grossly inferior in status to metaphysics and epistemology but more respectable still than the lowest of branches, aesthetics.) Postmoderns, in whatever varied and variegated guise they might come,[5] are generally—indeed, unanimously, dare we say—in agreement that, consequent upon the death of capital-P Philosophy (to use Rorty's expression), i.e., metaphysics (onto-theo-logy), "ethics" is now also quite dead.[6] Paradoxical though it might seem, it is precisely because ethics (in the traditional philosophical or epistemological sense of the term) is dead that *the question of ethics* has become so all-important.

Indeed, it is important to note that the demise of "ethics" or moral epistemology, understood along foundationalist lines, does not entail the dissolution of what might more appropriately be referred to as *the moral*.[7] What the demise of traditional ethics does mean is that the *phenomenon* of the moral-ethical needs to be reconceptualized, and in a thoroughgoing, *post*metaphysical manner.

If there is one thing that serves to unite postmoderns, be they "continentals" or "analytics," it is their refusal to subscribe any longer to foundationalist and essentialist myths. Everyone agrees that the existence, indeed, the very survival of "civilization" is contingent upon people interacting in a genuinely ethical manner (within and between nations), but postmoderns do not believe that traditional philosophical ethics, of either a deontological or consequentialist sort, has anything of genuine, i.e., practical, relevance to contribute to the new postmodern, global civilization now coming into being (a state of affairs sometimes referred to as "postcolonialism"). This is because traditional philosophical ethics is, by its very nature, foundationalist and essentialist (or, as some would say, Eurocentric).[8]

Whatever form it came in—deontological, consequentialist, or what have you—traditioanl (Western) ethics always assumed that, given the right philosophical *method* or calculus (adhesion to the categorial imperative, the maximization of utility, etc.), *the* single correct answer to any ethical dilemma could in principle always be determined in a quasi-algorithmic fashion. For modern philosophers, ethics was indeed nothing more than applied general theory (applied metaphysics). But as postmoderns are now acutely aware, all theory is, to one degree or another, "culture-laden." Practice(s), postmoderns therefore maintain, must always take priority over the logocentric theories of world-legislating metaphysicians. This naturally spells the end of ethics, in most of the traditional philosophical senses of the term (with the partial exception of the Aristotelean). No theory, purely as such, can claim unconditional univeral validity (all theories are, in some sense, culture-relative). As Charles Scott has remarked, "The question of ethics does not lead to a new ethics," i.e., a new ethical system.[9]

Does this situation entail the intellectual bankruptcy of all claims to universality in ethical matters? It is important to remember that ever since its inception in ancient Greece, philosophy has claimed for itself a universal vocation. To destroy or "deconstruct" that claim would, accordingly, mean nothing less than the destruction of philosophy itself (as those postmoderns who could appropriately be labelled "antiphilosophers" realize full well). If we take the postmoderns/postfoundationalists/post-metaphysicians seriously, do we have to reject the philosophical enterprise itself? Is philosophy in this postmodern age at, or nearing, its end? Perhaps what is above all in question in the question of ethics is the question of philosophy itself—of the very *possibility* of philosophy.

While the positions taken up by many postmoderns do indeed, as modernist critics commonly allege, seem to entail both relativism and nihilism (the rejection of any sort of universal values whatsoever), other postmoderns (hermeneuticists in particular) have argued that this is not at all—or need not at all be—the inevitable outcome; they have argued that the rejection of absolutism need not entail relativism and that the age-old notion of universalism can be revived (reconfigured, as Paul Ricoeur might say) in a properly postmetaphysical form. This is chiefly where the debate now lies—between, on the one hand, the Habermasians and the poststructuralists and, on the other hand, the hermeneuticists, on one side, and *both* the Habermasians and the poststrucuralists on the other. If the preceeding sentence is complex, it is because the current situation is itself highly complex (befitting a postmodern age of pluritextuality). There is no single debate over the ethical question but rather a host of overlapping debates focusing on a host of different aspects of the problem, as the contributions to this volume make clear. What is ultimately at question in the question of ethics, nevertheless, is the whole question of postmodernism, its significance and its legitimacy. Can one even continue to speak—meaningfully—of a *postmodern philosophy*? Or is that not simply a *contradictio in adiectivo*?

The debate over the question of ethics, as it continues in the present volume, is broached first by Richard Kearney, who claims that in these postmodern times we are living in a "Civilization of Images" that is rendering the human subject less responsible for his or her imagination—consumers and copiers of images rather than authors of inventive images. Images have become simulacra, endlessly copying and imitating other images in what has been called a parody/pastiche/simulation. Kearney's task is to see whether Levinas's work is instructive vis-à-vis the ethical implications of this image dilemma in contemporary poetics. Levinas would have us assume an ethical responsibility for the other, a responsibility that breaks through the circular game of mirroring and stakes a claim for radical otherness. But, asks Kearney, how can such ethical responsibility resist the ideology of simulacrum? How can we retrieve an ethical dimension of *poiesis* from the faceless civilization of the images that dominate our experience? The key lies in the experience of the Face in Levinas. Face-to-face conversation becomes for Levinas the ethical model of relationship par excellence. Kearney wonders, however, whether Levinas is privileging conversation over imagination as the proper mode of ethical openness. He argues that Levinas speaks against only the abuse of imagination, one which incarcerates itself in a blind alley of self-reflecting mirrors. Taking cues from the work of Paul Ricoeur, Kearney wants to forge an alliance between an ethics of responsibility and a poetics of imagination. He wants to take some initial steps towards developing "a critical hermeneutics of the postmodern imagination." He maintains that Levinas failed to see that the free play of imagination is indispensable for both poetics *and* ethics. Ethics and poetics converge at the juncture of the I and the other, in the words that are received from, and given back to, the other.

For his part Robert Bernasconi takes some initial steps toward staging a detailed confrontation between Levinas and the tradition of ethical inquiry with the aim of clearing up some of the confusion between Levinas and this tradition. Bernasconi attempts to supplement Levinas's work by exploring certain aspects of the tradition—responsibility, guilt, conscience—that pass into Levinas's thought, while others are ignored. Bernasconi argues that Levinas's aim in drawing a distinction between guilt for acts committed and guilt that precedes being itself (the already fallen) is to "disrupt the dominance that linguistic usage and legal community have had on the language and boundaries of ethics." This is an ethics that puts ethics itself in question. It is Levinas's recasting of the ethical question in ontological terms that makes his thought so important.

Joseph Margolis's essay engages in the always instructive exercise of categorizing philosophers along a new set of axes. His claim is that a creeping philosophical optimism (moral, epistemological, scientific) now dominates Western thought as the beneficiary of classical pragmatism and that any such optimism is destined to fail. For Margolis, this is "a sign of the profound failure to come to terms with the self-imposed cognitive limitations of late pragmatism." Reason has been displaced by "reasonableness." Margolis claims that the moral theories of MacIntyre, Rawls, Putnam, and Habermas all founder along similar lines, that is, with regard to their allegiance to optimistic notions such as reliable progress as the telos of reasonableness and a general presumption of some decisive but arbitrary and unexamined invariance within the flux of nature. This way of understanding philosophical positions, he maintains, cuts across continental/analytic "boundaries." Margolis concludes that the idea of arriving at universally necessary or categorical constraints of reasonableness by one privileged means or another is without merit. The best philsophical path, for Margolis, "lies with the conceptualization of all the standard questions under epistemically reduced conditions." Linking various theses—Apel's, Habermas's, Putnam's—by their adherence to the general principle of reasonableness means that Margolis can subject them all to a common critique.

Habermas's discourse ethics is also subjected to interrogation by Tom Rockmore. Rockmore portrays Habermas as trying to reformulate an acceptable version of Kantian cognitivism by means of a nonfoundationalist theory of discourse ethics intended to "reach Hegelian goals with Kantian means." Notwithstanding repeated attempts by Habermas to explain his views, the impression remains that much work still remains to be done. Habermas has had considerable difficulty stating his theory. The result is a series of statements that frequently leave the reader unsure of what exactly he is ruling out, or what in. As Rockmore sees it, discourse ethics stands or falls on two doubtful assumptions: (1) normative claims to validity have cognitive meaning and can be treated *like* claims to truth, and (2) justification of norms requires that a real discussion be carried out and thus cannot assume a strictly monological form. Rockmore sees no particular reason why unrestrained discussion should result in truth. In Rockmore's view, Habermas fails to redeem Hegelian insights with Kantian means. The difficulties of discourse ethics seem to reflect back on the theory on which it depends, that is, Habermas's theory of communicative action.

Caroline Bayard focuses her attention on yet another major participant in the ongoing dispute over the question of ethics, Jean-François Lyotard. Bayard argues that, contradictions and transformations in his thought notwithstanding, Lyotard has over the past four decades developed a series of ethical questions that have demonstrated remarkably continuous links. They have emphasized the concept of responsibility, while denouncing the serious *aporia* inherent in both Western and Christian culture. There is, Bayard says, some irony in Habermas's accusation that Lyotard is jeopardizing the heritage of modernity, since few philosophers have been more concerned than Lyotard with modernity and with Western culture's indebtedness to it. Lyotard's call for an obligation for specific individual intervention is clearly in line with much of modern ethics (Lyotard's ethics have shifted from an explicitly universalistic position to what Bayard calls a postmodern one), but his postmodern position is lucid and clear, allowing us to determine what can be salvaged from modernity and whether the "Ruins of the Past" can be transformed into a living heritage.

Appealing to the work of Ivan Illich and Michel Foucault, Barry Allen questions whether knowledge can ever be evaluated without regard for its consequences. He argues that the "self-evident proposition" that there has been a historical rupture with our past, forever dividing us postmoderns from the modern period, is simply not true. The so-called "postmodern" period is merely more of the same. There have been only quantitative differences in the industrial economy of goods and services and in the techno-scientific economy of the production of knowledge. Alluding to Illich, Allen argues that inquiry or the production of knowledge can turn counterproductive. This "paradoxical counterproductivity of knowledge" produces a state of affairs in which "people who are supposed to know . . . are making choices that are more stupid than would otherwise have been imaginable." But this is neither a critique of knowledge nor a call for greater ignorance. As Allen points out, it is not knowledge that makes us stupid. He argues that we ought to be free to ignore such knowledge, to regard its pretensions with skepticism or irony, and to resist its debilitating claim to know our "true needs." He calls for a kind of "epistemic asceticism" which would doubt, not the truth of what is alleged to be knowledge, but its usefulness.

Addressing himself to postmodern thought as instanced in Jacques Derrida, M. C. Dillon argues that postmodernism's rejection of both natural (biological-empirical) and supernatural (onto-theological) grounds for ethics leaves it open to the charge of moral relativism, and perhaps nihilism as well. All that seems to be left after the smoke clears is a kind of overarching metavalue of tolerance without much in the way of support. The traditional structure of sexual morality, for instance, based on the telos of reproduction, the distinction between the natural and the perverse, and the institution of marriage, does not survive the critique of natural law morality. Some social norms, practices, and laws are demonstrably superior to others, Dillion believes, and this superiority can be measured in terms of responsiveness to our emergent understanding of the lived body and its relations to other bodies and the ecosphere at large.

Focusing on the work of Richard Rorty, Evan Simpson and Mark Williams seek to elaborate and reconstruct, in terms that stress the role of reasoning or inference, the notion of a moral language. While Rorty is correct on their view in maintaining that there is no single set of ethical principles that will yield correct, universally binding moral judgments, the aim, nevertheless, of most modernist ethical theories has been the construction of a "moral Esperanto." Rorty defends a contrary view when he claims that moral principles are abbreviated versions of a range of institutions, practices, and vocabularies of moral deliberation rather than justifications for them. For Rorty there is an irreducible plurality of moral languages or vocabularies. For Simpson and Williams, this practical conception of ethics is defensible against naive charges of relativism and conservatism; neither relativism nor conservatism, they argue, is altogether undesirable, nor even avoidable.

As, in part, a response to Rorty's "antitheoretical" and "ethocentric" position, Paul Fairfield outlines a conception of ethical theory that takes its bearings from the tradition of hermeneutical philosophy. The objective of what he terms a hermeneutical ethical theory is to provide critical reflection with a set of principles to serve as constraints upon local practices and traditions. He argues that ethical theorizing must arise from within the realm of practice, specifically from the universal practice of hermeneutic dialogue. The practice of dialogical understanding, he maintains, contains an implicitly normative dimension which it is the task of ethical theory to render thematic. When we think through the ethical implications of the communicative process, what are generated thereby are principles of universal right reminiscent of the liberal virtues. After a brief discussion of the antitheoretical position in ethics, Fairfield formulates a conception of theory that takes its bearings from Gadamer's analysis of hermeneutic experience while bearing an important methodological resemblance to Habermas's communicative ethics.

In his contribution to this volume, Thomas Busch explores the phenomenological roots of contemporary hermeneutical ethics. Emphasizing the importance of the lived body (as, in his own way, Dillon did), Busch maintains that there exists an incipient communicative ethics in Husserl, Sartre, and Merleau-Ponty. He also maintains that an instructive lesson is to be learned from these three phenomenologists concerning the direction such an ethic would have to take. Husserl viewed science as the telos of history which originated with the Greeks and whose theoretical attitude first "bracketed the natural attitude." This was the origin of the notion of one identical truth valid for all, a truth in itself. This telos is where philosophy finds its vocation, mission, and ethical responsibility. For Busch, Merleau-Ponty and Sartre, in contrast, see an ethics of mutual recognition and respect in the communicative situation. Sartre, however, sees only two alternatives: transparency, where the interlocutors reveal all that they stand for, or secrecy. Sartre sees no "thickness, ambiguity, plurivocity, excess, interpretivity of an inevitable sort in language itself." Busch concludes that "Merleau-Ponty offers an understanding of communication that is the most faithful to finitude, to the linguisticality, sociality, historicality of rationality and truth." And for Busch this makes Merleau-Ponty's philosophy a better indicator of where communicative ethics should go, that is, in a conversational and non-utopian direction.

A similar line of argument is taken up by Gary Madison, who attempts to show how Merleau-Ponty's "philosophy of the flesh" contains an incipient ethics that could rightly be called an ethics of communicative rationality and which is of a properly postmodern sort. What makes Merleau-Ponty's thought especially pertinent to current debates over the question of ethics is that, while being conscientiously antifoundationalist and antiessentialist, it does not for all that renounce philosophy's traditional claim to universality, as so many contemporary positions do. Instead of endorsing, *faute de mieux*, relativism and cultural incommensurability (the denial of transcultural rationality), Merleau-Ponty seeks, in a thoroughly postmetaphysical fashion, to reconfigure universality as *transversality*. Madison also argues that Merleau-Ponty's ethics of reciprocity and recognition offers a promising alternative to both Habermas's *Sprachethik* and Levinas's "ethics of the Other." Madison then proceeds to show how

Merleau-Ponty's ethics calls forth a particular politics and how this politics is a direct anticipation of the postmodern politics of democratic civility championed in our times by Vaclav Havel.

Combining an interest in hermeneutics with a concern for feminist issues, Morny Joy discusses Luce Irigaray's "ethics of sexual difference." She sees Irigaray's "amorous discourse" as an ideal of an ethically based exchange that has distinct resonances with a type of ethics that is based on *phrōnesis*, one that she regards as informing hermeneutics. Joy explores the convergences and disparities between Irigaray's ideas and the implied ethics of hermeneutics in an attempt not only to reveal the subtle dynamics of both but also to formulate new ethical insights. Following Ricoeur, Joy sees hermeneutics as encouraging us to respect "the dialogue that we are" by not imposing our understanding on the text but by receiving from the textual other an enlarged perspective of ourselves and of the world in which we live. The other in general cannot be seen simply as an extension of a narcissistic project; it must be viewed as the only way in which I can, in a reciprocal relationship, fulfill my ownmost possibilities. Faithful to Merleau-Ponty, Irigaray (according to Joy) sees the "flesh" as the key to understanding ethics, especially any form of ethics which does justice to love, as well as abstract concepts such as "the good." Joy's article proposes some features that might inform an ethics based on "amorous exchange."

In his contribution to this volume, Charles Scott addresses one of the longstanding issues in ethical theory: transcendence. He seeks to put thoroughly in question the sense of transcendence that is our philosophical heritage in order to maximize the struggle in it, to interrupt the powerful suggestion of unity that the sense of transcendence often carries with it. The connection, Scott argues, between transcendence and unity in our lineage is "troubled." This occurs when difference grows in value or when human individuality without transcending human nature goes against the sense of transcendence. Scott believes that "traditional metaphysics is defined in part by efforts to maintain, articulate, and upbuild the sense of transcendence." The question of ethics for Scott arises not out of questionable values but out of ethics as such. Universalization as movement incites somthing like tribal wars, struggles for cultural domination. This is also why Scott offers no alternative ethics. The way to maintain the question of ethics is to focus on dangers like universalization. Not waiting for the Light, but encouraging more transformation without transcendence is perhaps part of the solution (if solution there be) to the question of ethics.

In a postmodern, post-Cartesian age there are few, if any, things that can be said to be certain (certainty is a strictly Cartesian concept). The nonviability of the modernist, Cartesian quest for certainty notwithstanding, there is nonetheless, even in our uncertain postmodern times, one thing that can be said to be certain: A viable ethics can only be (to allude to the title of a book by Simone de Beauvoir) an *ethics of ambiguity*. Ambiguity—difference, otherness, plurality—is something that, ethically, we must, in our theoretical lives, learn how to live with. There is no other option. As Zygmunt Bauman has observed:

> What the postmodern mind is aware of is that there are problems in human and social life with no good solutions, twisted trajectories that cannot be straightened up, ambivalences that are more than linguistic blunders yelling to be corrected, doubts which cannot be legislated out of existence, moral agonies which no reason-dictated recipes can soothe, let alone cure. The postmodern mind does not expect any more to find the all-embracing, total and ultimate formula of life without ambiguity, risk, danger and error, and is deeply suspicious of any voice that promises otherwise. . . . The postmodern mind is reconciled to the idea that the messiness of the human predicament is here to stay. This is, in the broadest of outlines, what can be called postmodern wisdom.[10]

Exactly what the option in favor of ambiguity (the rejection of "totalism") entails is, however, a matter of ongoing debate or interpretation. As the "Levinasians" so strenuously insist, the "Other" must always be respected, but, as phenomenological hermeneuticists insist with equal vigor, so also must be the self (the "subject" or, as Ricoeur would say, the *soi-même, ipse*).[11] For it must not be forgotten that respect for the other is contingent upon respect for one's own self (as Rousseau long ago pointed out). No one who does not respect his or her own integrity—who is lacking in what Ricoeur calls "self-esteem"[12]—will ever respect the integrity and well-being of others.[13] This is why that particular version of postmodern ethics that goes under the heading of phenomenological-hermeneutical insists so strongly on the old Hegelian notion of *Anerkennung, mutual* recognition, recognition of one autonomous self by another autonomous self. "Selves" can become—and be—"autonomous" selves, genuine moral *agents*, only to the degree that their autonomy is "recognized" by their own "others." As one postmodern feminist writer remarks: "The self is a relational self: a self capable of autonomy has an autonomous self-concept, and this self-concept can come into being only as it has been fostered and encouraged by the object relations in which the self has been engaged."[14] Such, in sum—*l'apprentisage de la liberté d'une manière intersubjective*—is the only viable formula for a genuinely postmodern society, which is to say, for democracy, i.e., a regime or mode of human coexistence centered around the ethical imperatives of respect and recognition. What is inevitably in question in the postmodern question of ethics is the question of the ethical and political *subject*, of democratic citizenship.

The reader of this volume will, of course, find no definitive answers to what a viable ethics might be in a postmodern age. But he or she will, we are convinced, find in this book many questions worthy of thought in this regard. To come to know what is possible and what is not, what is desirable and what is not, is no mean accomplishment.

1

The Crisis of the Image: Levinas's Ethical Response

Richard Kearney

La littérature est l'aventure unique d'une transcendance
enjambant tous les horizons du monde (. . .) La littérature
rappelle l'essence humaine du nomadisme. Le nomadisme
n'est-il pas la source d'un sens, apparaissant dans une lumière
que ne renvoie aucun marbre, mais le visage de l'homme? . . .
[L]'authenticité de l'art doit annoncer un ordre de justice.

—Emmanuel Levinas, *Sur Maurice Blanchot*

Kierkegaard attributed the crisis of the "present age" to the fact that
human subjects were lacking any passionate commitment to thinking. Today, more than a century after Kierkegaard, one is tempted
to add that we are also lacking a passionate commitment to *imagining*. We
live in a civilization of images where the human subject is deemed less
and less responsible for the working of his/her own imagination. The citizens of contemporary society increasingly find themselves surrounded by
simulated images produced, or reproduced, by mass media technologies
operating outside their ken or control. Human subjects are considered
more as copiers and consumers of images than as authors.

In all this, the predominant role of the image becomes one of
parody. The image ceases to refer to some *original* event—in the world
or consciousness—and becomes instead a simulacrum: an image of an
image of an image. In our *société de spectacle*, as Debord put it, the imaginary
circulates in an endless play of imitation where each image becomes
a replay of another which precedes it. The idea of an "authentic" or
"unique" image becomes redundant.

I have analyzed this so-called postmodern dilemma of the image as parody/pastiche/simulation in some detail elsewhere.[1] My task here is to inquire whether the work of Emmanuel Levinas, one of the foremost ethical thinkers in Continental philosophy, has anything to teach us about the ethical implications of this dilemma in contemporary poetics.

In his 1972 essay "Idéologie et Idéalisme," Levinas offers this apocalyptic account of our society of simulation, where the Same reigns supreme: "The contemporary world—of science, of technology, of leisure —sees itself as trapped . . . not because everything is now permitted, and thanks to technology possible, but because everything is the same. The unknown immediately becomes familiar, the new normal. Nothing is new under the sun. The crisis written of in Ecclesiastes is not one of sin but of boredom. Everything becomes immersed and immured in the Same . . . [E]verywhere the machinations of melodrama, rhetoric and play accuse and denounce. Vanity of vanities: the echo of our own voices, taken as response to the few prayers which remain to us, everywhere fallen back onto our own feet as after the ecstasies of drugs. Except for the other whom, in all this boredom, we cannot let down."[2]

What Levinas suggests here is that the best response to the collective solipsism of Western culture is the assumption of ethical responsibility for the other. Such responsibility breaks through the circular game of mirrors, which perpetrates the reign of sameness through blank parody, and stakes a claim for radical otherness. But how can such ethical responsibility resist the ideology of the simulacrum which pervades our social imaginary? How, if at all, can we retrieve some ethical dimension of poiesis from the faceless civilization of images which dominates our experience?

I Representation and the Face

There are a number of texts where Levinas undertakes an analysis of the aesthetic imagination, notably "La Realité et son Ombre," "Sur Maurice Blanchot," "La Transcendance des Mots" (on the writing of Michel Leiris), "Agnon/Poésie et Resurrection," "Paul Célan/De l'être à l'autre" and "L'Autre dans Proust."[3]

In "La Realité et son Ombre," written largely in response to Heidegger's ontological poetics of dwelling, Levinas begins by warning us against becoming engulfed in a "spellbinding world of images and shadows"— a world where enigma and equivocation rule and realities are evaded (RO 117). He reminds us of the ethical motivation behind monotheism's proscription of idolatrous images of death (RO 115). But he does not go so far as to suggest that the artistic imagination should be censored for ethical or religious reasons. He is calling for a mode of critical interpretation capable of retrieving art as "a relation with the other" (RO 117). And he commends the practice of such a reflective hermeneutic in avant-garde writing as a critical defense against "artistic idolatry." "By means of such intellectualism," writes Levinas, "the artist refuses to be an artist only; not because he wishes to defend a thesis or a cause but because he needs to interpret his own myths" (RO 117).[4]

Levinas endorses such critical self-interpretation. In *Noms Propres*, he praises Agnon for his invocation of a certain "Hebraic saying" which "unravels the ultimate solidity beneath the plasticity of forms that western ontology teaches" (NP 18). And he contrasts the captivating power of "imaginary presence" to Agnon's poetry of "resurrection" which goes beyond the idolatrous tendency of images and opens us to the "irrepresentable as an endless fission of all that has dared to tie itself into a substrate" (NP 21). So also in his texts on Celan and Proust, Levinas endeavors to develop a similar ethics of writing and reading, based on the simple observation that their writing clears a path "toward the other" (NP 63). This entails, in Celan's case, a body of poetry which allows for an alterity exceeding the imagination of the author himself. Celan, he claims, is a poet who "concedes to the other . . . the time of the other" (NP 63).

But what, we may ask, is the motivation of Levinas's critique of poetic imagination? Some answer, I suggest, is to be found in his contrast between the "face" and the "image" in *Totalité et infini*.[5] Here again, we find Levinas deeply suspicious of the enchanting power of images once they cease to be answerable to the other. The face is the way in which the other surpasses every image I have of him/her. As such, it is irreducible to a series of qualities that might be formed into some kind of noematic representation, correlative to a noetic intention. Or as Levinas puts it: "The face of the other destroys and surpasses at every moment the plastic image that it leaves behind . . ." (*TI* 51). The face transcends every intentional consciousness I have of it. It *expresses* rather than *represents*. And so Levinas describes it as that which I receive from the other rather than that which I project upon him. Face to face conversation becomes for Levinas the ethical model of relation par excellence. For it is here that the other comes to me in all his/her irreducible exteriority, that is, in a manner that cannot be measured or represented in terms of my own interior fantasms.

Is Levinas not therefore privileging conversation over imagination as the proper mode of ethical openness to the other? Is he not, indeed, condemning imagination out of hand as a subjective intentionalilty which reduces alterity to its own remembered or anticipated fantasies? Or, worse, as that perverse agency of one-way voyeurism which he identifies with the figure of Gyges whose ring enabled him to see but never be seen by others?

While this is partly the case, it is not the whole story. Levinas's suspicion of images is not directed against the poetic power of imagination per se but against the use or abuse of such power to incarcerate the self in a blind alley of self-reflecting mirrors. In other words, the exercise of a poetic imagination open to conversation with the other (as Levinas claims is the case with Leiris, Celan, Jabes, and Blanchot, among others) is already one that allows the face to break through the plastic form of the image which represents or intends it. Such a poetic imagination responds to the surprises and demands of the other; it never presumes to fashion an image adequate to the other's irrecuperable transcendence. An ethical imagination would, consequently, be one which permits "the eye to see through the mask, an eye which does not shine but speaks" (*TI* 38). It would be one which safeguards the *saying* of the face against the attempts of subjective fantasy to reduce it to the subterfuges of the world.

That is why, in Levinas's words, the face is that transcendence of the other which "break; through its own plastic image" (*TI* 128). And that is why an ethical poetics is one which responds to the face with the question "Who?" (opening us to the alterity of the other person) rather than the question "What?" (reducing such alterity to an impersonal system of substances, structures or signs). Moreover, it is just such a poetics of responsibility to the other which refuses the consumerist status of imaging as imitation without depth or reference. It challenges the claim by certain postmodern commentators such as Baudrillard that we are condemned to a culture of "simulation" without origin or end sublimely "irreferent" to the other.[6] Faced with the postmodern crisis of endless self-mirroring, wherein the face of the other is dissolved into a play of sameness with itself, ethical language bears witness to the infinity of the other. And it is this infinity which testifies to "my responsibility, to an existence already obligated to the other, beyond the play of mirrors" (*S* 158). "Over and against all the fashionable talk about the 'end of man;' such a poetics of responsibility remains committed to human conversation with the other, to the possibility of imagination recovering its hermeneutic power to speak one-for-the-other and to listen to the powerless cry of the stranger, the widow and the orphan—a cry which, in demanding that I respond and speak to the unseen other (*le tiers*) is already a demand for justice" (*S* 215).

For Levinas, not surprisingly, the best poetry is unfinished poetry— like Celan's, whose exposure of nothingness within is in fact a recognition of otherness without. A poetry which is always an "interrupted breath" (*"une souffle coupée,"* as in *Atemwende*) because haunted by the recognition that its own saying can never be said, completed, closed off. Celan in this respect remains for Levinas the poet who lent his voice to those who have no voice, who—like Beckett—was devoted to the failure of complete communication, to the impossibility of ending, to the refusal to bring *saying* to a full stop in the *said*. A poetics responsible to the other is therefore one which resists the temptation to mask the face behind an anonymous game of vertiginous repetition (*S* 270). It insists instead that language always expresses more than any plastic representation can suggest. Ethics is there to remind poetics that the other can never be captured in an image or imitation. And no matter how pervasive the persuasion that there is nothing beyond the image but other images, I will argue that the ethical ear of hermeneutic imagination refuses to be taken in.

II Toward an Ethics of Imagining

If a certain reading of Levinas's opposition of face to image in *Totalité et infini* might lead us to believe that ethics is opposed to any poetic functioning of imagination, a reconsideration of this argument in the light of what Levinas has to say in qualified favor of poetics in his texts on Celan, Proust, Blanchot and others would seem to redress the balance. Here it becomes clear that it is not the speaking and expressive power of poetic imagination that Levinas objects to, only its power to fetishize or idolize images by setting them up as a self-referential play of imitation. Bearing this important distinction in mind, it soon becomes evident that Levinas does suggest the possibility of an ethical reading of the contemporary crisis of poetics. We return therefore to our original question of how to form an alliance between an *ethics of responsibility* and a *poetics of imagination*.

Although Levinas never addresses this task directly, there are suggestive hints in certain texts. Before examining these, however, I would like to take an example not mentioned by Levinas himself but relevant to this problematic. I refer to the attempt made by Claude Lanzmann in *Shoah* to portray the horrors of the Holocaust in cinematic images. Here we have an instance of a practical endeavor to combine an ethics of responsibility with a poetics of imagination. Lanzmann seeks to present the irrepresentable in and through the audiovisual medium of film. He is trying to recount what cannot be recounted, to demonstrate the impossibility of reproducing the event of the holocaust in some kind of linear narrative while reminding us of the unforgettable—though usually forgotten—character of this event. To this end, Lanzmann refuses to portray the holocaust in terms of spectacle or sensation. He shows no images of burnt bodies or SS Commandants. He resists the temptation to imitate the inimitable in terms of dramatic reproduction or documentary newsreel. We do not see the victims—for to do so would, Lanzmann believes, be to reduce them to "objects" of genocide. What we do see are faces of some survivors who bear witness to the impossibility of representing in images that which they witnessed at first hand. In short, it is the use of cinema to express the irreducible otherness and unimaginableness of the holocaust which actually succeeds in reminding us that we have forgotten how unimaginable it was, and that we must not be allowed to forget this forgetfulness.

This cinematic *via negativa* combines an ethical and poetical function. It uses images against themselves to suggest what they fail to capture (by virtue of their failure to do so). *Shoah* provokes what it cannot evoke. To Adorno's question whether poetry can be written after Auschwitz, it answers that it cannot, but that we cannot stop trying. It is in that sense that we may describe it as a poetics committed to an ethics of responsibility. As a former disciple of Levinas's, Jean-François Lyotard, observes:

> To represent "Auschwitz" in images, in words, is a way of forgetting it. I'm not just thinking here of B movies and soap opera series and pulp novels or testimonies. I'm also thinking of those representations which can and could best make us not forget by virtue of their exactness or severity. Even such efforts represent what should remain unrepresentable in order not to be forgotten precisely as forgotten. Claude Lanzmann's film *Shoah* is perhaps a singular exception. Not only because he resists the use of representation in images and music, but also because he hardly offers a single testimony where the unrepresentable character of the extermination is not indicated, even momentarily, by an alteration of voice, a tightening of throat, a tear, a sob, the disparition of a witness out of frame, an upset in the tone of the narrative, some uncontrolled gesture. So that we know that the witnesses are surely lying, or "playing a role," or hiding something, however impassive they may appear.[7]

We are concerned here with self-negating imagination: one might even be tempted to add: self-deconstructing imagination. For at issue is a functioning of images which debunks its own claim to representational presence. We are confronted with a series of cinematic signifiers which refuse to be tied to a "transcendental signified"—intentions without fulfillment, as phenomenology would put it, *visées à vide*. And such a poetic refusal of intuitive closure, completeness, or certainty would seem to approximate to an ethical form of deconstruction. This supposition, or suspicion, becomes even more compelling when one considers Levinas's account of deconstructive thinking in *Idéologie et Idéalisme* as "signifiers playing in a game of signs without signifieds . . . a conceptual disillusionment with the possibility of positing sense, with Husserl's 'doxic thesis,' a denunciation of the rigor of logical forms as repressive, an obsession with the inexpressible, the ineffable, the un-said sought after in the mis-said, in the lapsus . . ." Are these not the very conditions of Lanzmann's *Shoah*? Or at least of Lyotard's reading of it? One is tempted to respond in the affirmative. But then we read Levinas's own concluding remark on such deconstructive discourse and are given pause. "Such;" writes Levinas, "is the painful rupture of modern discourse, exemplified by its most sincere representatives, but already trading on the false coin of primary truths and fashionable cant" (*TI* 31).

Although Levinas does not mention any poststructuralist thinkers by name, it is difficult not to associate such a description with philosophers such as Lyotard, Foucault, and Barthes. But the important issue here is not who's who in Levinas's description but how Levinas is to retrieve an ethical poetics from a deconstructive discourse on imagination. How, in other words, is he going to make a distinction between the "painful rupture of modern discourse" as ethical irrepresentability, on the one hand, and as mere fashionable cant, on the other? I think we find some hint of a solution in a passage in *Totalité et Infini* where Levinas speaks of a primary mode of expression where the signifier as face transcends all signifying systems and allows the other to present itself to us. Such language of proximity, which precedes linguistic signs, is actually an ethical language of the face as "original expression," as the "first word—you shall not kill" (*TI* 157, 173). This is a language which can break through the "neutral mediations of the image" and impose itself on us in a manner irreducible to the form of its manifestation (*TI* 174).

But to admit as much is surely to admit that the face has nothing really to fear from mediating, or mediated, images as long as we who respond to such images respond to the underlying language of the face which speaks through them? The face is only threatened, is it not, by images which would have us believe that the language of poetics can definitively divorce itself from the language of ethics? If this be the case, then Levinas's ultimate position would appear to be that poetic imagining is fine as long as it remains answerable to an ethics of alterity. Indeed such answerability could itself be seen as compatible with, and complementary to, a certain gesture of deconstruction. I refer here to the *dismantling* of the claim of modern subjectivism (idealist or existentialist) that the transcendental ego or existential imagination remains the origin and end of all value. The deconstruction of such a transcendental self might be said to serve an ethics of alterity.

Levinas appears to suggest as much in certain passages which acknowledge an ethical motivation behind anti-humanist critique of the self. The following admission from "Un Dieu Homme?" is a case in point:

> The contemporary anti-humanism which denies the primacy of being enjoyed by the person taken as an end in itself has perhaps opened a space for the (ethical) notion of subjectivity as substitution . . . the infinite patience, passivity and passion of the self (*soi*) whereby being empties itself of its own being.[8]

Viewed in this way the deconstruction of the humanist subject as locus of self-identical sameness can be seen as releasing a different kind of self, an ethical subject open to alterity and transcendence, open to that eschatological order of creation, still to come, announced in Genesis, a creation in which, Levinas insists, "everyone has a part to play."[9] But such a deconstruction of the humanist self in the name of eschatological poetics is only ethical, for Levinas, to the extent that it acknowledges that "responsibility as response is the primary saying; and that transcendence is communication which implies, beyond the simple exchange of signs, a 'gift,' an 'open house' " (*II* 33).

III Primary Sayings

This would certainly seem to be Levinas's thinking in his readings of Proust, Celan, Blanchot, and Agnon. It is time to have a closer look at some of these. In one of his essays in *Sur Maurice Blanchot*, entitled "The Servant and the Master" (first published in 1966), Levinas praises Blanchot's writing for what he calls a "moral elevation, an aristocracy of thought." What he means by this is a cold neutrality in Blanchot's language which expresses the inexpressible—that experience of *desastre* which he identifies with our contemporary culture of absence and death. "Objectivizing consciousness is replaced by a sense of being that is detached from cosmological existence, from any fixed reference to a star (dis-aster), a being that strains towards obliteration in an inaccessible non-language" (LR 150). What fascinates Levinas here is a poetic *saying* which undermines the *said*. Blanchot uses images as ciphers of infinity, gestures of interminable waiting that can never be fulfilled. His words operate as intentional signifiers of a self which undoes its own self-centeredness, exceeds its own ontological ipseity, out of concern for something other, something beyond the said or the sayable, the imaged or the imaginable— what Levinas describes as a "first concern for justice" (LR 150). Indeed, one is tempted to add that what distinguishes deconstructive writing as "moral elevation" from that denounced as "fashionable cant" (*bavardage à la mode*) is just that: a concern for justice.

Levinas makes a similar case for an ethically responsible poetics in his readings of Proust and Leiris. He interprets the Proustian author's endless quest for the lost self as an encounter with the enigma of the other. The fact that Marcel never fulfills his desire for Albertine does not mean he does not love her. On the contrary, "to the extent that Marcel struggles with her presence as absence in the narrative, this struggle is love, in that it is directed not by being-towards-death but by the death of the Other, not by Dasein, but by the responsibility for the Other's death which creates his infinitely answerable 'I' " (LR 160). The Proustian drama of solitude and incommunicability is not about the retrieval of some ideal state of self-being. It is about an ethical relation with the other that remains forever other. The Proustian imagination is read by Levinas accordingly less as a quest for lost being than "as the relational space in which I am hostage to the other" (LR 160).[10]

"Moral elevation" of a parallel kind is to be found in the writing of the avant-garde author Michel Leiris. Here once again the linguistic imagination is never allowed to slip away into empty imitations but is constantly recalled to critical responsibility. Images ceaselessly undermine their own mesmerizing power generating a movement of transcendence towards the other. They become genuine speech, which for Levinas means a "moment of critique" which explodes the *imaginaire* of self-sufficiency and opens us to a relation with someone.[11] As Levinas puts it, "this need to enter into a relation with someone, in spite of or over and above the peace and harmony derived from the successful creation of beauty, is what we call the necessity of critique" (TW 147). At this point Levinas contrasts writing which approximates to *vision*—where form is wedded to content in such a way as to appease it—and writing which approximates to *sound* where "the perceptible quality overflows so that form can no longer contain its content" (TW 147). The necessity of critique is met by the later kind, epitomized by Leiris's own texts. Here a rent is produced in our imaginary world and words are uttered which "surpass what is given." The ethical imagination of writers like Leiris is, it appears, acoustic rather than representational.

Leiris's writing is praised accordingly as a textuality of verbal sound which privileges "the living word, destined to be heard, in contrast to the word that is an image and already a picturesque sign" (TW 147). Leiris invents a literature of bifurcations (*bifurs*) and erasures (*biffures*) which resist the idolatry of total meaning. Levinas explains: "Bifurcations—since sensations, words and memories continually turn a train of thought from the path it seemed to be taking towards some unexpected direction; erasures—since the univocal meaning of cacti element is continually altered." (TW 145–46) In this way, Leiris reminds us that responsible art is in the first instance an act of speech where we hear, and respond to, the words of the other. But these words of transcendence can only assume a presence amongst us, as trace of the other, precisely because they refuse to become flesh. Levinas spells out what he means by such an ethical *ascesis* of words as follows:

> The use of the word wrenches experience out of its aesthetic self-sufficiency, the "here" where it has quietly been lying. Invoking experience turns it into a creature. It is in this sense that I have been able to say elsewhere that criticism, which is the word of a living being speaking to a living being, brings the image in which art revels back to the fully real being. The language of criticism takes us out of our dreams, in which artistic language plays an integral part. . . . Books call up books—but this proliferation of writings halts or culminates at the moment when the living word is installed (TW 148).

IV Conclusion

Leiris thus serves for Levinas—along with Proust, Blanchot, Agnon, and Celan—as a poet who responds to the fetishizing power of contemporary images by producing counterimages, word-images which disclose how being for the other, in and through language, is the first fact of existence. And one is compelled to infer that it is just such a poetics of the "living word" that Levinas would recommend as antidote to the proliferation of mirror-images and mirror-texts which characterizes our contemporary culture. The best answer to the parodic imagination is an auditory imagination critical of images and open to what exceeds them.

But avant-garde literature is not the only poetical medium to testify to the ethical. The critique of our civilization of images does not necessitate, as thinkers from Adorno and Marcuse to Steiner and Henri imply, a retreat from the glare of popular culture to the inaccessible reaches of High Art.[12] Levinas also acknowledges the possibility of media images offering ethical testimony in his remarks on the news coverage of a dying Colombian girl buried up to her neck in mud after a avalanche in 1986.[13] TV viewers can respond to such an image in a purely sensational or voyeuristic fashion. But we can equally respond to it as a naked face crying out to us in powerlessness and destitution. The choice of response to such a media image is ours, but it is always an *ethical* choice. And it cannot in fact be otherwise, for it is a response, one way or the other, to the ethical cry of another. Even the decision to be voyeuristic or sadistic in viewing such suffering—a decision to *refuse* to respond to the ethical cry—is itself a form of response to the other, albeit negative. Before we are condemned to be free, we are condemned to be responsible.

Recognizing the ethical charge of media images is, I submit, a first step toward developing a critical hermeneutics of postmodern imagination. It is regrettable that Levinas himself never explicitly pursued this path—and that, furthermore, he adopts an elitist attitude to poetics in his privileging of avant-garde writing. The closest he comes, perhaps, is when he acknowledges in "L'Idée de la Culture" (1983) that contemporary culture in the broadest sense can serve as the "irruption of the human in the barbarism of being." "Culture is not a surpassing or neutralization of transcendence," he claims,

> rather it is an ethical responsibility and obligation towards the other, a relationship to transcendence as transcendence. One could call it love. Culture is obliged to the face of the human other, which is not a given of experience and does not come from this world.[14]

But what Levinas fails to address, it seems, is the right of art as art to explore a realm of imagination which, in Ricoeur's phrase, "knows no censorship."[15] So that even if one is prepared to admit that aesthetic images are derived from the primary expression of the face and remain in the end of the day answerable to the face, one still reserves the right of art to suspend judgment, however provisionally, while it explores and experiments in a free play of imagination. Levinas does not fully appreciate that if the ultimate origin and end of art is ethics, the rest belongs to poetics.

Without this alibi, however temporary, poetics would cease to play freely, would cease to imagine how the impossible might become possible, how things might be if all was permissible. Deprived of such lee-way we are ultimately left with Lenin's maxim that "art is the hammer of the benevolent propagandist," or Sartre's that "words are loaded pistols."[16] Polemics notwithstanding, such slogans are the kiss of death for art.

The free play of imagining is indispensable not only for poetics but also in a real sense for ethics itself. This Levinas failed to see. If ethics is left entirely to itself, or allowed to dictate to poetics at every turn, it risks degenerating into cheerless moralism. Ethics needs poetics to be reminded that its responsibility to the other includes the possibility of play, freedom and pleasure. Just as poetics needs ethics to be reminded that play, freedom and pleasure are never self-sufficient but originate in, and aim towards, an experience of the other-than-self, of being-forone-another. That is where ethics and poetics meet—in those words which the self receives from the other and returns to the other.

2

The Truth that Accuses: Conscience, Shame and Guilt in Levinas and Augustine

Robert Bernasconi

Although Levinas has long criticized the subordination of ethics to ontology within the Western philosophical tradition, he has addressed the ethical theories found within that tradition only rarely and never in much detail. This has led to a great deal of uncertainty about the convergences and divergences between what Levinas understands by ethics and what has previously gone under that name. The familiar observation that Levinas does not offer an ethics as such, but is concerned with the meaning of ethics,[1] does not remove the need to find precisely what it is in the face to face relation that warrants Levinas's decision to continue to use the title *ethics*. The employment by Levinas of terms like responsibility, guilt, and conscience provides some kind of clue, but ultimately only the staging of a detailed confrontation between Levinas and the tradition of ethical inquiry in the West will provide an answer to this question. Meanwhile, I would like to take one small step in this direction.

The situation is somewhat confused by the way that Levinas has largely followed the tendency, which has its most extreme form in Heidegger, of equating the Western philosophical tradition, at least in the first instance, with Greece. What is currently understood by ethics owes at least as much to the Jewish and Judeo-Christian traditions as it does to the Greek determination of ethics, although that fact is still largely concealed by the way in which subsequent concerns about obligations and prohibitions are read back into a text like Aristotle's *Ethics*. While it is apparent that Levinas's debt to Judaic sources is in part responsible for the way in which his ethics diverges from, for example, that of Aquinas or Kant, it is also true that, even though he regards philosophical ethics as contaminated by the systematic presentation that determines it, he grants that there are moments that are salvageable and that, as it were, transcend the framework in which they are found. One thinks here of Levinas's remark that if one could, *per impossible*, retain one trait from a philosophical system while neglecting the details of that system, he would take Kant's categorical imperative.[2] Are there other instances? What should one make of them?

A provisional answer to these questions can be found in an interview Levinas gave to Richard Kearney. Kearney put to Levinas the following question: "And yet you claim that the ethical and the ontological coexist as two inspirations within Western philosophy?" Levinas responded by listing four places where one can find "traces of the ethical breaking through the ontological."[3] The first two do not come as a surprise. Levinas referred first to Plato's idea of "the Good beyond Being" (*agathon epekeina tes ousias*) that he had employed since the Preface to *Existence and Existents* in 1947 to refer to the relation with the Other.[4] He then cited Descartes's "discovery" of the idea of the infinite, which had been prominent in Levinas's work since "Philosophy and the Idea of Infinity" in 1957.[5] These two references were of such importance for Levinas's self-understanding that they provided him with the titles of his two major books, *Totality and Infinity* and *Otherwise than Being or Beyond Essence*. In comparison with the references to Plato and Descartes, the other two references found in the interview are somewhat surprising. Levinas continued:

> And similarly supra-ontological notions are to be found in the pseudo-Dionysian doctrine of the *via eminentiae* with its surplus of the Divine over Being, or in the Augustinian distinction in the *Confessions* between the truth which challenges (*veritas redarguens*) and the ontological truth which shines (*veritas lucens*), etc.

In what follows I shall explore the way in which certain aspects of the traditional concept of conscience pass into Levinas's thought, while others are questioned, taking as my guide Levinas's endorsement of this distinction found in the Tenth Book of Augustine's *Confessions*. In other words, I shall attempt to supplement Levinas's ground-breaking work by tentatively adding something of what I find missing there.

Levinas had already appealed to this same passage from Augustine's *Confessions* in "De la signifiance du sens." This was an essay Levinas had written in response to a meeting of French and Irish philosophers in June 1979 on the topic of Heidegger and theology and included in a volume arising from the conference.[6] In the course of this essay Levinas again proposed an account of transcendence which conserves "an irreducibly ethical meaning." For Levinas, before the face of the neighbor, in a responsibility without guilt, "I find myself exposed to an accusation which the alibi of my alterity cannot annul" (HS 139; OS 92). It was in that context that Levinas recalled that, when Augustine's distinction was cited in the course of the conference, it was interpreted by some of the participants from a Heideggerian perspective.[7] By contrast, Levinas referred Augustine's phrase not to the Heideggerian question of Being posed in good conscience, but to the question "is it just to be?" that arises in bad conscience. Levinas did not develop this reference to the *Confessions,* but at the end of the essay he made an observation that could be taken as showing what he would want a reading of this text to avoid. Instead of attempting to derive the ethical from the religious, as some genealogical accounts do,[8] Levinas warned that to take the idea of God on its own or in isolation from the other human being and to make it the basis of a religious experience would be to forget the ethical circumstances of its meaning. The dangers of such abstractions are evident from the fact of wars of religion (HS 142; OS 95). Levinas frequently says, "it is through my relation to the Other, [that] I am in touch with God."[9] This establishes the direction of his reading of Augustine, which refers the religious to the ethical, and not vice versa.

One might possibly dismiss these references to Augustine's *veritas redarguens* in the Kearney interview and in his contribution to *Heidegger et la question de Dieu* as merely occasional, a kind of *ad hominem* argument to a Christian audience and as such of little bearing for the interpretation of his thought, were it not for a further text, "Notes sur le sens." In this lecture from 1979, that was first published in 1981, and reprinted in a revised version in *De Dieu qui vient à l'idée* the following year,[10] Levinas offered two translations of the phrase *veritas redarguens.* It is both the truth which accuses and the truth which puts in question (DVI 255). Whereas the second phrase clearly recalls the analysis of "Truth and Justice" from *Totality and Infinity* that persists in "De la signifiance du sens," the first phrase evokes the discussion of the accusation in *Otherwise than Being,* as is underlined by the surrounding analysis. The two senses of *veritas redarguens* span the two books which furnish the decisive formulations of Levinas's thought.

It would seem likely that what drew Levinas to the idea of a *veritas redarguens* in the first instance was its relation to the notion of accusation that had by this time become prominent in his thought. Nevertheless his understanding of it as a kind of truth opposed to "the ontological truth that shines" was doubtless also important to him.[11] Levinas had in a 1972 essay, "Vérité du dévoilement et vérité du témoignage," attempted something similar,[12] although when this essay was incorporated into *Otherwise than being* the distinction between the two kinds of truth was not developed. In fact Levinas probably recognized in Augustine's distinction something of his own attempt in *Totality and Infinity* to argue in the chapter "Truth and Justice" that "truth presupposes justice."[13] The underlying basis for this claim was set out in "Freedom Called into Question," which is the first section of the chapter.

Levinas had already claimed that to recognize the Other is to recognize a hunger and so to give. "The presence of the Other" amounts to a "calling into question of my joyous possession of the world" (TeI 48; TI 75–76). However, it was only in the chapter "Truth and Justice" that Levinas announced that to welcome the Other is to put in question my freedom (TeI 58; TI 85). He presented his account in terms of an interpretation of conscience, guilt, and shame. In developing his answer to the question of the relation between truth and justice in *Totality and Infinity* Levinas linked the notion of truth to that of intelligibility, whereby to know is to comprehend or even, employing an analogy from the moral order, to justify. However, in a complex analysis, Levinas recognized that the task of justification is a derivative one. The justification of facts only becomes important once they are perceived as obstacles to spontaneous freedom. The question then becomes that of how one is to understand this inhibition of spontaneous freedom, as it takes place in a being that distrusts itself, puts itself into question, or is critical (TeI 54; TI 82). Does this inhibition take place as a consciousness of failure, arising in the discovery of one's weakness, or is it a consciousness of guilt, arising in the discovery of one's unworthiness (TeI 54–55; TI 83)? According to Levinas, the former represents the predominant tradition of European thought, in which the spontaneity of freedom is only limited and not called into question as such. Levinas proposed the alternative whereby "the critique of spontaneity engendered by the consciousness of moral unworthiness . . . precedes truth, precedes the consideration of the whole, and does not imply the sublimation of the I in the universal" (TeI 55; TI 83). In focusing on the *veritas redarguens* Levinas subsequently presented Augustine as a forerunner of this second interpretation.

If the critique of spontaneity precedes truth, as Levinas claimed, then the story about the relation between the justification of facts and spontaneity with which Levinas began this chapter of *Totality and Infinity* had to be dropped before he could state his conclusion. With characteristic hyperbole Levinas recognized in its place the passage of consciousness "back to what precedes its condition" (TeI 56; TI 84). In this context

Levinas called it "justice." It has proved a misleading choice of words insofar as this is a term that he usually reserved for the condition in which the ethical encounter with the Other is 'corrected' by the third party. Here it seems clear that Levinas is describing the ethical encounter as such. "The Other is not initially a *fact*, is not an *obstacle*, does not threaten one with death; he is desired in my shame" (TeI 56; TI 84). Shame does not have the structure of consciousness (*conscience*), but of conscience (*conscience morale*) where I am no longer the subject: the structure of shame is such that the subject is exterior to me. This is the beginning of morality at the point in which freedom feels itself to be "arbitrary and violent" (TeI 56; TI 84). One cannot fail to notice the tension between the relative familiarity of the concepts employed—conscience, guilt, and shame— and the unfamiliar framework in which they are being presented. The question is whether Levinas succeeded in redetermining these concepts by finding the basis for moral conscience in the experience of shame before the Other.

One should not suppose that the interpretation of conscience in terms of shame in the face of the Other is as such already a departure from an ethical tradition that locates conscience within interiority. Philosophers in the West have by no means been unanimous in placing conscience at the heart of interiority. Conscience played only a minimal role in Greek ethics, but there is at least some evidence for supposing that *suneidesis* in the first instance meant "shared knowledge" and not knowledge with oneself in the sense of being a witness for or against oneself (*auto suneidena ti*). According to Hermann Fränkel, the Greek idea of conscience is of a superhuman power which remembers guilt in preparation for some punishment subsequently to take place. Solon wrote of Justice (*Dike*) that "she knows in her silence the deeds that were done or are doing; and in time she comes always to avenge."[14] The idea that conscience was something one shared with another human being is rare but not unprecedented in the mainstream of Western thought. So, for example, Hobbes in *Leviathan* maintained that both conscience and being conscious are shared forms of knowledge, a knowing together. The use of the word conscience for "the knowledge of their own secret facts" was for him metaphorical.[15] Similarly, Feuerbach in *The Essence of Christianity* wrote that my fellow human being is "my objective conscience; . . . he is my personified feeling of shame."[16] In these cases, far from the inner workings of one person's conscience being inaccessible to everyone else except God, the other human being *is* that person's conscience.

A conscience, so formed, not only ruptures interiority, in keeping with the claim that conscience is "the calling of consciousness into question and not a consciousness of a calling into question."[17] Such a conscience also questions itself. One of the questions which Levinas sets out to answer is that of how a self-righteous conscience, a conscience which has been quietened or put to sleep, might be disturbed. Hence Levinas can say that what is at issue in his work is "the overcoming of all good conscience" (TeI 261; TI 304). Levinas does not describe an executive conscience which instructs one what to do and what not to do. The Other does not provide the specific ethics which Levinas holds back from developing. Nor is Levinas's conscience the legislative conscience which accuses me by reminding me of what I should not have done in a particular case.[18] Levinas does not seem to be preoccupied with the question of how someone might be judged after the event. He does not address the problem of the ill-informed or ill-educated conscience that led Bonaventure and Aquinas to point to another more fundamental conscience, *synderesis*, as a natural disposition which was both indelible and infallible.[19] This made it possible to resolve the question of how someone brought up without proper moral guidance might still be held responsible for their failings. But as Levinas is not concerned with the predominantly legal problem of passing judgments that assign blame or exonerate, he takes the discussion in a quite different direction.

Levinas does not pursue the somewhat marginal tradition of Hobbes and Feuerbach, where conscience is a kind of shared form of knowledge. Instead, he turns to Augustine. The Tenth Book of the *Confessions* that Levinas cites is one of the central texts for understanding the develop-ment of interiority as a realm of investigation: "I labor upon myself. I have become for myself a soil hard to work and demanding much sweat."[20] The debate about the extent to which Augustine can be understood as anticipating Descartes, however misleading it might otherwise be, does at least have the merit of indicating how firmly Augustine has come to be placed within the tradition of interiority.[21] Nevertheless, this debate has focused more on Augustine's possible anticipation of Descartes's *cogito* than on the relation between interiority and God as set out in the Third Meditation and subsequently explored by Levinas in *Totality and Infinity*.[22]

Conscience, for Augustine, was not strictly an inner voice arising from the self in isolation. In his *Confessions*, Augustine was clear that it arose in the sight of God. Genealogically, interiority might be said to arise from religious experience. The question is whether religious experience can be traced genealogically to ethical experience, as Levinas seems to have wanted to suggest in the remarks in "De la signifiance du sens" referred to earlier. Or, if Levinas is not precisely proposing a genealogical inquiry, it is perhaps a kind of *Destruktion* of the tradition parallel to Heidegger's in *Being and Time*, except that the primordial yet forgotten experiences to which it is directed would be ethical rather than ontological.[23] The association between conscience and shame is paramount in this process.

The immediate context of the phrases quoted by Levinas is provided by Augustine's question "why does truth engender hatred?" The phrase "truth engenders hatred" is borrowed from Terence,[24] but is here used in the context of the rejection of religious truth by those taken up by other things. Augustine wrote in response:

> Itaque propter eam rem oderunt veritatem, quam pro veritate amant. Amant eam lucentem, oderunt eam readarguentem. Qui enim falli nolunt et fallere volunt, amant eam, cum se ipsa indicat, et oderunt eam, cum eos ipos indicat.

> Therefore, they hate the truth because of the same thing which they love in place of the truth. They love the truth when it enlightens; they hate it when it reproves. Since they do not wish to be deceived, and they do wish to deceive, they love it when it reveals its own self, and they hate it when it reveals themselves.[25]

It seems apparent from the context that Augustine was not explicitly proposing a distinction between two different kinds or orders of truth. At the very most he proposes that the truth that accuses me and puts me in question has a different structure from the truth that simply illuminates the world. But that does not exhaust the extent to which these pages of Augustine can be seen as anticipating Levinas.

It is sometimes said that the anthropological question was posed for the first time in the Tenth Book of the *Confessions*. Whether or not this is true, it is important to recognize that Augustine puts "the question of man" to God.[26] More specifically, he poses the question in the context of a public confession. Confession in Augustine is at the same time a confession of faith, an act of praise, and a confession of sin. These senses are united in the following passage from Book Four: "Let proud men, who have not yet for their good been cast down by you, my God, laugh me to scorn, but in your praise let me confess my shame (*dedecora mea*) to you" (IV.1.1). The same multifaceted character of confession is evoked at the beginning of the Tenth Book. Augustine confesses before God in his heart and before many witnesses in his writing (X.1.1). The basis for what follows is that Augustine comes to know the abyss of human conscience (*abyssus humanae conscientiae*) in his being ashamed (*erubescam de me*) before God (*coram Deo*) (X.2.2).[27] Augustine's account of conscience may indeed open the realm of interiority, but it is important to recognize that this is accomplished by returning conscience to its roots in the experience of shame.

One can contrast Augustine's *veritas redarguens* with Philo's account of conscience as an accuser in *De Specialibus Legibus*. Philo had read in Leviticus that if a thief's sense of guilt (*asham*) led him to make reparation this would be cause for reducing the penalties due to him. On the basis of this passage, Philo described how, if someone charged with robbery escaped conviction (*elenchon*) by his accusers, he would still be convicted inwardly by his conscience (*endon hupo tou suneidotos elenchtheis*).[28] The Greek term *elencho* was well suited for Philo's purpose of drawing the parallel between conscience and the legal sphere. *Elencho* appears originally to have had the sense of "putting to shame" and to have then been transferred to both argumentative refutation and the legal realm. The Latin term used by Augustine, *redarguo*, also had this double sense of refutation and conviction, but he succeeded in the *Confessions* in drawing it back from the condition of being proved guilty in the courts to its phenomenological basis in the experience of guilt or shame. This is why nothing could be more apt than that Levinas should appropriate Augustine's phrase when his own thought similarly makes the return passage from a legalistic language back to its phenomenological basis.

Nevertheless, Levinas uses phenomenology to go beyond phenomenology, or behind its back, as it were. The guilt that Levinas describes in *Otherwise Than Being* as "irremissible" (AE 139; OB 109) does not find its basis in the abuse of freedom. He explicitly denies that "the for-the-other characteristic of the subject" can be interpreted as a guilt-complex, because that would presuppose an *initial* freedom (AE 160; OB 124). Nor does guilt, as it is presented here, have anything to do with the apportionment of blame. It would seem that Levinas recognized that so long as responsibility and guilt are both understood legalistically, then one responds better by offering excuses, by establishing that one is in no way implicated or involved, than by giving of oneself. This is the force of the statement that one is responsible independently of any contract. As if addressing Nietzsche's attempt to refer the notion of guilt to debt and from there to "the oldest and most primordial personal relationship, that between buyer and seller, creditor and debtor,"[29] Levinas declares that one is in debt "from the start" (AE 110; OB 87). Against the narrative that derives the ethical relationship from what is allegedly more primitive, Levinas points to "the anachronism of a debt preceding the loan" (AE 143; OB 112). Nor is this a loan that one could ever pay off: "the more just I am, the more guilty I am" (AE 143; OB 112). This sentiment does not originate with Levinas, but the continuity of his thought on this subject is confirmed by the fact that this is a concealed quotation from *Totality and Infinity* (TeI 222; TI 244).[30]

Totality and Infinity presented responsibility and guilt as intertwined (TeI 178; TI 203). In his most recent works Levinas has preferred to write of a "guiltless responsibility," but the inconsistency is only apparent, as this passage from "Ethics as First Philosophy" confirms:

> Responsibility for the Other, for the naked face of the first individual to come along. A responsibility that goes beyond what I may or may not have done to the Other or whatever acts I may or may not have committed, as if I were devoted to the other man before being devoted to myself. Or more exactly, as if I had to answer for the other's death even before *being*. A guiltless responsibility, whereby I am none the less open to an accusation of which no alibi, spatial or temporal could clear one.[31]

Whether he described responsibility as without guilt or as arising in guilt, the aim was the same in both cases. It was to disrupt the dominance that the linguistic usage and interests of the lawcourts and tribunals have had on the language and boundaries of ethics through the process of accusation and establishing guilt in the sense of legal responsibility.

Levinas's appeal to the phenomenon of shame can be understood in some measure as part of that same corrective process, even though Levinas took up the analysis of shame in an ontological setting before he articulated a clear concern for ethics. So "Evasion," an essay from 1935 that is conventionally regarded as Levinas's first attempt at original philosophy, culminates in an analysis of shame. However, what is most remarkable about this analysis is that it makes no mention of the Other before whom one is ashamed. It is "our presence to ourselves which is shameful."[32] By contrast, in "Transcendence and Height," an essay from 1962 which presented the theses of *Totality and Infinity* to an audience of his peers at the Société Française de Philosophie, Levinas provided an analysis in which shame arises in the welcome of the absolutely other (TH 96). The absolutely Other is the Other who opens the dimension of height (TH 90). According to Levinas, it is this dimension that is lacking from the account of guilt provided by the philosophy of existence. Like Levinas, Heidegger conceived of guilt as prior to any indebtedness.[33] For both of them, it arises from "commitments that were never contracted" (TH 97). Nevertheless, according to Levinas, Heidegger's failure to recognize the dimension of height, led him to an account of ontological guilt with "tragic and not ethical overtones" (TH 97). In effect, Levinas's position is that the structure that the philosophy of existence overlooked can be found in both Augustine's *Confessions* and Descartes's *Meditations*, where the dimension of height opened up interiority. Elsewhere and specifically in the context of an elucidation of the perfection of the infinite in Descartes, Levinas characterizes shame as freedom's discovery of itself as "murderous and usurpatory in its exercise" (EHH 176; CP 58).

Levinas does not draw a systematic distinction between shame and guilt, and he certainly does not use either term in a conventional sense, but Levinas's focus on shame as arising in the face of the Other who approaches one from a height at least captures one of the dominant senses of shame. There seems little place in Levinas for the internalization of moral prohibitions that is usually associated with guilt.[34] It would not be entirely wrong, therefore, to understand Levinas as attempting to reject the ethics based on guilt in favor of one founded on shame.[35] However, more significant is the fact that in Levinas, neither guilt, nor shame, when he evokes them in developing his own account, are tied to an accusation focused on a specific deed. It is this that enables Levinas to differentiate the Christian doctrine of original sin from his own account of "an accusation preceding the fault, borne against oneself despite one's innocence" (AE 144; OB 113). To emphasize this, Levinas goes as far as possible in freeing the notion of accusation from the idea of responsibility for some specific deed that one has wilfully chosen:

> Obsessed precisely with responsibilities that do not go back to decisions taken by a freely contemplating subject, and thus accused with what it never did, . . . ipseity "takes on itself," in the absolute inability of slipping away from proximity, from the face, . . . (EHH 233; CP 123)

By the same token, it is because the self is accused beyond any fault, before freedom and so in an unavowable innocence, that one is marked by the "original goodness of creation" and not by the state of original sin (AQ 156; OB 121).

For Levinas, the truth that accuses does not dictate what one should or should not do.[36] Nor does it say what one should or should not have done. It simply establishes a responsibility that one cannot evade: the impossibility of ever knowing what the right thing to do is combined with the impossibility of being indifferent so that one must do something, if only by refraining to do anything. An example is found in "Judaism and Revolution," one of Levinas's Talmudic commentaries from the collection *Du Sacré au Saint.* This text examines the question of the evil committed in the attempt to combat evil. Levinas's question is not whether one should use violence in such circumstances: "Unquestionably, violent action against Evil is necessary."[37] Nevertheless, there are certain responsibilities that the one using violence to combat evil must recognize. The first, which might seem particularly strange unless one recalls questions that Levinas posed in "Loving the Torah more than God," is to understand the meaning of the absence or silence of God (DL 193; DF 145). The difference between revolutionary action and police action at the service of the established

State lies in the fact that the proponents of the former are the ones who question the absolute claim of politics by asking about the cause of evil. It is hard not to be suspicious of Levinas when one reads his attempt to solidify the distinction between the two kinds of action: "It is not enough to be against a cause, one must be in the service of one" (SS 38; NTR 110). Is not being in the service of a cause itself often the cause of evil? And do not fascists and police states also have causes? But while being suspicious of what Levinas is saying, it is important also to recognize that the whole passage is about exercising suspicion on oneself. This, it emerges, is the second mark distinguishing revolutionary action from police action.

> Revolutionary action is first of all the action of the isolated man who plans revolution not only in danger but also in the agony of his conscience—in the double clandestinity of the catacombs and of conscience. In the agony of conscience that risks making revolution impossible: for it is not only a question of seizing the evil-doer but also of not making the innocent suffer. (SS 38–39; NTR 110)

It should be recognized that because the need for violence against violence is predicated on the absence of God, the revolutionary who employs it cannot claim to be doing God's work. He or she is acting in the dark. Hence "Judaism and Revolution" ends with questions and uncertainties: "What is exposed here is the full range of the anxiety that comes with the power of man over man" (SS 52; NTR 118).

The codes of behavior that direct one how to act, the debilitating sense of guilt that can arise when one obsesses about specific misdeeds, and the good conscience produced by casuistry, all serve to alleviate the fundamental feeling of unease that arises when one is put in question. Much of what passes for ethics are simply different ways of evading the truth that accuses. The truth of ethics, the truth that accuses, does not bring conviction in the sense of self-certainty, so much as a form of anxiety, even if that term can only be used in this context with caution. Augustine's differentiation of the truth that accuses from the truth that illuminates prepares for Levinas's subordination of the ontological order to the ethical, but, more importantly, it points to his attempt to free ethics from its dependence on a legalistic model. To this extent the anxiety of conscience that accompanies the welcoming of the Other amounts to more than "an ethics of ethics." It is an "ethics of suspicion" or even "an ethics against ethics."[38] Such an ethics finds its inspiration less in the *veritas lucens* than in the *veritas redarguens*.

3

Moral Optimism

Joseph Margolis

I f you ask me to identify the salient, single most vulnerable theme of contemporary Western moral philosophy, I should say it was *moral optimism*. I take the term as a term of art. I do not mean we believe we have good reason to believe our world is on the edge of a notably good life. On the contrary, "moral optimism" in the philosophical sense is, in its recent public manifestations, a kind of whistling in the wind, a nervous testifying that our rational competence in moral matters is (despite a deliberate scaling-back of cognitive presumption) fortunately *not* at risk to anything like the Nazi or Stalinist excesses that (we are now pleased to say) have been satisfactorily exorcised. At the end of the Gulf War, for example, President George Bush was heard to say that the Americans (therefore, the world) had banished from the West's political space every moral ideology that threatened the preeminence of liberal capitalism, and that capitalism could now be happily counted on to prevail in the foreseeable future.

Bush's confidence was an unguarded expression of an optimism of the political opportunist's sort: it's not exactly what I had in mind. Nevertheless, at a deeper level of analysis than Bush would wish to probe, the philosophical optimism I am speaking about *does* lurk and occasionally shows its face. Bush shares, however inchoately, that deeper optimism with such skillful philosophers as Alasdair MacIntyre, John Rawls, Hilary Putnam, and Jürgen Habermas. *They* are "moral optimists" in the full sense intended; and, for my money, Bush is the political pawn who, through the cunning of history, obliges us to read more carefully the lessons of that philosophical tribe. I see this as the sign of a profound failure to come to terms with the self-imposed cognitive limitations of late pragmatism.

Mind you: Aristotle and Kant and Hegel, who, in various ways, are the tutors of our quartet, are *not* "optimists" at all. On the contrary, *optimism*, as I understand the notion, is a legitimate orientation signifying: (i) the displacement of *reason* or rationality by *reasonableness*, by way of (ii) displacing the autonomous, objectivist competence of the first (reason) in favor of a punctuated or contingently expanding consensus formed under the auspices of the second (reasonableness). The process of serious inquiry—in any sector of interest: science as well as morality— *is* "optimistic," *if* whatever otherwise may be supposed to be the native (essential or a priori) competence of reason can now be instantiated or approximated (empirically, phenomenally, pragmatically) by some form of reasonable consensus (social or psychological) that repudiates the first's epistemic presumption. In this sense, for instance, Bernard Williams is definitely not a moral optimist, because he is not prepared to invest in measuring universal reasonableness or any approximation of the cognitive projects otherwise invented in the name of moral reason.[1] Karl-Otto Apel is similarly *not* an optimist, because *he* is an out-and-out Kantian, a complete apriorist about moral matters (albeit a curious Peircean Kantian).[2] (He has no worries about the cognitive privilege of practical reason.) On the other hand, at least in matters of scientific method, Karl Popper and T.S. Kuhn (ambiguously) and Imre Lakatos *are* optimists, whereas Paul Feyerabend and Arthur Fine are not.[3] I am convinced that a "philosophical optimism"—whether of the moral or scientific or epistemic sort—now dominates Western thought as the beneficiary of classical pragmatism; and that, despite that fact, it must fail and is particularly transparent in its moral guise.

Optimism may be seen to take two characteristic forms—across the philosophical board: (a) that of claiming a naturalized but reliable progress as the telos of reasonable inquiry, and (b) that of presuming some decisive but arbitrary or unexamined invariance within the flux of nature. I claim that the moral theories offered by MacIntyre, Rawls, Putnam, and Habermas founder, along the lines of (a) and (b), or a combination of the two. But, more than that, a very large army of contemporary theorists ranging over many different kinds of philosophical inquiry can be shown to be similarly infected. Thus, to pique your curiosity, I suggest that Hans-Georg Gadamer's hermeneutics depends on a weakness of the (b)-sort, in the same sense in which (in the analytic tradition) Donald Davidson's advocacy of supervenience (regarding the mind/body problem) and Alvin Goldman's advocacy of reliabilism (in epistemology) also do.[4] (I am not claiming that Gadamer is a pragmatist.)

I cannot pursue these parallels here. I mean only to draw your attention to the ubiquity and uniformity of what I am calling "philosophical optimism." It suggests the importance of tracing the narrower career of moral optimism, which, as I say, is sweeping Western moral theory. I should add that optimisms of the (a)-sort yield various forms of *liberalism* (in moral and political matters), or of *progressivism* (more generally, in either moral or scientific matters); and that optimisms of the (b)-sort yield various forms of (what I call) *traditionalism*.[5] MacIntyre, Gadamer, and Rawls, I say, are traditionalists; Habermas, Putnam, and Popper are progressivists. (The distinction fits "continental" and "analytic" philosophies with equal aptness, a fact that is instructive in its own right.)

I

Let me begin, then, with Putnam's theory. It is the least ramified and most transparent of those mentioned; but, for that reason, it helps to expose the cognate weaknesses in the more complex views of the others. Plainly, the others are much more influential in moral matters than Putnam is. Putnam, I may say, is quite explicit about his own agreement with the views of Habermas and Apel. He is a self-styled pragmatist who—in a spirit at once Kantian-like and Peircean (together with Habermas and Apel, who are also "Kantian" or "Kantian-like" and "Peircean")—holds that: (1) the rationale for truth in both moral and scientific matters rests with the life of an inquiring community; and (2) objectivity in accord with (1) may be vouchsafed without retreating to any cognitive privilege. In my idiom, Putnam believes that something like the Kantian and Peircean goal can be rescued by replacing a priori reason by a consensual, actual, praxis-centered reasonableness. Putnam retreats from a universalized ethic (in one sense), and he fails to distinguish satisfactorily between Habermas and Apel (since Apel *is* a Kantian apriorist but Habermas is not); but he confirms, nevertheless, the remarkable convergence between the pragmatist possibilities of a Peirceanized Kant developed, across the Atlantic, between himself and Habermas—between the most recent American and German efforts at reunifying certain strands of Western philosophy:

> Habermas and Apel claim—and I agree [he says]—that the notion of
> a warranted or justified statement [of, say, a moral or scientific sort]
> involves an implicit reference to a community. . . . It must, in short, be

a community which respects the principles of intellectual freedom and equality.[6]

Putnam understands this theme to be Kantian. I cannot entirely agree with his reading of Kant, because, in effect, he takes Kant to be an "optimist." He is perhaps right in construing Kant to have (in effect) defeated Thomas Aquinas (and, in our time, MacIntyre), since: "according to the medievals, as Alasdair MacIntyre has reminded us, we possess a capacity to know the human 'function' or the human 'essence'; whereas (*pace* . . . MacIntyre) Kant understands that this will no longer wash. In the *Grundlegung* he says explicitly [says Putnam] that one cannot build an ethic upon this notion of Happiness, because too many different things can be made out to be the content of that notion. . . . The situation is dark because reason does not give us such a thing as an inclusive human end which we should all seek (unless it is morality itself, and this is not an end that can determine the content of morality)" (MFR, 48–49).

Here, Putnam fails to signal the fact that Kant *does* protect the privilege of reason, in the moral sphere, in a way quite different from MacIntyre's or the medievals'; by that error, Putnam affirms that, although the "content of morality" cannot be "determined," it can be legitimated—in a way that brings Kant and pragmatism together. Putnam fails to appreciate, therefore, that Habermas believes that consensual reasonableness *can* approximate to the Kantian presumption about pure practical reason (also, that Apel directly invokes a priori reason), and that Habermas and Apel rest *their* confidence on the recovery of a "universal ethic" from the exercise of "reasonableness" (Habermas) or "reason" itself (Apel).

Having recovered (to his own satisfaction) Habermas's and Apel's contribution to our understanding of science and morality—the matter of "implicit reference to a community," "the loss of essences," and the mutual respect for one another (the sense of liberal equality) entailed by those conditions—Putnam merely opposes conceding that "one can derive a universal ethic from the idea of reasonableness, or from the (Kantian as well as Peircean) picture of truth as idealized rational acceptability, but [he also insists] a different weaker but still important conclusion [may be derived]" (MFR 55; see also 50, 52, 54).

Here, the picture becomes murky, because, if I am right in my reading of Putnam, he fails: first, to appreciate the import of Kant's adherence to the essential, universal powers of a priori reason; second, the decisive respect in which Apel simply invokes Kant's presumption (as somehow embedded in social existence and reflection) and the respect in which Habermas believes *he* can save its would-be achievement (eschewing Apel's apriorism) by the contingent processes of a continuous, consensual, and dialectically responsible reasonableness; *and* third, the troublesome sense in which he himself, despite his opposition to a "universal ethic," is caught up in the same "optimism" Habermas is.

On the first score, Putnam misses the crucial point. He takes Kant to be mistaken, it is true, in supposing that "moral philosophy is impossible without transcendental guarantees that can be given only if we posit a noumenal realm" (MFR 42). But he does not seriously question the conceivability *of* a "noumenal realm," or, more exactly, the conceivability of *that* conceptual power by which what *is* universally binding on "pure practical reason" (*not* mere consensual agreement among reasonable creatures) *can* actually be specified.[7] In this spirit, Putnam treats the prospects of an objective science and morality in the same way. Thus, he argues: "what the relativist fails to see is that it is a presupposition of thought itself that some kind of objective 'rightness' exists."[8] It is difficult not to construe this as transcendentally intended, though it is not meant to be privileged or a priori. In any case, it is an *obiter dictum.*

Putnam closes *Reason, Truth and History,* in which the charge against the relativist appears, with the following sentence: "The very fact that we speak of our different conceptions as different conceptions of *rationality* posits a *Grenzbegriff,* a limit-concept of the ideal truth" (RTH 216). *The Many Faces of Realism* seems now to be a confession that that confidence is no longer defensible; but the later text is not consistent on the matter, and *Realism with a Human Face* confirms that Putnam has no intention of abandoning the idea of "truth as idealized rational acceptability."[9] The fact is, Putnam is an "optimist" about both science and morality, largely, but not completely, in accord with Habermas (MFR 53–56). Put more frontally: to be attracted to a "Kantian-like" program and to abandon Kant's own apriorism (or any surrogate: Apel's, for instance) is, effectively, to subvert the very possibility that truth, goodness, rationality, legitimation, or any similar normative concept *could* vouchsafe an invariant—any discernibly invariant—"regulative" function. There cannot be a *Grenzbegriff* of Putnam's sort (or Habermas's, for that matter) if a "Kantian-like" constructivism cannot fall back to apriorist assurances. For, on the argument, any would-be regulative function of truth or reason would then be a contingent artifact of a contingently "constructed" world. That is indeed the essential argument and insight of *The Many Faces of Realism,* but for some curious reason Putnam has not yet reconciled these opposed contentions. The issue takes a local form, but its import is hardly local.

By contrast, Kant consistently applies the categorical imperative to the contingencies of human life, but he does not satisfactorily explain or legitimate the presumption of its categorical force. The categorical imperative appears to be nothing but an invention—offered within the confines of the phenomenal world (on the strength of what is supposed to be our transcendental understanding of our own constituting role in the structuring of the experienced world)—*of what creatures thus confined* might *imagine* the noumenal powers of reason to be. The best Kant could possibly do here is christen a particular model of reason as *that* very conception that, construing our own subjective powers to be noumenal (though they are plainly not), would, "noumenally," then bind our deliberate actions (in the phenomenal world) unconditionally, categorically.

Kant's entire undertaking in moral philosophy, therefore, cannot be more than an earnest charade. (That ought to be the pragmatist's conclusion.) If, for instance, along Hegelian, phenomenological, or hermeneutic lines, we admit the possibility that our conceptual powers are themselves artifacts of preformative social and historical forces *and* applicable only within *their* terms (*praxis*, in Marx's sense), then both the "conceivability" of the noumenal powers of reason and the presumption that rational self-legislation cast in terms of universalized maxims can claim categorical force are clearly failed (naive, possibly incoherent) undertakings.

Now, then, to clinch the bearing of this finding on Putnam's other mistakes: if the first error be conceded, then Putnam cannot possibly appreciate the sense in which Habermas *is* an "optimist" in supposing: (a) that *he* can retire the presumptions of a priori reason (à la Apel as well as Kant), and yet (b) recover (at least progressively or by approximation), through the consensual processes of communicative exchange within actual societies, *the universally valid, categorically binding, formal moral constraints* that Kant assumes apply to action (by way of a priori reason); or, if the second error be conceded, then Putnam cannot be expected to appreciate the sense in which: (c) *he* himself, despite rejecting "moral essences" and the necessity of forming a conception of the "noumenal realm," is, because of his (own) pluralism, *a victim of the same presumption (but not the same particular doctrine) that grips Habermas.*

Putnam apparently believes that a plurality of valid but limited (possibly nonconverging) moral options *is not* sufficient to disqualify the explicit universalism of Kant, Apel, or Habermas. He himself requires a universalism by which to legitimate the non-universalized (plural) visions of the morality *he* offers in place of this recent Frankfurt School's option.

Putnam criticizes Kant's insisting on a uniquely correct or true account in morality as well as science. "What we require in moral philosophy," he says, "is, first and foremost, a moral image of the world, or rather—since, here again, I am more of a pluralist than Kant—a number of complimentary moral images of the world" (MFR 52). By the expression "here again," Putnam means to remind us that, more or less along W.V. Quine's lines—in the matter of the "indeterminacy of translation" and the (rather doubtful) import of the Löwenheim-Skolem theorem—realism must be reconciled with the finding (ineluctable, on Putnam's view of his own "internal realism") that we cannot expect to vindicate a uniquely correct account of the way the world is: "realism is *not* incompatible with conceptual relativity" (he says).[10]

But Putnam has never satisfactorily defended his longstanding conviction that truth has "a regulative function" that disciplines our epistemic beliefs and conjectures in the sciences. Truth has a regulative function, he claims, namely, that of "*idealized* justification [of truth-claims], as opposed to justification-on-present-evidence." In this regard, Putnam opposes Michael Dummett's "anti-realist" thesis, since, for Dummett (it seems), "one can *specify* in an effective way [*now*] what the justification conditions for all the sentences of a natural language are."[11] (Here, the irony is that Dummett has the seeming advantage of a naive realism. That is, his "anti-realism has no particular epistemic force": it plays the part only of the procedural caution.)

By this maneuver, Putnam distinguishes between truth and justification, since justification but not truth is a matter of degree and may be lost; justification is idealized but its idealization cannot be stated once and for all; and the conditions for truth itself cannot be given in terms of any theory of meaning. Putnam's most careful reading here is this:

> (1) that truth is independent of justification here and now, but not independent of *all* possibility of justification . . . (2) that truth is expected to be stable, or 'convergent'. . . . In my view, [he says,] as in Quine's, that justification conditions for sentences change as our total body of knowledge changes, and cannot be taken as fixed once and for all.[12]

Putnam regards this as compatible with the thesis (his reading of the applicability of the Löwenheim-Skolem theorem) that "*the same objects* [in the actual world] can be what logicians call a 'model' for incompatible theories [indefinitely many interpretations of *those* objects, compatibly with 'internal realism']" (RTH 73–74). But the careful reader must remember that *truth* and realism thus construed are "expected to be stable, or convergent"; that the argument is meant to hold in moral matters as in science; *and* that, according to his latest adjustment, this is no longer a reliable supposition in the way it was once supposed to be.[13] Putnam yields on privilege, but tries to recover the benefits of privilege "by other [by pragmatist] means." That is what I understand an "optimist" to be committed to—an untenable position.

II

I have been pressing Putnam because his account of the "idealized" (regulative) function of truth—in both science and morality—undermines the pretense that the processes of *reasonable* consensus (under the conditions of actual social life) *could* ever be counted on to yield an approximative recovery of the (strictly *non*consensual) universality of (anything like) Kant's supposition regarding "pure practical" *reason*. Putnam abandons altogether the "'Objectivist' picture of the world" (in Husserl's sense of "objectivist") and holds instead that "The deep systemic root of the [philosophical] disease [he means to root out] is in the notion of an 'intrinsic' property, a property something has 'in itself', apart from any contribution made by language or the mind" (MFR 8). He concedes that "Internal realism is . . . just the insistence that realism is *not* incompatible with conceptual relativity"; but, against the "relativist," he still insists that realism continues to oppose (opposing Richard Rorty in particular) the thesis that "there is no truth to be found . . . 'true' is just a name for what a bunch of people can agree on' " (MFR 17–18).

Still, Putnam no longer speaks of what is "stable" or "convergent" in the way of truth (or justification); he even draws a parallel between science and ethics in exposing the "mistake of supposing that 'Which are the real objects' [in the world] is a question that makes sense *independently of our choice of concepts*" (MFR 20). He now says flat out:

> the enterprise [of distinguishing disjunctively between appearance and reality, between "what is 'simply true' and what has only 'assertibility conditions'; or the cut between what is already true or false and what is an 'extension of previous use' (albeit one that we all make in the same way), or between what is a 'projection' and what is an independent and unitary property of things in themselves"] isn't worth the candle. The game is played out. We can make a rough sort of rank ordering (although even here there are disagreements), but the idea of a 'point at which' subjectivity ceases and Objectivity-with-a-capital-O begins has proved chimerical. (MFR 28; see also 26)

I take this to signify the collapse of Putnam's (the "optimist's") thesis with respect to *both* morality and science. So that when Putnam announces that "the value of Equality is, perhaps, a unique contribution of the Jewish religion to the culture of the West"—for instance, most notably, in the "principle": "There is something about human beings, some aspect which is of incomparable moral significance, with respect to which all human beings are equal, or whose contribution to society is the least, are deserving of respect"—he *can claim no possible legitimative basis for his dictum,* except his own adherence to a certain favored ethnocentric (liberal) conviction (which, unfortunately for his own view, pretty well commits him to something like Rorty's more candid ethnocentrism).[14] Putnam is either unwilling or unable to acknowledge that the defeat of (postmodernist) ethnocentrism is not tantamount to ensuring a ("Kantian-like") *Grenzbegriff.*

I take the expression, "deserving of respect" (in the moral context), and (earlier) the view that "truth is expected to be stable, or convergent" (in both the moral and scientific contexts) to be coy acknowledgements that Kantian universality (noumenal *or* consensual) is now impossible to justify; and, therefore, *that reasonableness cannot be taken to instantiate in a punctuated way, or to approximate asymptotically, the privileged pronouncements of reason.* In that sense, the defeat of Putnam's thesis is, or entails, the defeat of both Apel's and Habermas's thesis (though the connection may not be entirely obvious). If so, then we have gained a powerful finding with very little effort. Of course, the champions of Habermas will insist on another inning, one in which Habermas's own texts are directly examined. Fair enough.

III

I shall not explore Apel's apriorism in any depth. I take note of the fact that Apel's characterization of the a priori (not his strategy for recovering it) is thoroughly Kantian. Apel rejects the "scientistic notion of normatively neutral or value-free 'objectivity' " and (like Peirce) affirms that "logic—and, *at the same time,* all the sciences and technologies— *presupposes* an ethic as the precondition for its possibility." "The logical validity of arguments cannot [Apel says] be tested without, in principle, positing a community of scholars who are capable of both intersubjective communication and reaching a consensus . . . . the *validity* of solitary thought is basically dependent upon the justification of verbal arguments in the actual community of argumentation."[15]

The fundamental difference between Apel's and Habermas's legitimative strategy lies in this: Apel tries to draw out transcendental a priori rules (universally and necessarily binding on rational thought—theoretical as well as practical) *from* the very nature of community life itself; whereas Habermas claims that the practice of social communication requires a progressive strengthening of universal constraints on rational participation that are not a priori but pragmatically arrived at in the very process of reflecting on the ongoing objectives of such communication.

For the time being, this is sufficiently precise for our purposes. It helps to explain, for instance, the sense in which Habermas is an optimist but Apel is not. Apel construes the behavior of the "communication community" as falling (more strictly than it might for Kant) *within* the standard terms of reference of Kantian "experience." He therefore appeals to the reflexive powers of transcendental reason working within the boundaries of the "communication community." (He means to obviate noumena.) Habermas eschews all presumption of transcendental powers—but *not* (second-order) legitimative discourse that is both pragmatic and in some sense necessary.

I offer two provisional arguments on the legitimative issue. In accord with one, *if*, as I say, Kant's general strategy (employing phenomenal reason in order to discover transcendentally necessary, universally binding constraints within itself) fails to explain the modal necessity of what it claims to find, or fails to explain why the seeming necessity of what it alleges it finds should not be construed as an artifact of its own incompletely penetrable, variably preformed conditions,[16] then it is not clear why Apel's new argument regarding genuinely a priori constraints on communicative practices should hold any more convincingly. The other argument concerns Habermas's treatment of a challenge Hans Albert had put to Apel, that, by an interesting irony, applies to Apel but does not rightly apply to Habermas's weakened theory of legitimative discourse. The upshot of these paired considerations, I believe, is to segregate quite sharply arguments from the a priori powers of reason and the a posteriori powers of reasonableness and to jeopardize, by that disjunction, the claims of both Apel and Habermas.

The matter may be approached obliquely, by reviewing John Rawls's recent effort to extend the range of his own theory of justice into the space of the morality of politics. The issue seems quite daunting, but (as we shall see) it is actually, now, easier to resolve. For, as it turns out, the failure of Rawls's argument matches the failure of Putnam's and confirms the sense in which Habermas's "moral optimism" cannot possibly recover anything like the universality and necessity of a priori (or essentialist) arguments (suspect in their own terms). The weakness of Rawls's argument, therefore, helps to confirm the sense in which neither

Aristotelian nor Kantian forms of optimism can serve the purpose at hand. (It also betrays the subversive pragmatist theme.)

Albert's challenge permits us to link Apel's and Habermas's strategies perspicuously. Albert is right, I think, in supposing that *if* one seeks "an absolute foundation" for knowledge (of any kind), then *any* concession to "fallibilism" will prove fatal.[17] *If* transcendental reasoning is meant to yield such a foundation, then the best strategy for contesting Apel's extension of Kant's method becomes instantly clear; and, the impossibility of Habermas's securing anything like Kant's (or Apel's) finding by any means by which he explicitly abandons transcendental reasoning and (all) cognitive privilege becomes even clearer.

Albert himself subscribes to the Popperian analogue of a thoroughgoing fallibilism. He claims the "classical epistemologists" (he includes Apel and Habermas), pursuing "an Archimedean point of knowledge" with respect to both "the *attainability* and the *decidability* of truth," subscribe to the "principle of sufficient reason"—which states: "always seek an adequate foundation—a sufficient justification—for all your convictions" (TCR xvi, 13–14; see also 48). On Albert's assumption, transcendental arguments, all arguments pursuing (but not assured of) "an absolute foundation" for "*everything*" (in the way of truth-claims), must resolve the trilemma (Albert calls it "the Münchhausen trilemma"): that is, the need to choose between "an infinite regress," "a logical circle," and "the breaking off of the process [of justification]." "Since both a infinite regress and a circular argument seem clearly unacceptable," Albert suggests, "one is inclined to accept the third possibility." But that would involve "an arbitrary suspension of the principle of sufficient justification" (TCR 18).

On this, Habermas has the following to say, having already acknowledged that Kant's defense of the categorical imperative *is* doubtful— because *it* rests on a dubious "moral intuition" (a form of cognitivism) or because, by appealing to "the substantive normative concepts of autonomy and free will" (involving the conceivability of a noumenal order), it may well have "committed a *petitio principii*":

> I am not dramatizing the situation when I say that faced with the
> demand for a justification of the universal validity of the principle of
> universalization, cognitivisms are in trouble. The skeptic feels emboldened
> to recast his *doubts* about the possibility of justifying a universalist morality
> as an *assertion* that it is impossible to justify such a morality. Hans
> Albert took this tack with his *Treatise on Critical Reason* by applying
> to practical philosophy Popper's model of critical testing, which was
> developed for the philosophy of science and intended to take the place

of traditional foundationalist and justificationist models. The attempt to justify moral principles with universal validity, according to Albert, ensnares the cognitivist in a "Münchhausen trilemma" in which he must choose between three equally unacceptable alternatives. . . . The status of this trilemma, however, is problematic. It arises only if one presupposes a *semantic concept of justification* that is oriented to a deductive relationship between statements and based solely on the concept of logical inference. This deductive concept of justification is obviously too narrow for the exposition of the pragmatic relations between argumentative speech acts.[18]

I'm afraid Habermas is confused here, in spite of the fact that, beneath his countermove, there lurks a genuine discovery. For one thing, he misreads Albert's charge. He construes the point of the *third* option (of the trilemma) to be restricted to the rules of ordinary deductive inference. This could hardly be the way of transcendental (or his own "pragmatic") justification. Furthermore, the underlying problem *does* apply to the justification of both deductive and nondeductive inference (as Kant and Peirce—and Aristotle—realized). That is not a matter merely of a relation between statements: it concerns the structure of argument, practices involving a certain orderly use of statements.

Again, Albert does not limit his maneuver to deductive inference; he applies the trilemma to the *assertion* of the transcendental or pragmatic *legitimation* of *Apel's* and *Habermas's* (legitimative) "*conviction.*" It is true he offers the model of "self-evident" and "self-authenticating" statements, in addressing Apel's and Habermas's arguments. But he is clearly offering a model here. There's nothing wrong with that; for, on his own argument (the appeal to sufficient reason), his opponents require "an Archimedean point of knowledge." "The procedure is analogous [he says] to the suspending of the causal principle by the introduction of a *causa sui.*" (Habermas has not met the charge.) "But what [he asks] are we to make of a statement that cannot itself be justified, but must assist in justifying everything else; that is represented as certain, despite the fact that one can really doubt everything—including the statement—on principle; that is, an *assertion,* the *truth* of which is *certain* and therefore *not in need of foundation?*" (TCR 19)

Simply put: Albert is challenging the *assertion* of the "self-evident" or "self-authenticating" *practice* Apel and Habermas favor, with respect to their own legitimative *claims*—which range over *act* and *conduct* as well as *inference*! *They* are committed to a "dogma," Albert says. Surely, Habermas's demurrer is a conceptual howler: he fails to see that he *is asserting* that a certain pragmatic *commitment is* universally necessary at some critical point.[19] Still, Habermas does have a point: the legitimative question concerns "pragmatic relations between argumentative speech acts." It's only that neither Apel nor Habermas can escape the force of Albert's appeal to the principle of sufficient reason. Apel *might* succeed, *if self-evident legitimative principles obtained*; and Habermas might succeed, *if he could safely violate his own injunction to abandon Kant's and Apel's appeal to a priori privilege.*

Having said this, I am prepared to acknowledge that Habermas is entirely on target. He introduces (in order to dismiss) "the structure and status of the transcendental-pragmatic argument" in the form Apel and other theorists (in English-language philosophy) offer: notably, A. J. Watt, influenced by Collingwood, and R. S. Peters, who invokes a principle of equality or "fairness" that cannot fail to remind us of both Putnam's and Rawls's moral intuitions.[20] What (against Apel) Habermas means to show is that, although "a transcendental-pragmatic justification of the moral principle is in fact possible ['possible', in something like Kant's sense] . . . this justification of discourse ethics [Habermas's and Apel's moral program] cannot have the status of an ultimate justification and . . . there is no need to claim this status for it" (DE 82). This is meant to enable us to steer a middle course between the apriorists who claim that only "an ultimate justification" will do and the "skeptics"(Albert, the Popperians, and others who side with them) who claim that only "an ultimate justification" will do but that it cannot be supplied.

I shall come to Habermas's argument in a moment. But, by way of anticipating its inherent weakness—which, you remember, I offer as an instance of the general weakness of the pragmatist's "approximation" of apriorism (meaning, by that, to couple the characteristic strategies of Putnam and Habermas and to suggest the analogous weakness of theorists like MacIntyre and Rawls), all in the name of "moral optimism"—I break off here for a short detour before examining Rawls's recent (failed) attempt to extend his own account of "justice as fairness" in support of an "optimist's" defense of political liberalism.

My point is that the essential weakness of Rawls's new argument betrays the impossibility of approximating the apriorist's (or essentialist's) "ultimate justification" by less than apriorist (or essentialist) means, *and* that nothing less than such means *could* ensure *universally necessary* constraints on moral and practical conduct. Habermas is bent on supplying such (impossible) means. Watt's formula (which I shall look at very briefly) is instructive in this regard, because, following Collingwood, Watt does not deny the historical variety of discursive practices. Still, Watt argues *to* the "presuppositions of a mode of discourse" that he takes to yield invariant principles. Of this he says (Habermas quotes him):

[We are] to accept the skeptical conclusion that these principles are not open to any proof, being presuppositions of reasoning rather than conclusions from it, but to go on to argue that commitment to them is rationally inescapable because they must, logically, be assumed if one is to engage in a mode of thought essential to any rational human life. The claim is not exactly that the principles are *true*, [but] a mistake is involved in repudiating them while continuing to use the form of thought and discourse in question.[21]

In this, Watt shows Habermas the way to accept Albert's objection and to outflank him at the same time. But Watt *is* an apriorist. *He* holds that, whatever the contingent variety of discursive practices that obtain historically, there *are* universal principles "essential to any rational human life" that can be directly drawn from such variety. Habermas believes *he* can draw out what *is* universally binding in *our* "mode of discourse" without prejudging the import of the flux of discursive practices.

The claim is an interesting one; but you can see that it may be poised for self-destruction. In any case, it catches up the line of argument Habermas objects to in Apel. Habermas's thesis is that the skeptic (Albert) "can join the ranks . . . of the neo-Aristotelians and neo-Hegelians, who point out that discourse ethics does not represent much of a gain for the real concern of philosophical ethics, since discourse ethics offers at best an empty formalism whose practical consequences would even be disastrous." For his own part, he gamely insists—adopting the Hegelian thesis that "morality is always embedded in . . . ethical life (*Sittlichkeit*)"— that "discourse ethics is always subject to limitations [of determinate historical practice], though not limitations that can devalue its critical function or strengthen the skeptic in his role as an advocate of a counterenlightenment" (DE 98–99; see also 95–96).

What Habermas means is this: (i) there *are* universally necessary constraints on discourse ethics (and, presumably on the Peircean argument, on science as well); (ii) such constraints cannot (and need not) be "derived" in the a priori or essentialist manner, on pain of cognitive privilege, or of claiming what has already been discredited in Kant (as by Apel), or risking the formalism Hegel exposed, or falling victim to Albert's trilemma, or the like; and (iii) such constraints *can* be reclaimed pragmatically, by testing "counterexamples" drawn from actual discourse—by demonstrating "that there are no alternatives to the presuppositions [the champion of discourse ethics] has made explicit" (DE 97). My own charge is that that strategy won't work and that a scan of Rawls's analogous strategy shows us why it won't. (But bear in mind Habermas's wording: "there are no alternatives"; and compare Rawl's wording with Habermas's.)

IV

The failure of Rawls's project is entirely straightforward. It rests on a marvelously astute intuition of Rawls's about what he needs for his own project, what he must avoid if he is to avoid apriorism, essentialism, cognitive privilege of every sort, and what, also, he cannot successfully disjoin from what he must avoid. He begins by citing an imperious pronouncement of Bossuet's, viz.: "I have the right to persecute you because I am right and you are wrong."[22] Of course! Of such views, Rawls says:

> Since many doctrines are seen to be reasonable, those who insist, when fundamental political questions are at stake, on what they take as true but others do not, seem to others simply to insist on their own beliefs when they have the political power to do so. Of course, those who do insist on their beliefs also insist that their beliefs alone are true: they impose their beliefs because, they say, their beliefs are true and not because they are their beliefs. But this is a claim that all equally could make; it is also a claim that cannot be made good by anyone to citizens generally. So, when we make such claims others, who are themselves reasonable, must count us unreasonable. And indeed we are, as we want to use state power, the collective power of equal citizens, to prevent the rest from affirming their not unreasonable views.

Rawls's guiding political principle is this: "It is unreasonable for us to use political power, should we possess it, or share it with others, to repress comprehensive views that are not unreasonable" (PL 61). (I take this to be a version of the principle of sufficient reason.)

Now, I ask you: is Rawls's principle true (confirmable by some discerning power of reason) or (only) reasonable? If it is true, then Rawls is a Bossuetian and has contradicted himself. If it is reasonable but not true (not the sort of thing that could be straightforwardly true), then, *if it is indeed true that it is reasonable* (but not true), then Rawls is still a Bossuetian and has contradicted himself. And if it is reasonable and not true, and not even true that it is reasonable (that is, not true that it meets any valid criterion of what, in terms of rational or universal consensus, *is* [truly] reasonable), then Rawls is no more than a partisan or ideologue who happens to favor liberalism *but* cannot show, in any rational or reasonable way (except as an ideologue), that it *is* unreasonable to oppose his own conception of reasonableness or to "repress [what he claims] are comprehensive views that are not unreasonable." *If* this third alternative is coherent, or at least not "pragmatically" paradoxical or self-defeating, as charged, then both Apel and Habermas must be wrong in what *they* claim.

The third option does not violate Albert's trilemma, but it makes a much poorer thing of Rawls's theory than Rawls would be willing to accept.

The curious thing is that Rawls argues in a way that is not altogether distant from Habermas's strategy: his notion of "reflective equilibrium" is not at all "monologic," as Habermas insists, though it is certainly not "discursive" in Habermas's sense.[23] What I mean is this: there is no way to specify "reasonableness" *objectively*, if there are no objective moral truths about human life—either about what is universally necessary for (invariant) human *reason* (Kant) or for (invariant) human *nature* (Aristotle); both Rawls and Habermas (in their different ways) eschew the a priori claims of (pure) reason and the discovery of the essential requirements of the good life; and, in doing that, they each disqualify the possibility of *an objective reasonableness* that may be drawn out of the contingencies of social experience. If we can't know what is morally true in some realist or objectivist sense, then we cannot know what is *objectively reasonable* in the way of justice or a fair treatment of our fellows either. On the argument, both Rawls and Habermas are (however admirable) ideologues committed to a liberal policy that neither can show to be universally binding in any (now-) pragmatic sense in which societal life may be said to be organized in a morally appropriate way. (The problem is the same as Putnam's.)

The question Rawls poses at the start of *Political Liberalism* is this: "How is it possible that there may exist over time a stable and just society of free and equal citizens profoundly divided by reasonable though incompatible religious, philosophical, and moral doctrines?" (PL XVIII). Notice three features of this subtle question: first, Rawls *posits* the exclusive (liberal) objective of a constitutional society of "free and equal citizens," he does not "derive" the notion *as* a universally binding moral (or political) objective though he once supposed he had done so (in *A Theory of Justice*); second, he acknowledges that *that* citizens who are "free and equal" *may be* "divided by reasonable though incompatible . . . doctrines" is not, and cannot be judged, "unreasonable"; and, third, he raises the Kantian question about (the "possibility" of) *that* posit, *not* about what *is* universally or rationally binding in the moral or political way.

Now, Habermas seems to be committed to something like these same constraints, *in* that he repudiates Apel's apriorism and means to adhere to the painstaking practice of testing any and all "counterexamples" as they arise in a society's evolving experience. Fine. But he differs from Rawls in this: (a) he makes no preliminary posit of a liberal objective, he assumes he can draw his own version of such a doctrine ("discourse ethics") *as* universally necessary, *from* slimmer resources; and (b) he means to avoid the instant universalized rule Rawls aims for (Rawls's formalism, which would, in effect, be aprioristic if it were not ideological), by admitting that his own provisionally necessary rules are always at risk in the *next* emergent phase of communicative life.

I shall allow myself only two further remarks about Rawls's project. For one, Rawls tries, in leading us to the rules of liberal societies, to define what he means by "reasonable." He does not "define the reasonable directly [but, rather,] specif[ies] two of its basic aspects as virtues of persons": "Persons are reasonable in one basic aspect when, among equals say, they are ready to propose principles and standards as fair terms of cooperation and to abide by them willingly, given the assurance that others will likewise do so" (PL 48–49).

This must be construed in terms of what, earlier, I cited as Rawls's guiding political principle; in particular, the "reasonable" is meant to extend to "all [or at least part of all] recognized values and virtues within one rather precisely articulated system" (said, by Rawls, to be "fully comprehensive" or "partially comprehensive" [PL 13]). The latter distinction (a "precisely articulated system") cannot fail to affect the scope and viability of the "reasonable": which is to say, the "reasonable" cannot fail to be ideological; although Rawls means it to be relatively objective, universal, *and* binding within the liberal context. He also contrasts the "reasonable" and the "rational," meaning (by the latter) "a distinct idea from the reasonable," one that "applies to a single, united agent (either an individual or corporate person) with the powers of judgment and deliberation in seeking ends and interests peculiarly its own" (PL 50; Rawls takes the distinction to be close to Kant's).

The "second basic aspect" of the reasonable rests with "the willingness to recognize the burdens of judgment and to accept their consequences for the use of public reason in directing the legitimate exercise of political power in a way the rational is not" (PL 53–54). But that very "willingness" bears directly on the *aporiai* of liberalism which defeat the "possibility" of ever specifying the universally binding constraints *of* the liberal state *within* the posited boundaries of liberalism itself. Thus, consider one of the "burdens of judgment"—the one Rawls freely acknowledges, drawn from Isaiah Berlin. Berlin affirms compellingly: "Some among the Great Goods cannot live together. That is a conceptual truth. We are doomed to choose, and every choice may entail an irreparable loss."[24] If I understand the matter rightly, this means that the "reasonable" can *never* be objectively discerned as universally binding; it can only be convenient or fortunate for those involved. It can never be categorically necessary, or such that its rejection yields a self-defeating paradox.[25] To move at once to the inference I want: Habermas cannot possibly escape a similar verdict.

V

I now turn to Habermas's strategy. The decisive thing is to locate Habermas's distinctive legitimative program. It is not like Apel's search for "ultimate justification," so it is not aprioristic or cognitively privileged. On the other hand, it is not concerned with merely escaping contingent contradictions, contingent paradoxes, or contingent incoherences. I can offer you a pretty example of what Habermas has no interest in, in developing the second possibility. Habermas himself is clear about the matter, for he cites, approvingly, G. Schönrich's conditional criticism of P.F. Strawson's philosophical method—that is, *if* Strawson's method *were* to be offered in the way of yielding a priori truths about an inescapable conceptual scheme. Schönrich says that it would be impossible for Strawson to reach any such finding, "since it is in principle an open question whether the subjects of cognition will change their way of thinking about the world [so as to depart from Strawson's schema] at some point or not" (DE 95–96). Schönrich is right—and the point is apt: Strawson's metaphysics is hardly unavoidable.

I have myself elsewhere argued that Strawson's account of "basic particulars" happens to be incoherent (but not because Strawson presumes his metaphysics to be ineluctable). It fails simply because, on the theory, persons and physical bodies are both "basic particulars" (hence, not proper parts of one another); and yet Strawson holds that, as a rule, only one individual thing (that is not a part of another) can occupy one place in the real world at any given time. Necessarily, on the thesis, a person and a physical body *may* and *can*, contrary to what Strawson says, occupy the selfsame place. There is no logical "out." But there is also no universally necessary reason why two distinct individual things could not (be admitted to be able to) occupy the same place.[26] Habermas is right to ignore the matter, but it affects his own argument in the deepest way. For he too needs a "sufficient reason" for holding that changes in "our way of thinking" will not undermine our would-be rational principles.

What *Habermas* is bent on identifying are what he sometimes calls "performative contradictions," which are meant to explicate the following programmatic desideratum, viz.: "the identification of pragmatic presuppositions of argumentation that are inescapable and have a normative content" (DE 96–97). (Strawson's claim, therefore, could not possibly serve as a reassuring exemplar. I contend that nothing can.)

Habermas offers little in the way of explanation in his own voice, but we can work well enough with what he says. For one thing, the new formulation is meant to replace his earlier search for the lineaments of "an ideal speech situation." He still believes his earlier "intention" was "correct": "the reconstruction of the general symmetry conditions that every competent speaker who believes he is engaging in an argumentation must presuppose as adequately fulfilled." This notion leads to various schemes of "communication rules" at various levels of intervention— where enabling provisions are supplied for ruling "out all external or internal coercion other than the force of the better argument and thereby also neutralize all motives other than that of the cooperative search for truth."[27] (We must bear in mind, of course, that "uncoerced" agreement can be discerned only relative to the "coercion" of one's *Lebensform*. This is as true for the "optimisms" of Putnam, Rawls, Kuhn, Popper, and Habermas as it is for Peirce. That is, the meaning of "coercion" is itself an artifact formed within our own enabling *Lebensform*.)

The vision is a noble one. No doubt about it. But it takes only a moment to grasp the sense in which Habermas's program is a fair analogue of Rawls's search for the conditions of reasonableness. Thus, *if* there are no definable rules by which the "truth" may be discerned—or approximatively approached by progressive or self-corrective measures (recall the collapse of Putnam's program!)—and if, for most complex (nondeductive) arguments, there is no rule for determining "the force of the better argument," then the entire project must fail. Furthermore, there *is* no compelling sense in which, lacking such rules or acting contrary to any sincerely posited candidate rules, communication need utterly fail, or need fail to produce results that may count as an improvement on earlier claims and beliefs.[28]

In fact, the usual paradigms of "performative contradiction" are surely no more than hothouse cases or profoundly problematic. Apel, whom Habermas follows here, offers, as exemplars, the "denial" of the cogito and the self-refuting "arguments" of the skeptic.[29] I don't deny that, on Apel's (and Habermas's) reading, the Cartesian doubter and the Popperian skeptic "contradict" themselves "pragmatically"; but I see no reason to suppose that those famous puzzles need be construed in just the fortunate way Apel foists on us. (I see a rather close parallel, here, with Kant's notorious account of the incoherence of the would-be rational suicide.)

Consider some of the would-be pragmatic rules. Habermas reviews a list of "presuppositions of argumentation" offered by Robert Alexy, which he says operate on various levels. (Alexy addresses the "Münchhausen trilemma" in a way congenial to Apel's and Habermas's general outlook.[30]) The following is a fine specimen:

> 1.2 Every speaker who applies predicate F to object A must be prepared to apply F to all other objects resembling A in all relevant respects. (DE 87)

Now, this is surely a vacuous rule; also, a perniciously misleading one. Yet it seems innocuous enough. For, consider that to be properly eligible for "predicate F" means nothing more than to "resemble A in all relevant respects." The trouble is—this is what is pernicious, not merely vacuous—there is no reliable rule for determining *when* particular things resemble one another in "all relevant respects." There is no known algorithmic solution to the problem of "real generals."[31] Rule 1.2 either has no ethical import or has ethical import on something like Peirce's view that logic is an ethical science. But what of

> 2.1 Every speaker may assert only what he really believes. (DE 87)

Surely, there is no way of ensuring the pragmatic necessity of 2.1, unless one falls back to Kant's view of pure practical reason. It may be an ingredient in an "ideal speech situation"; but then, this single instance confirms the divergence between such a vision and pragmatically necessary performative rules of discourse.

Alexy goes on—apparently Habermas approves:

> 3.1 Every subject with the competence to speak and act is allowed to take part in a discourse

and

> 3.2 Everyone is allowed to question any assertion whatever. (DE 89)

Here, of course, the aporia that Rawls inadvertently concedes (while deliberately recognizing the fairness of Isaiah Berlin's "burden" on moral and political judgment) surfaces in a new and troubling guise. For, surely, 3.2 is preposterous in real-time terms and 3.1 is clearly open to the worst possible abuse. (The numbering, I may say, is intended to convey the sense [drawn from Alexy] that Habermas has surveyed the principal runs of pertinent questions affecting the pragmatics of discourse [DE 86–89].) Alexy himself goes on blithely enough; for instance, to

> 5.2.1 The moral rules that form the basis of the moral conceptions of the speakers must be able to withstand scrutiny in a critical, historical genesis;
> 5.2.2 The moral rules that form the basis of the moral conceptions of the speakers must be able to withstand the scrutiny of their individual history of emergence;

and

> 5.3 The factually given limits of realizability are to be observed.[32]

Rule 5.3 means that where debate has a practical payoff, one may have to act without having arrived at an entirely satisfactory solution. (This is a reasonable companion to Berlin's aporia, *not* a universal principle reliably operative in the liberal context.) The other two rules presuppose that the "rational justification" of moral norms *is* possible and that the contingencies of history must be assessed and, where necessary, discounted. (None of this is explained or vindicated.)

I therefore conclude, without further ceremony, that the whole idea of arriving at universally necessary or categorical constraints of reasonableness or of the pragmatics of discourse or of anything of the kind, *without the presumption of a priori or privileged cognitive resources,* is utterly without merit. I cannot say this forcefully enough: it is what I take "moral optimism" to entail. I see no possible escape. Very few philosophers, of course, now presume to recover any form of cognitive privilege. No known attempt is compelling or even promising. A fortiori, no moral optimism, having weakened our cognitive resources, could hope to remedy that loss by "pragmatic" means.

Pragmatism is the philosophical scruple of pursuing legitimative questions under cognitive resources no longer privileged in any way. "Moral optimism" is its immediate casualty among pragmatists and non-pragmatists alike who attempt to reclaim older normative assurances no longer viable. It has a wider application, of course, for instance in subverting all those philosophical strategies that, more or less in sympathy with W.V. Quine's "Epistemology Naturalized,"[33] are now called "naturalistic" or "naturalizing." I say only that "naturalizing" is, in a deep sense, the reverse of "optimism": optimism illicitly recovers the privileged claims of an older stratum of philosophical confidence; naturalism pretends to be able to gain valid results without legitimative resources of the relevant sort. There are pragmatists of both kinds, as you may imagine. But the best philosophical path lies between the two: lies with the reconceptualization of all the standard questions under epistemically reduced conditions. The defeat of moral optimism without disallowing second-order moral questions points the way.

4

More Hegelian Doubts about Discourse Ethics

Tom Rockmore

The longstanding, implicit ethical motivation of philosophy in general is manifest in the ongoing effort to work out a viable theory of ethics. Recently, the issue has been joined in a triangular debate between neo-Aristotelians, or communitarians like Sandel and neo-Thomists like MacIntyre, neo-Kantian cognitivists, and skeptics. In Germany, in related ways Karl-Otto Apel and Jürgen Habermas have been trying to reformulate an acceptable version of Kantian cognitivism, Apel through a foundationalist program and Habermas through a nonfoundationalist theory of discourse ethics intended, as he says, to reach Hegelian goals with Kantian means.[1] This paper will examine Habermas's project in the light of this stated intention.

I The Ethical Inspiration of Philosophy

Habermas's theory is motivated by the traditional philosophical concern with practically relevant theory that has been raised again in a forceful manner in response to the events in our troubled time. The widespread failure of intellectuals to act in responsible ways casts doubt on the traditional notion of intellectual responsibility.[2] In principle, intellectuals have a comparative advantage in discerning the true, and knowing the true and doing the good are inseparably linked. Yet this dual conviction is severely challenged by the attraction of such major philosophical thinkers as Heidegger to Nazism[3] and Lukács to Stalinism. If we simply judge by the results, it is unclear how we can continue to make unrestricted claims for the social usefulness of even the most brilliant intellectuals. For their own actions in the deepest crises of our time call into question the fabled link between the true and the good and even their very capacity to discern the true.

The resultant crisis in the notion of intellectual responsibility tends to obscure the consistently ethical impulse intrinsic to philosophy. The very early, pre-Socratic cosmological speculations are not ethical or at least not clearly ethical at all. But at least since Socrates, the ethical theme, widely conceived, has never been absent from later philosophy. The Socratic claim that the unexamined life is not worth living was immediately transformed into the Platonic claim that philosophy is the condition of the good life that runs throughout later philosophical theory. This theme is powerfully restated in Kant's unsupported affirmation that critical philosophy, centered on pure reason, is intrinsically concerned with the ends of human being. It is restated for our time from a post-Kantian phenomenological perspective by Husserl and Heidegger, in the former's insistence on transcendental phenomenology as the defense of socially-indispensable reason and in the later Heidegger's claim that thinking beyond philosophy is equally indispensable.

Habermas's concern with ethics follows from his earlier interest, from the Marxist angle of vision, in the link of theory to social practice. Habermas began as a second-generation member of the Frankfurt School variety of neo-Marxism. He later left that behind in a qualified return to Kant. His early work within the framework of the Frankfurt School presupposes the distinction between traditional and critical theory that is never wholly absent from his later work. As originally drawn by Horkheimer, this distinction separates roughly between forms of theory that are socially irrelevant and socially relevant.[4] According to critical social theorists, traditional theory raises unsustainable claims for the socially indispensable nature of philosophy that go back in the tradition at least to Plato. With respect to Kant, critical theory can be regarded as attempting to make good on the Kantian claim for the intrinsic social relevance of a pure theory that is intrinsically practical.

Habermas's writing combines a continued interest in the concerns of critical theory that he seeks to realize through a qualified return to Kant. Although Habermas has since abandoned the effort to formulate the promise of socially useful theory from the Marxist angle of vision, however conceived, he is still committed to the reconstruction of theory that can do so from a neo-Kantian perspective. The considerable interest of his more recent effort to formulate a theory of discourse ethics lies in the implicit promise, not only to answer Hegel's objections to Kant, but also to redeem the promissory note of theory, in the Kantian sense, as intrinsically practical.

II On the Background of Habermas's Ethical Theory

A view of ethics developed in isolation from more general considerations stands or falls on its own merits whereas the difficulties of a view that depends on a wider theoretical framework reflect back on it. Rawls,[5] to whom Habermas is in part responding in his ethical theory,[6] is typical in this regard. In writing since his monumental *Theory of Justice*, Rawls specifically insists on the importance of eschewing wider considerations in order to formulate a minimal framework for politics in independence of any overarching theoretical commitment.[7] In that sense, he resembles many other writers on ethics in English, who concentrate mainly or even wholly on the ethical problems in isolation from more general considerations. On the contrary, European thinkers, like their Greek predecessors, more often tend to derive their specifically ethical views from more general theories.

Like Kant's moral theory, Habermas's theory of discourse ethics is not autonomous but rather follows from his wider theory. To grasp Habermas's turn to ethical cognitivism, it is useful to say a few words about the origins of his theory. Habermas's neo-Kantian approach to ethics is consistent with his diagnosis, attempted reformulation, and finally his rejection of Marx and Marxism. Marx is a contextualist. Habermas's retreat from historical materialism over Hegel toward Kant presupposes a turn from contextualism to anti-contextualism that is presupposd in his theory of discourse ethics.

Habermas's complex intellectual itinerary reflects the political reality of his life and times. Born in 1929, he was a teenager at the end of the Second World War. When he began to publish in the early 1950s, in Europe Hegelian Marxism was thought of as representing a viable political alternative that later crystallized under the heading of Marxist humanism. This political commitment was widely attractive to intellectuals in France until the student revolt in 1968.

Habermas's retreat from Marxism parallels the retreat of so many other intellectuals from social commitment to a more neutral theoretical level following the discouragement about the real possibilities for practical political engagement. As the political facts about so-called real socialism became increasingly known, an increasing disillusion with this practical alternative affected European intellectuals in general. Merleau-Ponty is a typical example. After his early commitment to Marxism, in which he tolerated a certain terrorism on the basis of humanism,[8] he began to judge it more critically in terms of its practice.[9]

In Habermas's writings, this disillusion is apparent in a gradual retreat from the neo-Marxism of the Frankfurt School, his first intellectual home, toward a particularly austere form of neo-Kantianism. Habermas's retreat from Marxism parallels the retreat of so many other intellectuals from practical commitment, linked to the optimism about broadly left wing Hegelian Marxism following the end of the Second World War, to a more neutral theoretical level following the discouragement about the real possibilities for practical political engagement. His later writings exhibit few obvious remaining links to Marxism other than the residual concern, also illustrated by many more standard types of philosophy, for instance Kant and Hegel, with the general issue of the link between theory and practice.

As befits a social theorist, Habermas's concern with the link of theory to practice has always been rather theoretical. His early work, roughly until the end of the 1980s, was closely linked to his effort to provide an intellectually viable form of what he called historical materialism, a term he applied indiscriminately to Marx and Marxism, whose views he tended to conflate.[10] The evolution of his theory, at least until the *On the Reconstruction of Historical Materialism* [1976],[11] is directed toward the reformulation of that Marx and Marxism as a putative alternative to traditional theory, the same project that underlies the work of the Frankfurt School variant of neo-Marxism.

Among students of Marx and Marxism, Habermas is distinguished by the epistemological thrust of his writings. With the obvious exception of Georg Lukács, probably the most important Marxist philosopher,[12] most of the main students in this field are mainly content to make claims for Marx and Marxism that they do not attempt to defend. Most students of Marxism are largely ignorant of classical German philosophy, including Hegel's theory, to which they relate Marx's theory. In this respect, Lukács is an obvious exception. He advances a complicated argument for Marxism based on a highly original, but also flawed reading of Kant's thing-in-itself as representing a problem that cannot be resolved within the framework of German idealism. According to Lukács, whose closely follows Engels, a solution to the problem of classical German philosophy requires a transition from idealism to materialism, from philosophy to Marxist science.

Habermas differs from Lukács in eschewing Marxist arguments in order to apply the usual standards of epistemology in the broad sense to Marx and Marxism. His original diagnosis of what he regards as the epistemological deficit of historical materialism can be paraphrased as the claim that Marx's theory is self-referentially inconsistent since it fails to consider the conditions of its own possibility. This leads to a crucial distinction, presupposed in all his later thought, initially between work and interaction,[13] later reformulated as a distinction between work and communication, intended to recover the reflexive dimension. Habermas's own later theories of communicative action and discourse ethics presuppose this distinction that enjoys a dual role as the corrective to historical materialism and as the basis of his own replacement for that theory.

III A Sketch of Discourse Ethics

Habermas's theory of discourse ethics has emerged in a series of papers in recent years in the wake of his efforts to extend his theory of communicative action. The most important statement so far is in a lengthy paper entitled "Discourse Ethics: Notes on a Program of Philosophical Justification" (MCCA 116–94). This discussion has been subsequently clarified in another, equally lengthy paper: "Remarks on Discourse Ethics."[14] Yet although Habermas has repeatedly tried to explain his view and to deflect criticism of it, the impression remains that much still needs to be done.

In part because of Habermas's difficulty in stating his theory in clear, simple terms, and in part because of what sometimes seems to be a tendency to refer to nearly every possible book or article in the literature, it is difficult to grasp even the basic moves in Habermas's theory. The result is a series of statements that leaves the reader unsure of what Habermas is ruling in or ruling out. Even the main contours of his position remain unclear in the series of references to a bewildering series of theories that tends to replace detailed or even careful exposition of the basic concepts.

Consider the following typical, lengthy passage in which he depicts discourse ethics as an alternative to Aristotelian ethics and utilitarianism while making good on Kantian moral theory:

> . . . discourse ethics takes its orientation from an intersubjective interpretation of the categorial imperative from Hegel's theory of recognition but without incurring the cost of a historical *dissolution* of morality in ethical life. Like Hegel it insists, though in a Kantian spirit, on the internal relation between justice and solidarity. It attempts to show that the meaning of the basic principle of morality can be explicated in terms

of the content of the unavoidable presuppositions of an argumentative practice that can be pursued only in common with others. The moral point of view from which we can judge practical questions impartially is indeed open to different interpretations. But because it is grounded in the communicative structure of rational discourse as such, we cannot simply dispose of it at will. It forces itself intuitively on anyone who is at all open to this reflective form of communicative action. With this fundamental assumption, discourse ethics situates itself squarely in the Kantian tradition yet without leaving itself vulnerable to the objections with which the abstract ethics of conviction has met from its inception. Admittedly, it adopts a narrowly circumscribed conception of morality that focuses on questions of justice. But it neither has to neglect the calculation of the consequences of actions rightly emphasized by utilitarianism nor exclude from the sphere of discursive problematization the questions of the good life accorded prominence by classical ethics, abandoning them to irrational emotional dispositions or decisions. (JA 1–2)

This passage reads more like a series of conclusions than a careful description of the theory itself. Yet in the mass of verbiage, at least three things are clear. First, it is apparent that Habermas means to engage the current alternatives as well as the entire prior philosophical discussion of ethics. Second, at least in principle we understood his intention to defend morality against ethics, or Kant against Hegel, while analyzing justice from the moral perspective in a manner that remains socially useful. Third, according to Habermas in some undetermined manner we can derive a theory of ethics on the basis of the presuppositions of discussion in general.

In Habermas's most detailed statement of discourse ethics to date, he typically begins by posing his theory as an alternative to Alasdair MacIntyre's neo-Aristotelian position. Habermas, who seems to have *After Virtue* in mind,[15] simply ignores the concern with religion and religious philosophy, specifically with Thomism, that has become central to MacIntyre's recent writing,[16] which he regards as an effort to extract a universal core from the Aristotelian concept of praxis. For Habermas, this effort must fail for two reasons. On the one hand, something like the *polis* can no longer respond to the pluralism of modern life. On the other, although universal assent can be secured through what he calls rational will formation, philosophy can no longer attempt to decide the substantive questions of justice or an authentic life (JA 150, 176).

In previous writings, Habermas stresses the importance of completing what he regards as the unfinished project of modernity, understood as a view of autonomous reason that peaks in Kant's critical philosophy.[17]

Following this line of argument, Habermas opposes his theory to Mac-Intyre's view that the Enlightenment project of a secular moral theory devoid of metaphysical and religious assumptions has failed (MCCA 43). He aims to make good on this project by following the cognitivist line of argument leading away from Kant according to which "practical questions admit of truth" (MCCA 57). He associates this task with the work of such others as Kurt Baier, Marcus Singer, John Rawls, Paul Lorenzen, Ernst Tügendhat, and Karl-Otto Apel. Yet certainly this generalization is false for Rawls, who bases his theory of justice on consensus, while eschewing the further step, essential to Habermas's view, that consensus yields truth.

Habermas's discussion, which is broken down into three main divisions, includes a series of propadeutic remarks to defend the neo-Kantian cognitive approach he favors against value skepticism, an account of universalization as a rule of argumentation intended to make agreement possible in moral argumentation, and an analysis of the bases of discourse ethics in action theory. The discussion of value skepticism is intended to allay skeptical doubts about the cognitivist program that assumes the objective decidability of questions of value. In this respect, Habermas seems close to the Kantian view that ethics is a science yielding objective, in Kant's terms apodictic, knowledge.[18]

The review of value skepticism rests on the cognitivist insight, underlying Habermas's approach, of an analogy between normative claims to validity and truth claims (MCCA 56) that is basic to the Kantian approach. For Habermas as for Kant, good actions depend on true choices since, following a line of argument that goes back to the ancient Greeks, the good follows literally from the true. The problem is how to arrive at moral truth. In place of the monological approach of the categorical imperative, Habermas invokes a plural subject intended to make moral argumentation and agreement possible (MCCA 57). He rejects the Kantian procedure that relies on the conception of the categorical imperative on the grounds that at this late date truth is the result of a cooperative endeavor, as in Peirce's view that truth is what the community of informed observers tells us it is. In his revised form of universalization, the universal will toward which Kant aims is captured in the general acceptance of "the consequences and the side effects it [i. e. every valid norm] can be anticipated to have . . ." (MCCA 63). It follows that only such norms are valid upon which the participants in the discussion can agree (MCCA 64). Hence, Habermas assumes that intersubjective discussion can yield valid norms.[19] But he disclaims anything like Apel's effort at ultimate justification (MCCA 77, 82–98) and reiterates his conviction that moral questions yield to rational decision procedures based on discussion.

iv More Hegelian Doubts about Discourse Ethics

It is obvious that Habermas's theory of discourse ethics depends on a theory of practical reason. The conception of reason that is a red thread in the German idealist tradition from Kant to Hegel, including later Marx, is central to an understanding of Habermas's ethical theory. One of the immediate results of the great French Revolution was the philosophical realization that human reason needs to be understood from a historical angle of vision, as rooted, according to Hegel, in the historical moment, in short from a contextual angle of vision.

Habermas's ethical theory can be understood in the first instance through the alternative between contextualism and anticontextualism. Hegel's critique of Kantian morality results in a move from anticontextualism to contextualism that is reversed in Habermas's neo-Kantian theory of discourse ethics. In his retreat from Marx and Marxism toward Kant, Habermas moves from the postrevolutionary approach to reason in context, as in the Hegelian view of spirit, toward a quasi-Kantian, prerevolutionary view of reason as wholly undetermined and decontextualized, reason as devoid of context. His cognitivist view of ethics is possible only from something like a Kantian view of reason. Like Kant, Habermas bases his view of right action in a theory of pure practical reason, or pure reason that is intended to be practical.

In his discussion, Habermas tries to counter doubts from the perspectives of communitarianism, skepticism, and Hegelianism. The most interesting objections for his theory and for his theoretical trajectory come from the Hegelian side. Hegel is known for his sharp critique of Kantian morality. There is probably no criticism raised against Kant's theory of morality since Hegel that is not anticipated in the latter's discussion of the Kantian moral theory.

Habermas's view raises questions on a number of distinct levels concerning its resistance to Hegelian criticism and its ability to reach Hegelian goals with Kantian means. The first step is to clarify the discussion beyond the stage reached in Habermas's texts. Although he proclaims his intention of reaching Hegel's goals, he never goes so far as describing them. For our purposes we shall construe these, following Ritter,[20] as destroying the illusion of the sufficiency of subjective morality and of incorporating morality and ethical life within right that is the foundation of ethical life. It will suffice to recall that Hegel insists that the system of right, or the legal framework of society, makes possible the actualization of the free will. According to Hegel, the freedom of the will, presupposed in morality, is only realized in ethical life within the wider legal context.[21]

Hegel's critique of Kant turns on his preference for spirit, or a thicker view of reason, over the very thin Kantian conception of pure reason that is central to the latter's moral theory. For Hegel, pure reason is not practically relevant, inadequate as a guide to the good life; for only reason that is located in the social context, or spirit, remains linked to it. Habermas's response is in effect an argument that a version of the thin Kantian view of reason, or reason as divorced from context, is adequate as a guide to moral action in a modern version of the good life.

If Hegel is correct, then a moral theory of the Kantian type is not practically useful. Habermas is aware of the need to respond to Hegel's critique of Kant in order to make good on the Kantian project. He takes up possible Hegelian doubts in a special discussion that in in effect concedes all the Hegelian criticisms of Kant while asserting that his own theory is immune to them. Hegel, as Habermas points out, opposes both abstract concepts of justice and individualism in his view of ethical life. A constant theme, present even in Habermas's principle of universalization, is that we can and must be attentive to possible consequences in the process of coming to agreement. Yet this very un-Kantian move, necessary to deflect the force of Hegelian critique directed against any claims for the utility of a cognitive approach to morality apart from and prior to experience, implies that, despite Habermas's explicit claim, the revised theory is finally not very Kantian at all.

v The Cognitive Approach to Morality

As concerns Habermas's discourse theory of ethics, special attention should be paid to his cognitive approach to morality and the consensus theory of truth it presupposes. Discourse ethics, Habermas claims, "stands or falls" on the twin assumptions that "normative claims to validity have cognitive meaning and can be treated *like* claims to truth" and that "the justification of norms and commands requires that a real discourse be carried out and thus cannot occur in a strictly monological form" (MCCA 68). Both assumptions are doubtful.

Habermas's choice of language is unfortunate. He does not clarify but only blurs the relevant issue in stating that normative claims must be able to be treated, as he says, like claims to truth. It is not clear what he is saying. Everything hinges on the meaning of the word "like" in this context. Either normative claims are or they are not truth claims. The concept of a quasi-truth claim is difficult to evaluate since it is unclear what is at stake.

If normative claims are truth claims, then we require an acceptable decision procedure to justify norms submitted to the process of justification. Kant, whom Habermas has in mind, makes a stronger claim than Habermas in holding that universalizable principles of action are not only justified but in fact true. For Kant, to be true means to be universal and necessary. If a principle of action, or maxim, is universal and necessary, then it can be regarded as and in fact is true from the Kantian perspective.

Kant's cognitivism in ethical matters is based on his normative view of knowledge as requiring universality and necessity and on his related view that practical theory requires knowledge. The latter follows from an analogy between physics and ethics, or natural and moral philosophy, two sciences which, Kant holds, must respectively yield laws of nature and freedom.[22] If ethics is like physics, then there must be laws governing the ethical realm just as there are laws governing the natural realm. The problem is to derive such laws through the principle of universalizability.

Kant's view of law is at least questionable. If the analogy between physics and ethics holds, then we can assume that there is a single set of ethical principles in the same way as there is a single set of physical laws. Kant never considers the possibility that there could be two or more different laws with respect to the same set of objects, or at least two different, equally valid interpretations of the same set of phenomena, for instance the wave and the corpuscular views of light. If that is the case, then even nature can have more than one series of natural laws.

The case is certainly more complicated for the moral domain where conflicting intuitions, based on different backgrounds, hold sway. Kant assumes but never actually shows that moral questions yield to a cognitive approach. If there were more than one possible universalizable principle of action, then mere universalizability would be insufficient to provide moral knowledge. Or, to put the point differently, there could be more than one way to analyze the same case, more than one candidate for moral knowledge. It is not difficult to find counterexamples that undermine the idea of a univocal analysis yielding moral knowledge in the Kantian sense. An instance is a situation in which the possibility of lying is rejected on the grounds that lying is never correct and embraced on the grounds that there is a further good to be attained that is more important than the lie itself. This is an illustration of a standard objection to the Kantian moral theory, according to which there can be no univocal analysis of concrete cases. For as in the example proposed, scrutiny of moral situations from different points of view yields different results.

If Habermas were to answer Hegel's doubts about Kant in his own theory, then he would need to provide a full list of them. Habermas's limited catalogue of Hegelian complaints is actually too limited. In the *Phenomenology of Spirit*, Hegel, who criticizes virtue ethics as well, raises precisely this objection against moral cognitivism in his remarks on "Reason as lawgiver" and "Reason as testing laws." Hegel's point is not only that the attempted general laws are empty, since they apply equally well to all cases, but that each any law is as good as any other law. "The criterion of law which Reason possesses within itself fits every case equally well, and is thus no criterion at all."[23]

Habermas, who does not consider this Hegelian objection, can only meet it in part. Unlike Kant, the deontologist, who is unconcerned with consequences, moral claims are not empty since he builds them into the problem of universalizability. For Habermas, those affected must consider the direct and indirect effects of adopting different norms (MCCA 65). Yet attending to consequences does not handle the further problem of the different perspectives from which an analysis can be carried out. Different perspectives can be either hermeneutical, following from genuine disagreements about how to understand the particular situation, or valuational, concerning the evaluation of relative consequences. In either case, they raise difficulties for the cognitive approach to ethics, which is result-oriented as a condition of action. This general problem can in practice be overcome through abstracting from the particular circumstances, as Kant does. Yet this approach has the disagreeable result, discerned by Hegel, that the resultant theory applies to no particular case or to all in the same way.

VI Consensus As a Criterion

In his moral theory, Kant rests his case on the rational action of the isolated subject that generalizes the principle guiding action prior to so acting. In abandoning the monological Kantian procedure, Habermas hopes to ground the cognitive approach to ethics in his consensus theory of truth, where rational consensus replaces the categorical imperative. The idea of consensus is a basic feature in social contractarian forms of political theory from Rousseau to Rawls. Rousseau's idea of the general will, which underlies Kant's categorical imperative as valid for everyone, finds a distant echo in Rawls's notion of an overlapping consensus meant to found the minimal political framework.

Following Rousseau, who holds that the universal will is always right, Kant justifies the principle, or maxim of an action, on the grounds of its universalizability. If an idea is universal, if it potentially applies to everyone, then it should be acceptable to all rational beings as a principle of action. Yet since the Kantian procedure is concerned with what is right, not with what is useful, it wholly disregards possible consequences.

This is the basis of Hegel's complaint against Kant, which can be roughly paraphrased as the observation that what is right, or morally correct, is only incidentally useful. Aware of this objection, Habermas in turn recasts right as useful in a quasi-utilitarian manner in his idea that we can agree on norms as valid if and only if they can be accepted as such by others concerned with consequences of all types. In other words, his theory relies on rational consensus from a utiliarian perspective for its decision procedure.

For Habermas, consensus is basic to his view of discourse ethics. Now consensus is a problematic concept, especially as the basis of an ethical theory. In an important book, Nicholas Rescher has recently criticized consensus from the angle of vision of democratic pluralism. He argues strongly, correctly in my view, that consensus is at best one factor in determining how to act.[24] Certainly, the idea of political consensus at any cost opens the door to forced consensus, even totalitarianism, and appears to deny the very possibility of legitimate dissent that seems to become inconceivable and certainly undesirable. Orwell and the very real forms of totalitarianism in our own troubled century speak in different, equally powerful ways to the dangers of enforced consensus in politics, science, and other areas of life.

The alternative is consensus that is freely obtained, hence unconstrained. Yet it may simply be unavailing to hope that consensus can in practice be freely achieved. To see this point, we need look no further than the intellectual tradition. Intellectual inquiry occurs in a process of debate that, reputedly like psychoanalytic treatment, is intrinsically interminable. There is no reason to hold that it will lead either soon or ever to a final conclusion, acceptable to all parties. It is not irrational, but rational, not an illustration of bad faith but an illustration of good faith, to continue to disagree, even on fundamental matters, since the various discussants judge from differing, different, often incompatible points of view. In the intellectual arena, disagreement is not abnormal but normal. In fact, to the extent that further progress through debate is possible at all, it presupposes disagreement among the parties to the discussion. Now if Habermas were correct, then we should expect that a consensus would form about the correctness of his theory. Yet that is hardly likely and no one, not even he expects it.

In a wide variety of fields, consensus is simply not a meaningful criterion. Certainly, there is no consensus in literary criticism, or poetry, or in philosophy. Peirce argues for consensus among informed observers as the operational criterion of what is considered to be true at a given moment. Yet even physics, now often taken as the standard of what is true, as in the writings of the Vienna Circle, tends to tolerate a fair amount of disagreement, for instance in the debate about the interpretation of quantum mechanics. Kuhn has shown that scientific consensus is unstable, and gives way from time to time to a new consensus.[25] Fleck has further shown that at least in science, what appears to be consensus is based on factors that are not and cannot be made wholly rational.[26]

It is at least arguable that a lack of consensus in the academy as well as in the political arena is more useful than its achievement. J. S. Mill argues cogently that a society that contains different, conflicting points of view is better off for it. Discussion that would not otherwise terminate in agreement tends to be richer for the disagreement. Research on different theories, particularly the kind that challenge basic assumptions, advances the discussion.

VII Rational Consensus and Cognitive Truth

There is a further problem in the presupposed link between rational consensus and truth. The association of consensus and claims to truth goes back in the tradition to Socrates' dialogical practice. Socrates simply presupposes that through unconstrained discussion, constrained only by reason, the discussants can and do arrive at the truth.

This idea is highly problematic. There is probably no substitute for free and fair discussion. But while we may choose, perhaps must choose, to take such discussion as the acceptable framework for arriving at truth, it is a significant error to equate agreement with truth. In the history of philosophy, as in other disciplines, there have been times when a large consensus temporarily formed around the claims of a particular theory only later to dissolve. This phenomenon is even more common in the political arena. National Socialism came to power in Germany through a democratic election. The communists won the free election in Czechoslovakia in 1948. At one time there was a wide consensus about the wisdom of the American intervention in Vietnam. The widespread phenomenon of the development and then later disappearance of a consensus is sufficient to alert us to the perils of conflating the certainty arising from agreement among some or all concerned with truth.

It is questionable to correlate truth and consensus in more than an accidental sense. It is fairly obvious, since there can be a consensus without truth and truth without consensus, that consensus and truth are unrelated. Later writers tend to take a more cautious view of the cognitive claims of consensus. Peirce's pragmatic view that truth is what the informed community of scientists agree on acknowledges that we can never assume that our current beliefs are not subject to further revision. This doesn't prevent us from employing some kind of community standard for justifying our claims, such as relying on science, as Sellars and then Davidson recommend, against folk science. But it does prevent us from claiming that consensus of any kind is more than a justification as opposed to a valid truth claim, where a truth claim refers to claims that something is true without limit.

Yet even if we concede that the social process of discussion is not necessarily productive of truth, Habermas's theory is in trouble. Rawls's well-known theory of justice as fairness presupposes an overlapping consensus that, since it already tacitly exists among members of a pluralistic, democratic society, simply needs to be uncovered. Habermas has a very different form of consensus in mind that does not already exist but must rather be produced. But, as the current debate about universal health reminds us, there is simply no reason to hold that consensus can ever be produced on fundamental issues.

Habermas indicates his desire to limit the scope of discourse ethics, as he says, to "narrowly circumscribed questions of morality that focuses on questions of justice" (JA 2). Yet in a democratic political system—where issues cannot simply be decided on political grounds, although political, even ideological considerations are probably never absent—discussions about basic issues, particularly issues of justice, tend to be protracted, even intractable. In practice, the kind of narrowly circumscribed questions of morality focusing on justice that Habermas targets cannot simply be decided by rational debate. A recent instance among many is the ongoing debate about a woman's access to abortion, which some regard as a basic, fundamental right, on a par with, say, freedom of speech, and others view as equivalent to murder.

Consensus is not easier to reach in the legal arena than elsewhere. Often, the Supreme Court, Congress, and the President disagree on a particular issue. The Supreme Court of the United States is concerned with interpreting the United States Constitution in a debate that has already lasted more than two centuries and the end is not in sight. Although a consensus is occasionally reached on a particular issue, even that is subject to revision as the composition of the Court changes. To put the point bluntly, there has never been and probably never will be a so-called rational consensus concerning such questions.

VIII On Habermas's Self-misunderstanding of the Kantian Nature of Discourse Ethics

Habermas's announced effort to redeem Hegel's intentions with Kantian means suggests both that his own theory is Kantian in certain relevant ways and that it attains Hegel's goals in ways different from Hegel's theory. This claim is doubly doubtful. Habermas seems to be laboring under a self-misunderstanding about the nature of his theory that is mainly Kantian in name only. It is obviously Kantian with respect to the broadly cognitive approach to morality as part of the wider problem of knowledge. Yet the non-Kantian, even anti-Kantian aspects of discourse ethics, beginning with its name, are so striking as to raise the question of why Habermas claims allegiance to Kant at all.

Thomas McCarthy, Habermas's most important American student, carefully says no more than that Habermas's theory is closer to the Kantian tradition than to others.[27] Among the differences between Habermas's theory and Kant's, five are particularly important, as concerns its status as an a posteriori, nonmonological, consequentialist theory of ethics restricted to clarifying the conditions under which the participants can rationally decide moral and ethical questions (JA 179). To begin with, Kant is concerned with a theory of morality, not a theory of ethics. The choice of the term "discourse ethics" can arguably be justified on the grounds of Habermas's aim, as he insists, to realize Hegel's own aim. But that is not Kant's aim.

It is more difficult to justify other differences between Kantian morality and discourse ethics while maintaining the Kantian status of the latter. Habermas repeatedly describes Kant's moral theory as mono-logical and this description has been accepted without comment in the discussion of Habermas's theory of discourse ethics. Yet strictly speaking Kant's approach is not monological at all, since he assumes a distinction between a rational subject and an individual. Kant's antipsychologism, as Husserl, for instance, clearly realized,[28] prevents any attempt to iden-tify the transcendental subject = X with an individual human being (CPR B404, 331).

Habermas's adoption of a plural subject for norms affecting every-one is less controversial than the transference of normative justification

from the a priori to the a posteriori plane. Obviously, Kant's own deontological theory is not and ought not to be regarded as consequentialist.
Habermas's apparent consequentialism enables him to evade some of the
criticisms raised from the Hegelian angle of vision that properly accuses
the Kantian theory of irrelevance to practical life. But Habermas's justified interest in consequences obviously runs against the deontological
nature of Kant's theory. In opting to consider the consequences of the
adoption of a given norm, Habermas may be prudent if he wishes to
deflect Hegelian criticism. But he leaves behind a theory that derives what
should be done while neglecting what is done or its limits (CPR B375,
313). While Aristotelian ethics and utilitarianism consider consequences,
Kant's does not. Yet the necessity that Kant sees as a requirement for
claims to know cannot follow from practical consensus that at best can
yield no more than universality.

Habermas specifically limits his theory of discourse ethics to clarifying the conditions of the rational decision on moral and ethical questions.
This limitation is clearly at odds with Kantian morality that is intended to
be practically useful. Despite his emphasis on consequences, Habermas
is strangely not concerned with the practical questions of daily life, but
rather with the theoretical questions that derive from them. For this
reason, a doubt subsists as to the extent of his commitment to the real
consequences of the adoption of particular moral norms. Further, there is
an obvious consequence with respect to the utility of Habermas's theory.
In restricting ethics to a mere clarification prior to the decision making
process in concrete situations, he in effect deprives the theory of any real
practical value.

IX Conclusion

For the reasons given above, Habermas fails in his endeavor to redeem
Hegelian insights with Kantian means. Rather, he falls back into the acknowledged problem of the cognitive approach to ethics that on anything
like the Kantian model or its more recent formulations sacrifices social
utility for epistemological concerns. He fails in this endeavor for two reasons. On the one hand, his theory is not particularly Kantian, not more so
than, say, Hegel's own theory, which, on Hegel's own testimony, is inspired
by the critical philosophy. On the other hand, despite the announcement
of his intentions, the theory of discourse ethics fails to redeem Hegel's
insights. On any reasonable interpretation, Hegel is concerned with the
practical relevance that, as his critique shows, is lacking in Kant's view

of morality. Yet this is a goal that Habermas precisely disclaims in his restriction of discourse ethics to the more theoretical, but less practically relevant task, useless for everyday life, of the clarification of the bases of morality and ethics.

Two inferences follow immediately. First, and fairly obviously, the difficulties of discourse ethics reflect back on the position from which discourse ethics follows. Discourse ethics presupposes the theory of communicative action emerging from Habermas's critique of historical materialism from a Kantian angle of vision. His critique presupposes his distinction between work and interaction, or work and communication. His failure to demonstrate either the relevance of discourse ethics or communicative action from which it derives suggests that strengthening the epistemological viability of social theory, the general project which motivates his critique and attempted reformulation of Marx and Marxism, requires abandoning its social relevance. To put the point otherwise, when social theory respects traditional epistemological norms, it loses its social interest.

Second, and somewhat less obviously, there is a lesson to be drawn with respect to the link between morality and ethical life. The importance of Habermas's effort to redeem Hegelian insights with Kantian means is partially obscured by his somewhat artificial separation between neo-Aristotelianism, or communitarianism, and Hegelian criticism. Hegel remains in many ways an Aristotelian, not incidentally through the contextualism that separates his view of ethical life from Kantian morality. Marx is sometimes seen as a left-wing Aristotelian. From this perspective, discourse ethics can be regarded as the latest stage in the dispute launched by Aristotle's critique of Plato. Against the Platonic view of ethics as a pure science, Aristotle objects that politics includes ethics.[29] A successful reformulation of the Kantian theory of morality that overcame Hegelian objections to its utter uselessness would go a long way toward redeeming the ancient idea that pure theory is the legitimate ground of social life. Conversely, Habermas's inability to bring this off only strengthens the contrary conviction that pure theory is useful only for philosophers and other scholars.

The focus of this paper is squarely on Habermas's announced effort to redeem Hegel's aims with Kantian means. I have not specifically addressed the viability of the theory of discourse ethics. Nonetheless, I am skeptical about the prospects for Habermas's project. I shall conclude with a rapid remark about why I think that the prospects for anything like a cognitive approach to ethics is unlikely to succeed. The point can best be put by drawing attention to the relation between the so-called cognitive approach to ethics and the conception of the subject.

Habermas's theory of discourse ethics presupposes his cognitive approach to the ethical domain that in turn presupposes an abstract conception of the subject. Philosophers like Kant, Husserl, and most recently Habermas are typically concerned with an ahistorical theory of knowledge that fails to respect the historical nature of human being for which it is allegedly indispensable. Yet since human beings are historical, knowledge is dependent on a historical process. If claims to know depend on the knowing subject, then they must be made from within the historical flux.[30] To be sure, Habermas is not unaware of this problem. Despite his evident sympathy to Kant whom he sees as incorporating the best features of the Enlightenment project, Habermas concedes that to attempt to derive a socially relevant theory out of reason itself is no longer plausible. Yet he continues to privilege epistemological objectivity over social utility in his cognitive approach to ethics. My suggestion, to conclude, is that rather than abandoning social relevance to retrieve epistemological objectivity we need to combine both aspects through a theory formulated from the angle of vision of the historical subject.

5

Lyotard's Ethical Challenges: Meditations for the End of a Century

Caroline Bayard

Lyotard's writings from 1948 to his 1993 volume of theoretical essays, *Moralités postmodernes*, obviously cover a large historical and hermeneutical spectrum. A half-century is no flimsy fragment of time and would require several historically grounded, contextualized decodings were one to do full justice to the breadth of the investigations carried out by its main player. The first difficulty North American readers encounter when confronted with such a rich body of texts published from the mid 1950s until the 1990s (not all of them accessible in English) is directly related to the sheer size of this corpus.[1] The second has to do with the contradictions that arose between Lyotard's Marxist, Third-Worldist tenets in *Socialisme ou Barbarie*, his subsequent passion for deconstructing both Marxist and Freudian categories in *Dérives à partir de Marx et de Freud* and Nietzschean categories in *Des dispositifs pulsionnels*, to the philosophical, cultural, and sociological transformations registered in his *La Condition postmoderne*—still his best known work in North America, although it was translated into English only in 1984).[2]

In *La Condition postmoderne* Lyotard challenged the complex legacy inherited by Western cultures from their Enlightenment forebears, thus encountering substantial opposition from critical theorists, most notably Jürgen Habermas, and as I will show later, from feminist theorists, particularly Linda Nicholson and Nancy Fraser and Nancy Hartsock. Retrospectively speaking it is relevant to note that both critiques—feminist and Habermasian—were considerably nuanced by subsequent interventions from the latter parties. Other feminist critics, most notably Cecile Lindsay, suggested that Lyotardian foresight had *not* been negligible in furthering feminist scrutiny of the aporias of Western cultures on the subject of feminist theory. And Habermas partially retreated from his 1981 charge against Lyotard when in the nineties, in the wake of German reunification, he modified his previous positions on the pristine and unimpeachable nature of the Project of Modernity, just as Lyotard retreated from his positions of the early 1980s.[3]

Lyotard's ultimate ethical and political stand during the Gulf War (against the nonaligned countries' position), as well as his famous essay on open, postmodern, liberal societies in the wake of the demise of the Berlin Wall, of Marxist utopias, of any scientific utopia, explicit in *Moralités postmodernes,* can be singled out today as the last phase in a complex rostrum of Lyotardian positions.[4] It also constitutes the focus of the present essay and should be situated within a general critique and reappraisal of liberalism by West European theorists. It has already been explicitly foregrounded by political and social theorists both in the two Europes and in North America.[5] As such, it nevertheless needs to be placed in the broader context of Lyotard's development and ensuing transformations. While I am arguing that Lyotardian positions are not easily translatable into uncomplicated or rudimentary terms of reference, I am also proposing that during almost five decades this philosopher generated, formed, and provocatively articulated ethical inquiries that manifest continuous conceptual links with one another. I am further submitting that Lyotard focuses upon his readers' sense of responsibility as much as he alerts them to the limits intellectuals' interventions betray in a postmodern context at the end of this millennium. These limits do not free social and political actors from obligations, nor do they emancipate them from an attentive accountability to their community on moral, political, or individual levels. Yet as Lyotard insists, the locus occupied by responsible individuals in the nineties is considerably different from that circumscribed by Zola, Sartre, and Foucault in successive and different moments of their shared European history.[6] While he asserts that intellectuals are neither moribund, nor superfluous (as Jean Baudrillard has unhesitatingly suggested), their place and trusts (both *what* they trust in and what observers trust them *for*), need to be recircumscribed attentively as one takes into account those major paradigmatic transformations that characterize postmodernity in a post-totalitarian era. In this specific context, which constitutes a substantial part of Lyotard's meditation on the end of our century, it is relevant to draw on those intersections emerging between Western Europe and the "Other Europe," or between postmodernity and post-totalitarianism. European and North American scholars—Richard Rorty,

Peter Beilharz, Gillian Robinson and John Rundell, Richard Bernstein— have reflected upon those issues after the fall of the Berlin Wall. They are useful to mention here as they situate Lyotard's interrogations and dissatisfactions *within* a larger historical framework and epochal setting. But such interrogations and dissatisfactions while they surged up in his writings well before *Moralités postmodernes,* nevertheless aid readers in interpreting the end of modernity, the beginning of the postmodern era. The purpose of the present essay is to illuminate the antecedents of *Moralites postmodernes,* the process it followed as much as the junctions it established with a specific historical, epochal moment.

Links between Different Moments: Lyotard's Peregrinations during the Past Fifty Years

The political realities of Algeria in the late fifties, a country attempting to shake off—at great cost—the French colonial yoke, provide us with the first possible glance at Lyotard's writings. Read four decades after their first publication in *Socialisme ou Barbarie,* both "The Situation in North Africa" and "A New Phase in the Algerian Question" allow readers to appreciate Lyotard's intuitions about the burning cauldron of a war of independence that—given the million French settlers who had been living in Algeria for five generations, identifying with neither the French government in Paris nor a Parisian culture which for all practical purposes was both removed from and alien to them—also had the ambiguous accents of a quasi-civil war.[7] Lyotard, who taught philosophy at the French lycée of Constantine between 1950 and 1954, did not terminate his engagement with the complex war of independence raging there until 1962. In 1962 and 1964 he was to write two essays that strangely prefigured those developments Algeria faces in the mid 1990s when a worn-out, rigid National Liberation Front (FNL), the party in power for the last forty years, has lost the trust of the majority of Algerians and while a brutal fundamentalist movement with substantial support from the population attempts to secure political power.[8] As terse, brief assessments of the early years of the FNL, these essays crystallize key elements of what would become an explicit political reality in 1994–95. Also, they prefigure the bitter historical judgment Lyotard would enunciate in 1983 in a different context.[9] In fact, both "Algeria Seven Years After" and "Algeria Evacuated" foretold the dangers of a bureaucratic apparatus as well as the inability of Algerian workers to build autonomous political organizations during the first decade of their independence years, and less than ten years after they had fought a war which had been costly not only in terms of human losses, but also in that of economic and managerial structure destruction.[10] It is interesting to note that it was in June 1989 that Lyotard wrote *La guerre des Algériens*, a moving appraisal of what this specific war meant to him as a witness (although not as direct participant, a distinction he is extremely sensitive about), as well as a retrospective judgment of what *Socialisme ou Barbarie* had meant to its contemporaries between 1950 and 1963 and what it symbolized decades later. Lyotard rejects the suggestion that this journal would have been only the theoretical mouthpiece of militants, workers, and intellectuals banding together to carry on the marxist critique of reality, or "the hybrid offspring of Parisian intellectuals." Some thirty-one years later, in fact, he looks upon this involvement precisely as "An analysis which refused to surrender unconditionally to the state of things [thus] carrying resistance by other means, on other terrains." Acknowledging, in accordance with his deeply anti-utopian, postmodern mistrust of revolutionary fervor, the materiality of the "intractable," Lyotard insists that while in 1989 a radical alternative to capitalist domination has to be abandoned, nevertheless this does not imply that one must give up the principle of resistance, inventiveness, creativity, and self-government, nor abandon a passionate scrutiny of that which should and will remain, in different forms, the "intractable," however much Western societies and political wavelengths have obliterated it of late.[11]

Where did he invest his philosophical energies after leaving *Socialisme ou Barbarie* in 1963? The simplest way to summarize—without grossly oversimplifying—his intellectual development from 1968 to the late seventies would be to note that the student revolution which briefly bloomed in Paris in May 1968 was the watershed sustaining and nourishing his critique of Western societies from the late sixties to the end of the next decade, a time at which he published *La condition postmoderne*, subtitled "Rapport sur le savoir," and a reflection on "knowledge in advanced societies." He was thus the first to identify and qualify the phenomenon known as "postmodernity" in Western societies apart from Anglo-American reflections on this subject.[12] But Lyotard in the early seventies had already provided a philosophical context that was able to encourage a deconstruction of Freudianism and Marxism, as well as an attentive scrutiny of Nietzschean thought. Lyotard, his intellectual companions, and his critics (the latter with a particularly acerbic style) have commented on such an evolution. I will not elaborate on these heterogeneous developments, except to mention that 1968 as an historical encounter with history, as a philosophical fragment, cannot be isolated from Lyotard's own maturation as a thinker, when he continues to analyze this particular epoch and defines it as a watershed of his own development as a philosopher. He does so even as late as 1993 when he reflects upon those phenomena in *Moralités postmodernes*.[13]

A Process for the 1980s

I believe it is relevant to recognize that precisely in this last decade Lyotard's writings negotiated heterogeneous interrogations which moved from the Kantian sublime and the aesthetic issues raised by the latter (as testified in Lyotard's *Leçons sur l'analytique du sublime,* to challenging Heideggerian thought and Philippe Lacoue-Labarthe's complex and mistaken engagement with the German philosopher (as one can judge from Lyotard's *Heidegger et les juifs*).[14] Such intellectual operations also eschewed Lyotard's acknowledgment of the aporias of modernity in *Le Postmoderne expliqué aux enfants*. This process was going to take him through *L'Inhumain,* particularly through the famous essay "Réécrire la modernité." Taking all of these writings into account, although not following a narrowly defined chronological order, I will assess his writings from the 1980s, then primarily concentrate upon his analysis of postmodern ethics for the end of this century, their political directions and social aporias, particularly in the fragments he designates as postmodern moralities with *Moralités postmodernes*.

One of the lessons to be drawn from Lyotard's texts in the eighties appears to be his critique of the macro-legacies of Western cultures as one moves from *La Condition Postmoderne,* which challenges the stability of the master narratives in Western cultures, to *Le Différend,* which scrutinizes European and non-European cultures' reluctance and sometimes even incapacity to acknowledge the enormity of the grief and interrogations raised by the Holocaust after 1945. In this process, Lyotard has been one of the most consistent critics of such macro-legacies as Christianity's, and of their universalistic intent: as he reminds us in *Le Différend,* what else is salvation but the choice to save even those who have not selected to be saved? Another macro-legacy that he frequently parallels with the latter is Marxism, his past critical passion from *Socialisme ou Barbarie*.[15] It would be reasonable to conclude after reviewing Lyotard's state of the art (or participation in philosophical debates from the late 1940s to the mid 1980s) that he has been intensely alert to the multiple *differends* Western subjects had been active agents for. While this is in part an outgrowth of his work with the *Socialisme ou Barbarie* group, his indebtedness to Lévinas is also significant from the late 1970s on, specifically in *Le*

Differend, where he notes that obligation, identity, and otherness need to be rethought after the Holocaust.[16] It is important also to note that Lyotard's work in *Le Postmoderne expliqué aux enfants* sustains and continues such queries, particularly when he admits that these philosophical aporia had already been contained some decades ago in Theodor Adorno's desperate question: Can there be art after Auschwitz? But curiously in fact, or maybe paradoxically, Lyotard identifies, from the very first pages of *Le Differend* two philosophers who would have succeeded, in the first case in enunciating an epilogue for modernity (Immanuel Kant with his third *Critique*), in the second case, in articulating a prologue for "an honorable postmodernity" (what Ludwig Wittgenstein would have done with his *Philosophical Investigations*).

While Lyotard is explicitly contradicting Adorno's desperation there as much as his own in the same text, nevertheless he is clear that both references made here to an epilogue for Modernity and an honorable postmodernity lay the ground for further explorations of the first as well as of the latter. Both *Le Differend* and *Le Postmoderne expliqué aux enfants* explore these promises.[17] In doing so, Lyotard, if he recognizes the very impossibility of identifying and comprehending the incommensurable grief of the Holocaust, nevertheless does not conclude that ethics have become an impossibility. However, the end of *Le Differend* is a bitter statement on the improbability of a cosmopolitical history in the 1980s, as much as that of a political program capable of resisting capital's hegemony, though he qualifies the latter statement with a precautionary reminder that "although [in this case], one can still bear witness to it."[18]

I would add in this context that a contradiction quickly emerges from, on the one hand, Lyotard's judgments about the capitalist economy as genre, or that which does not allow the heterogeneity of genres of discourses, and even requires its suppression: "Time [being] at its fullest with capitalism [and] a verdict always pronounced in favor of gained time, [putting] an end to litigations [and] for that reason aggravating differends" in *Le différend,* and on the other, his later texts, which rationalize and vindicate liberalism.[19] For instance, also in 1989, he reminds us that capitalism does not constitute a world history, that nineteenth- and twentieth-century philosophies of history are obsolete, "liberal parliamentarism having been refuted in May 1968 and the doctrine of economic liberalism refuted in the crises of 1911 and 1929, just as the post-Keynesian revision of that doctrine had been in 1974–79."[20] Yet a close comparison of this analysis with subsequent ones appearing in *Moralités postmodernes* raises serious questions. Looking, for instance, at his essay "The Wall, the Gulf, the System," one can see that for Lyotard "liberal capitalism has triumphed over both fascism and communism and in doing so, while it initiates disparities, awakens divergences and favors alternatives, as a system, it continuously revises itself while integrating prevailing strategies."[21] Indeed, when he explains how the East German crowds voted with their feet for a certain system in the bipolar Yalta world, he acknowledges thus that they put an end to one of the two options still existing within this dual universe. Of course, he recognizes that there is *one* great absent missing from this picture: "something that cast its tragic light over the historical stage for a couple of centuries: the proletariat." But equally, whatever his nostalgia for the heroic times of *Socialisme ou Barbarie* may be, it is clear that Lyotard entertains no nostalgia for this particular ghost.[22] In the end, liberalism turned out to be the viable choice. And Lyotard admits this regretfully when he recognizes that the status of capitalist systems may be interpreted in much different terms when one identifies *both* liberalism and market economy as "parties which have triumphed over all their opponents."

But in fact, there are dissimilarities and shared perimeters in Lyotard's analysis. The central contradiction has to do with on the one hand, his suggestion in 1983 that gained time provokes the elimination of differends, hence that social, cultural, and communal homogeneity can be the only the choices of a hurried capitalism. Such a critique is reasserted more strongly in 1987, when in *Le postmoderne expliqué aux enfants* he appears to reject even a partial justification or moderate vindication of liberal practices as he enunciates a critique of their processes, virtually conflating them with totalitarian procedures: "there have been controversies between liberals and conservatives . . . but after two centuries we can say that neither economic, or political liberalism, nor various Marxisms can escape the accusation that they committed crimes against humanity."[23]

Yet, explicitly in 1993, after facing the Berlin Wall and East German intellectuals who ambiguously remind him of his own Marxist processes from the 1950s and early 1960s, also referring to the Gulf War, analyzed here with particular acuity given his long-standing interest in Arab cultures, he recognizes that transformations and changes hold a strong quality of liberalism as the promise of their survival: "the more open the system, the more efficient it is; closed and isolated systems are doomed to disappear."[24]

One explanation of Lyotard's fairly radical turnaround is that, while in 1983 he was still closer to a nuanced Marxist analysis than he could be after 1989, and in 1987 he was also still adopting a Third-Way approach (a preference he certainly was not the only one to entertain and one which received abundant succor from other French philosophers at that time), in 1993, as a philosopher and a postmodernist, he had nowhere else to go but to embrace, critically and with qualifications as much as irony, a liberal line. I would also add, not as a justification, but as a recognition of shared territories between both his positions from 1983 *and* 1989, that he never could be, even in 1993, an ardent, uncritical supporter of liberalism.

Looking, for instance, to his essay *La Guerre des Algériens,* written in June 1989, it is clear that in it he explicitly challenges on the one hand, the abuses that "a so-called liberal parliamentarian system can exert against its own people," and on the other hand, those subsequent tyrannies that may emerge from liberation movements, when he writes, "Proud struggles for independence end in young reactionary States."[25] What is to be remembered from both this essay and the subsequent *Moralités postmodernes,* however, is that to him, as well as to a substantial part of the post-post-Marxist Left in France, a post-Yalta world needs to keep in mind "the intractable voice which remains, even when Marxism is finished and especially when European wavelengths are occupied with vastly different voices, most of them indifferent to the legacy of social and political struggles of the oppressed."[26] What such moves signal also is that the system has—to a degree—digested the intractable, thus transforming the ruses of the system into a versatile, adaptable liberalism, considerably more worrisome even than he had predicted a decade ago.[27]

Although Lyotard never explicitly admits it, one can nevertheless summarize the situation in the following manner: his 1950s essays from *Socialisme ou Barbarie* candidly believed in Third World socialism, in a definite alliance between proletarian workers and the Algerian Fellahs. Yet, *Le Différend* in 1983 already recognized that the transformations or passages promised by great doctrinal syntheses only "end in bloody impasses," another way of saying utopias had been collectively rejected. What is more, in the same book, the economic genre's hegemony of overt discourses was presented as virtually indisputable (however much homogenizing it conducted in this process). "The Name of Algeria" was unreservedly and explicitly recognizing the demise of *any* Marxist project, as much as the reality that a "radical alternative to capitalist domination *must* be abandoned." His essential code, however, a few lines later, was the admission that the carrying of resistance, by other means, had always been and remained as that which was "intractable."

In his *Moralités postmodernes* in 1993, liberalism had won the day. Was this the end of the story? Did this mean that the affiliations explicit in "In the Name of Algeria" had disappeared? Did it mean that the activities in which he, with thousands of other people throughout the 1960s and 1970s, had immersed himself, had ceased to have any meaning?[28] Should one conclude that history modified Lyotard's judgment and made him effect a radical turnaround, as Chantal Mouffe recently suggested?

Such would not be my conclusion, and because Lyotard's situation is more nuanced than some commentators give him credit for, it is relevant to examine his positions throughout the eighties in order to interpret, as well as criticize, such transformations. Certainly his *Tombeau de l'intellectuel* focused on the issue of responsibility as that which foregrounds expectations much different from those traditionally enunciated these past two centuries by Voltaire, Zola, Foucault, and Sartre.[29] Yet, it also insisted that a strong answerability to injustices, an obligation to specific, individual calls for intervention. should prevail. Thus while Lyotard's reminder was a far cry from Enlightenment intellectuals' universalistic call to rally the barricades, still it was clearly grounded upon explicit obligations and particular intercessions. Such focus in fact had been elaborately scrutinized, not only in *Le Tombeau de l'intellectuel*, but also in *Au juste* and in *Témoigner du différend*. In another essay I analyzed how his writings concurred with another postmodern theorist such as Václav Havel.[30] In fact I would add today that Lyotard in both his 1983 and 1987 books was focusing already upon ethical, political, and community issues that were to capture the attention of other theorists such as Agnes Heller, Fehér Ferenc, and Zygmunt Bauman very soon after. It is true that the latter did not unconditionally concur with him on the role envisioned for intellectuals at the end of our century (nor did they agree with one another about such a responsibility), but a shared denominator stood out: universalistic positions had become untenable and master narratives decisively decimated for the majority of them. Although how they proceeded to adjust to a post-Yalta and postmodern universe differed widely, as it should among postmodernists anyway.

In Lyotard's case, intellectuals' responsibilities were tangible and concrete: they had to testify in favor of differends *and* they could not speak for them as Voltaire and Zola eloquently had. What they needed to do, however, was to ensure that such differends could be heard, and even permit a certain silence in order to be heard. But as the author of *Le Tombeau de l'intellectuel, Just Gaming, Le Différend,* and *Le Postmoderne expliqué aux enfants* reminded us: to imprudently designate a just cause in a conflict of ideas or powers usually leads onto the path of error so often trodden by Western European intellectuals.[31]

The question attentive readers will be tempted to ask is: What is left for intellectuals and citizens to do in the nineties, after the Berlin Wall signaled the end of the last of contemporary utopias, after the Gulf War pitted a large part of Western nations against a specific number of Arab nations? I interpret *Moralités postmodernes,* as much as those texts which came out in the eighties—as contrasted and contradictory they may be—as the humble endeavor to rethink the political. What I am explicitly hearing here is that a *different* kind of responsibility is now required from the participants of civil societies, one which, as a form of ethics starting with *La condition postmoderne,* through *Just Gaming, Le Differend, Le postmoderne expliqué aux enfants,* up to his last meditation on the end of the century in "The Wall, the Gulf, the Sun: A Fable," explicitly shifted from the explicitly universalistic positions of *Socialisme ou Barbarie* enacted in the 1950s and 1960s to postmodern enunciations in the 1980s and 1990s. As lucid and distinct postmodern enunciations, they not only further and enrich the challenges posed by other postmodern theorists, but they also posit a different way of articulating the political.

The Nineties: *Moralités Postmodernes* and the Gulf War; Women's Critique of Anti-Enlightenment Positions

Those among French intellectuals who still believed in leftist politics, and in ideals of justice—however heterogenous the latter may be—found substantial difficulties in accepting Lyotard's position on the Gulf War. What is more, a number of feminist theorists, as I mentioned at the beginning of this essay, seriously objected to those anti-Enlightenment positions he enunciated in the eighties, particularly from *La Condition postmoderne* onward. Both kinds of critiques should be looked at since they highlight, in the nineties, some of the problems encountered by Lyotard's positions as well as some of the intuitive resolutions he formulated at a time when such conclusions were not exactly celebrated.

If one looks at the first one (i.e. the Gulf War and the position he took, not only as a citizen, but also as a philosopher), it becomes clear that the stance he adopted in 1991, along with an avowed preference for open systems against closed ones, angered a considerable number of people, among whom one should count old intellectual companions who read in such determination the confirmation of his turn towards rightist politics.[32] Nevertheless it is relevant to note that both statements (petitions signed and addressed to *Libération*) were positions not deprived of subtleties, by philosophers who identified themselves as such, as well as qualified, by each side, by specific intercessions. On one side, there was the heterogenous coalition pitted against Saddam Hussein; on the other, enunciated on behalf of the dispossessed of the world, one could observe a South attacked by a rich North. For Gilles Deleuze, Pierre Bourdieu, and Etienne Balibar, the intervention led against Iraq was *not* the outcome of a collective outcry against injustice and lawlessness, but the product of two imperialisms, one international, led by the U.S. steering its vision of a New

World Order, the other local, led by Hussein, whose conspicuous objective was complete hegemony over the Arab world. As an international crusade, motivated by the control of an important part of the world's oil reserves, the West's intervention was a severe blow to democratic ideals, as much as an obvious regression for the freedom of Arab nations. But, on the other side, Lyotard's, Taguieff's, and Touraine's essay rejected the last interpretation of this military intervention, posited by Deleuze et al. as a war of the rich against the poor, of the North against the South. They designated it instead as the defense of the rule of law in a post-Yalta world suddenly destabilized by the disappearance of its binary balance. While none of the signatories denied the immense responsibility of Western nations who had constructed, abetted, and shaped Saddam Hussein (a position Lyotard was to elaborate upon in "The Wall, the Gulf, the Sun: A Fable"), nevertheless all recognized the need to attend to those exacting demands enunciated by an ethical politics in the nineties.[33]

While none of these two positions satisfactorily answered the issues at hand (i.e., geopolitical rationality and economic justice), it would appear looking back upon these conflicts five years later that with, on the one hand, Saddam Hussein still in power, actively butchering his own civilian population, on the other hand with those nations which had opposed Iraq in 1991, in 1995 on the issue of economic sanctions, that Lyotard's position *and* the contradictions resulting from it should be scrutinized attentively. Both his 1991 positions and contradictions witnessed in 1995 should be contextualized within the framework he set on the issue of justice in his earlier texts.

What had emerged earlier in *Le Différend* and *Le postmoderne expliqué aux enfants* was a philosophical argument waged on two opposing, contradictory tracks. On the one hand, he insisted upon the impossibility of accepting foundationalism in the 1980s, upon the dangerous determination of a utopian faith guaranteeing immutable and immovable laws, while reiterating the preposterousness of countering the irremediable opacity of language itself.[34] Yet, he asserted in the same texts that justice might prevail when one resists the behavior of philosopher-kings and Enlightenment tenets and practices an anamnesis salvaging the child in each one of us.[35] Without confronting him with binary solutions (either/or), one is tempted to suggest, after examining such discrepancies, that he is trying to have his cake and eat it, too: salvaging a postmodernity that, without becoming a new metanarrative, behaves in fact like one. Obviously such contradictions may be a source of creativity, but they justifiably frustrate his critics.

His challenges to foundationalism have aroused considerable interest amongst feminist critics, especially Linda Nicholson and Nancy Fraser, although as strong acts of defiance against Enlightenment principles, metanarratives, and foundationalism, they have equally been threatening to many of them. Seyla Benhabib articulated her doubts about such a frustrating eclecticism and a self-contradictory polytheism that proposes a vision of politics she views as "incapable of justifying its own commitment to justice."[36] Both *Au juste* and *Témoigner du différend* with their pagan desires and their heterogeneous intentions certainly lend themselves to such a critique. I might add, however that some ten years later Lyotard himself has rectified such preferences and conceded they presented unresolvable contradictions.[37] If paganism is not offering the alternatives it presented to European postmodernists in 1979, yet in 1995 Lyotard's choices appear to situate themselves on stronger grounds. Let us elaborate on these points. First of all, his mistrust of Marxist metanarratives appears abundantly justified by a number of events on the one hand, and by substantially heterogeneous philosophical interventions on the other. As for his mistrust of metanarratives, I would add that a number of feminists have joined him in rejecting essentialism as a philosophical possibility.[38] Thus it becomes inescapable that while Lyotard's theories have signaled fluctuating, heterogeneous affiliations between 1948 and the early 1980s, his rejection of metanarratives, on the other hand, was consistently enacted from 1979 on. As the expression of his tenacious insistence upon the importance of plurality and otherness, it situates him in a specific intellectual context. One which, while acknowledging the importance to resist totalitarianism, political oppression, invasions and closed systems (as his signing "A Necessary War" [*Une guerre requise*] testifies), refuses also to see such efforts as the be-all and end-all of philosophical, ethical, and political efforts. And such demands, reminders, such a quest for qualified alliances *and* difference, may well be what constitutes his distinctive locus at the end of the twentieth century.

Assessing the Locus of Lyotard at the End of the Century

How can one define the position and ethical identification of Lyotard in the 1990s? How can one delineate his role as philosopher and ethicist in the postmodern world, when one acknowledges the detectable presence of contradictions within his writings? Or when one examines the curious conflation of justice *and* indeterminacy, of the child in us *and* legitimacy, as if the two could coincide automatically, although he certainly strives to persuade us they do in "Mainmise"?[39]

Another question one will be tempted to ask is: How does Lyotard position himself vis-à-vis some of his contemporaries, those who have precisely contested his positions in the early eighties (such as Habermas), or those who have attempted to reconcile specific oppositions between his texts and Habermas's (as Wellmer did in 1991), or those who have chosen to arbitrate in this process (as Rorty did in 1986)? To a degree, *Moralités postmodernes* may well be the attempt to respond to these endeavors. But it also stands as an end-of-the-century effort to examine the virtues, worthiness, commendable contentions of liberalism, as well as its limits, drawbacks and weaknesses. As such, it situates Lyotard's thought at that historical locus and perilous time when politically speaking, friend and foe, Right and Left, differences, in fact are threatened with extinction. Different political philosophers have referred to such tendencies in the nineties, specifically on the terrain of European politics. They compared such contemporary conflations with others, practiced in different historical epochs.

One point needs to be clear from the outset: Lyotard stresses that there are no alternatives after 1989 beyond liberal democracy. On this particular terrain he defends himself from any revolutionary nostalgia smacking of leftist irredentism when he writes, "And I do not find it fair when Rorty or others read in my defense of differends echoes of leftism, of terrorism even. One thing is to look upon a discussion whose aim is to extend consensus as an important political task, another to reduce the purpose of language to such a discussion."[40]

Similarly, in an essay dedicated to his colleague and compatriot Gilles Deleuze titled, "Ligne générale," Lyotard reflects upon the dangerous abuses of the definition of "liberal democracy," as well as that of "special rights and minority rights" in North America. While he stresses that rules of liberal democracy are essential, as much as the defense of those rights which justify the necessary existence of Amnesty International, on the other the constant exhortation to observe and monitor conformity to these rights can become totally oppressive as one moves from the position of vigilante to that of proxy for a totalitarian order.[41] The intractable Lyotard was speaking about earlier, or what he called also in *Moralités postmodernes* "l'inhumain, la région inhumaine qui échappe tout à fait à l'exercice des droits," is also that which no democracy, liberal or other, can legislate about, unless it become a totalitarian order, as Lyotard to Deuleuze insists is "lyne générale." Recalling Kant, in the essay addressed to his American friends, or marked specifically by references to Rorty and Davidson, Lyotard also notes that the distinction brought by Kant's *Second Critique* had to do precisely with such: with moral law, with the unanimity such law should arouse amongst reasonable human beings.

But Kant had reminded us that such "acceptability" is not the content of that which is just, only its procedure: as it is only through a determination one proceeds to analogically, that one can begin to see moral obligation satisfied. And Lyotard summarizes such a process by adding that "If law were a knowable quantity (cognizable, discernible?), then ethics could be reduced to an epistemological procedure."[42]

How could one pretend to be a liberal democrat and appear in the presence of that unknowable? The elusive partner Lyotard is alluding to in his title is that "Other." Thus, to try to reduce the latter to a definition, as the term already does, or to a possible partner for a workable consensus, is already in his eyes a defeat for liberal democracy. So that the "grande Terre" Rorty is calling for is not really desirable in Lyotard's eyes. On such a territory, the latter discerns those metaconversations already practiced by a global empire through its pragmatics and communication procedures, a mistrust already formulated, as mentioned earlier, by the philosopher Michel Serres, or in Ignacio Ramonet's *Le Monde Diplomatique.*

Explicitly, Lyotard favors archipelagoes and heterogenous discourses over inland unifications, or (without abusing economic metaphors) heterogeneous markets and multiple contracts over "free trade/ GAAT deals." Divergences and misreadings are therefore essential, otherwise pragmatics will kill plurality and the dangers lurking behind liberal democracies become concrete realities. At a time when the nation-subject has absorbed considerable energy among Europeans, especially on those eastern borders of a Maastricht EU, Lyotard's rueful invocation of Heidegger's dreaded ghost seems wiser than a number of temptations, both East European (Serbian, in particular), or West European for that matter (de Benoît's intuitions on communities, their imperial roots in France, or the CSU resentments in Bavarian Germany), would reflect such nostalgia. In this context, it is pertinent to read how Lyotard in *Moralités postmodernes* reminds us of the ways the philosopher of *Sein und Zeit*, intensely preoccupied in 1933–1934 with historicity and togetherness, was keen to urge the German people, or Volk, to reach its *Entloschlossenheit* and preserve its authenticity. Lyotard ruefully reminds us here that Heidegger, as much as his Japanese contemporaries, should have been more aware of the importance of resisting the metaphysics of the empire, from the east or from the west.

Specifically in this context, Lyotard's analysis of the conference held in November 1941 in Kyoto, on the eve of Pearl Harbor, during which the Japanese philosophers Koyama Iwao and Kosaka Maasaki were exchanging views that the moral energy of a people, only capable of acquiring a subjectivity when it becomes a national body, could be relevant today to a number of Europeans while nationalism arouses a number of ugly demons again. To both these imperial philosophers in 1941, a natural community could only become a nation if it was capable of projecting its history and facing its future, thus fusing together the Nation-Subject and the organicity of the nation's Body. Of course Heidegger took this process one step further in the second part of *Sein und Zeit*, which as we all know carried the *Volk* one step closer to its destiny. When it comes to the nation-Subject, even the New Right idealogue in France Alain de Benoîst would reject this project, and the Bavarian CSU nominally repudiate it; but a number of East Europeans who do not spend an inordinate amount of time re-reading Heidegger do not operate models considerably different from those practiced by the worst and most nationalistic elements of West Europe.

In such a contemporary context, as a meditation on the end of the twentieth century, Lyotard's suggestion is quite telling about the locus he has delineated for himself: one that in this case confronts a number of his old demons, as well as attempts to defy more immediate ones. As he puts it in *Moralités postmodernes*, giving up on emancipatory ideals could also free people from the metaphysics of any empire, from east, or west, because the earth, by itself, does not have any pathways: pathways are made wherever human beings go through. In fact, when postmodernists started undermining such essentialism they were appealing for an open, radical indeterminacy. I might add today that, not just la Nouvelle Droite in France, with de Benoîst, but also the Bavarian CDU and various Serbian warlords might benefit from Lyotard's last coda, if they cared to hear it: "Both east and west, it is possible to resist vast Empires when one also frustrates and foils the need for identity."[43] Such attentive reminders would have been useful to imperialist philosophers in Kyoto in 1941 (although they were not heard and Japan plunged into the Second World War).

As reminders, they might foil today's European madness if one listened to small narratives, rather than focus over imperial grands récits: unfortunately, such is not the case, and Europe has not appeared ready to learn from its past, as *Praxis International* thoughtfully noted in 1994 while Sarajevo burned.[44]

6

Disabling Knowledge

Barry Allen

It is certain that no vexation or anxiety of mind results from knowledge but merely by accident; all knowledge being pleasant in itself.

—*Francis Bacon*

Where is the wisdom we have lost in knowledge? Where is the knowledge we have lost in information?

—*T. S. Eliot*

I

We moderns like to think of ourselves as exceptional, as having rationalized and disenchanted the world, definitively transforming the premodern cosmos into one of pure matter and mechanical interactions. All theories about our supposed "modernity" (Hegelian, Marxist, Weberian, Heideggerian, Habermasian, and so on) agree that Western societies turned some epochal corner, probably in the seventeenth century. Cartesian rationalism, industrial capitalism, experimental science, the bureaucratic state—all seem to prove the same self-evident proposition: A great divide or historical rupture irrevocably sunders modern and premodern societies; we are different from others, we have broken with our past.

Yet no one has really done that, we have never been "modern." That is not to deny the obvious differences (economic, scientific, technical, and so on) that distinguish the twentieth century from, say, the fifteenth. But do such differences add up to some sort of epochal shift or rupture with the past? Is it not possible that, on the contrary, our so-called modernity may be the cumulative, crescendo effect of innumerable small changes in the scale and scope of things that human beings have always been doing, as they remake their artifactual environment? Though we did no more than change the pace and reach of networks linking people, instruments, results, goods, and money, we changed the pace a lot. Today half our politics are conducted in scientific research, half of nature is an artifact sealing a social bond.

Whether one considers the industrial economy of goods and services, or the technoscientific economy of knowledge, what is characteristic of modern times is a quantitative difference in the degree to which inputs and outputs are integrated, labor divided, people and things linked in more far-flung networks of practices and instruments, documents and translations, centers of calculation, calibration, experimentation, and profit. Rather than being a historically exceptional, disenchanted, or uniquely technological society, we moderns have accumulated longer and more heterogeneous networks, so that now researchers and their reports, results, tools, and assumptions pass from place to place typically without interruption or discontinuity, all over the globe and into the surrounding atmosphere. And while the "innovation of longer networks is an interesting peculiarity," it is not sufficient "to set us radically apart from others, or to cut us off forever from our own past."[1]

One effect, unexpected and paradoxical, of the new scale in the production of knowledge is the appearance of an enigmatic counterproductivity for knowledge. The idea of specific (or paradoxical) counterproductivity comes from Ivan Illich, who introduced it to describe the way our major tools subvert the purposes for which they were engineered and financed. "At some point in every domain, the amount of goods delivered so degrades the environment for personal action that the possible synergy between use-values and commodities turns negative. Paradoxical, or specific, counterproductivity sets in . . . whenever the impotence resulting from the substitution of a commodity for a value in use turns this very commodity into a disvalue in the pursuit of the satisfaction it was meant to provide." Automobiles and highways are supposed to make people more mobile, but the system turns counterproductive when traffic jams and fuel shortages immobilize us. More hospitals, physicians, and health insurance are supposed to make us healthier, yet these systems also turn counterproductive when iatrogenic sickness—the pain, dysfunction, and disability resulting from technical medical intervention—comes to rival the morbidity caused by automobile and industrial accidents. "Only modern malnutrition injures more people than iatrogenic disease in its various manifestations." Hence the predicament Illich calls *medical nemesis*: The counterproductivity of high-intensity health-care is immune to its technical interventions, whose treatments unpredictably convert to new pathogens in a "self-reinforcing loop of negative institutional feedback."[2]

Paradoxical counterproductivity results from an excessive effort to replace the things that people make and do for themselves with commodities—goods or services that must be paid for, whether directly or indirectly. Cars replace legs, driving replaces walking, formal education replaces informal learning, professional medicine replaces vernacular or self-care. In each case, we are asked to buy (or receive from others) what people used to make or do for themselves. This destruction of nonmarket use-values is heralded as "economic development" and "modernization," which has its dilemmas, of course, but they can be solved by more of the same, by more thoroughgoing modernization, more substitution of more resource-intensive goods and services for vernacular skills and tools. Illich's argument is that there are inbuilt, unpredictable limitations past which the substitution of commodities for things produced by those who intend to use them for their own satisfaction turns counterproductive. The new goods turn into destructive nuisances that retain net value only for the provider of services. "Beyond a certain threshold of intensity, dependence on a bill of industrial and professional goods destroys human potential, and it does so in a specific way. Only up to a point can commodities replace what people make or do on their own. Only within limits can exchange-values satisfactorily replace use-values. Beyond this point, further production serves the interests of the professional producer— who has imputed the need to the consumer—and leaves the consumer befuddled and giddy, albeit richer."[3]

Inquiry, or the production of knowledge, can also turn counterproductive. The present-day scale and division of labor in the production of knowledge can render counterproductive the very knowledge that it produces and applies. The paradoxical counterproductivity of knowledge leads to people who are supposed to know (or those who rely on their advice) making choices that are more stupid than would otherwise have been imaginable. Knowledge turns from a morally neutral source of technical power to a strategy of political government that disables and stupefies those whom it is supposed to serve.

II

Knowledge is power, as Bacon said. What, if anything, does Foucault add with his idea of "power/knowledge"? For Bacon the identity of knowledge and power is not a fact but a hope, a wish, an imagined future. He does not claim that knowledge and power *are* the same, but that it should be so, that any knowledge properly worthy of the name *would* be powerful, as any real truths would be useful ones. His statement about knowledge and power is therefore not an analytical or critical thesis, but instead a persuasive effort to revise what counts as "knowledge." For Foucault, however, the relationship between knowledge and power is not a futuristic ideal but a worldly fact. As a matter of historical fact, he claims, "the exercise of power creates and causes to emerge new objects of knowledge and accumulates new bodies of information . . . The exercise of power perpetually creates knowledge and, conversely, knowledge constantly induces effects of power."[4]

It is among Foucault's undeniable accomplishments to have put "small power"—the "micro-powers" he describes in discussing the rise of what he calls "discipline"—on the agenda both for political philosophy and activism. These forms of power are increasingly more significant to our experience of government than the "big powers" which preoccupy modern political philosophy (Sovereign, State, Capital, Ruling Class). Yet disciplinary micro-powers typically do not operate with the mechanisms of coercion that history and theory alike have accustomed us to expect from dominating powers. Because of the new centrality of disciplinary micro-powers, and because of the key role of scientific or quasi-scientific knowledge in their operation and in their legitimacy, the relationship between knowledge and power acquires unprecedented political significance. To grasp both the effectiveness of disciplinary power and its high degree of legitimacy requires a theory capable of appreciating this relation in a new and better way than can the traditions of pragmatism or *Ideologiekritik*. Foucault's major contribution to modern political philosophy is to have sketched the main lines of such a theory. The point of speaking of "power/knowledge" is not to say that knowledge *is* power, or that there is nothing more to knowledge than service to power, or anything of the sort. The point is to emphasize the reciprocity which obtains between those specific forms of knowledge which "discipline" makes possible (roughly coextensive with the so-called human sciences) and the exercise of disciplinary power over conduct, an exercise of power which is extended and refined through the further growth of that knowledge.[5]

The knowledge and power that especially concern me here is the professional, disciplinary power/knowledge of those who impute needs to others for whom they alone have the right to prescribe. They have been called the dominant, domineering professions (Illich), and include social workers, economists, opinion researchers, primary and secondary teachers, and ("the most striking and painful example") physicians and allied health-care workers. Secure in a discipline's self-certified rationality and epistemological warrant, accredited experts typically receive the presumption of others (bureaucrats, magistrates, police, primary teachers, and so on) with whom they share some interest in the political government of conduct.[6] Such knowledge can be and routinely is an instrument for political effects of government, especially through the strategy of imputed needs. To elucidate the character of imputed needing I shall set it in context within a four-fold division of needs.

1. Mortal: Imminent needs which if not made less pressing must end, finally, all life projects.

Mortal needs are by definition compelling beyond normal liberty of self-government. If you are grievously wounded, your need is compelling; you have little liberty to choose whether or how help comes. Mortal needs are not so-called basic needs, and do not have to be specified in advance or limited to some small number that would be common to humans everywhere and always. It should be possible to recognize that there are moments of mortal need without getting bogged down in issues about what needs are primary or secondary, cultural or natural, universal or idiosyncratic, objective or subjective. Mortal needs are neither natural (if that excludes the local and contingent), nor conventional (if that means unconditioned by phylogenesis). They are no more all the same than we are.[7]

2. Telic: A perceived, conscious, articulated need arising from an acknowledged plan, project, or deliberate choice. Such needs are "telic" in the sense of having personal purposes as it were inside them. They are conceived, constructed, discovered, or disclosed in the light of broader personal aims, character, and identity.

3. Mimetic: Needing that is stimulated by the spectacle of others visibly wanting the same things or seemingly satisfied by them.

It is not necessary to follow Rousseau, and suppose that mimetic needing only shows up late after our original state, or to follow Heidegger, and regard such needs as evidence of a fall from some more authentic way of being human. Yet who doubts that the scope and intensity of mimetic needing has risen dramatically in the last century? A capacity for mimetic needing which might have remained largely dormant has instead been stimulated to reckless heights of consumption, and exploited as an economic source of "demand" for things we would otherwise never have dreamed that we needed.[8]

4. Imputed: Needing stimulated by another who imputes a need or identifies and prescribes for a personal deficiency.

Among the oldest prototypes for imputed need is the Christian's need for sacraments and pastoral care. At a time when a filigree network of clientage linked the men who governed the far-flung cities of the late Roman empire, Christians translated people's real need for patrons and friends into an imputed need for an invisible power, as in the cult of saints, the theology of sacraments, and pastoral care. Charity was a major instrument of episcopal power in the cities of the late Roman empire. After the conversion of Constantine (312 CE) the new style of urban government exercised by the bishops, self-proclaimed "lovers of the poor," advanced what Peter Brown calls "a new imaginative model of society." Against older pagan forms of urban solidarity the bishops cultivated "a very different, more basic bond of solidarity. The poor were nourished not because they were the fellow citizens of a specific city, but because they shared with great men the common bond of human flesh. . . . All men stood before God as the poor stood before the powerful on earth—as helpless beings, in need of mercy."[9]

The Roman church is a paradigm of an institution that is both individualizing and totalizing, and its pastors are a prototype of the "helping professions" of the welfare state. The invisible care administered through a sacrament (a technique whose use is restricted to licensed professionals) is the first model of an imputed and supposedly lifesaving need for something whose operation must be magical to all but the theologically sophisticated (for whom it is merely miraculous). The *Liber Regula Pastoralis*, written by Gregory the Great on his ascension to the See of Rome in 591, defines the pastoral office as "the government of souls" and "the art of arts." The pastor "espouses the cause of the people," coming to them "like a physician to a sick person." His power and knowledge must be both individualizing and totalizing. His interventions "should be adapted to the character of the hearers, so as to be suited to the individual in his respective needs." The director of conscience must move the minds of the whole people by moving the minds of each one separately. Knowing their singular differences the pastor plays them like the separate strings of a harp. "For what else are the minds of attentive hearers but, if I may say so, the taut strings of a harp, which the skillful harpist plays with a variety of strokes . . . And it is for this reason that the strings give forth a harmonious melody, because they are not plucked with the same kind of stroke."[10] Those who are drawn into a pastoral or caring relationship thus enter into a peculiar relationship of power: putatively salvific, continuous and coextensive with life, simultaneously individualizing and totalizing, linked to the production of knowledge of individuals which is cultivated for the sake of comprehensive social government, governing *all* by governing *each one*.

The Church thus first established the office of one who, by virtue of piety and expertise, has the responsibility to care for others, opening the frontier of imputed needing and accustoming Europeans to an institution of comprehensive care by professionals with expert knowledge and benevolent intentions. With the disintegration of Roman secular power, responsibility for local political administration increasingly fell to the church, which seems to have tried to adapt to the new purpose models of government with which it was already familiar. These models were monastic, pastoral, and charitable. Eventually, of course, many pastoral and charitable responsibilities were taken over by secular governments. A form of power which for more than a millennium had been linked to a specific religious institution spread out over the entire social body, as new claims of a pastoral nature to care for individuals spread and multiplied outside the ecclesiastical institution. Aims of health, welfare, and security take the place of the religious aims of the traditional pastorate and politics replaced religion as the instrument of this-worldly salvation. The Samaritan quality which informed the first ecclesiastical care of souls has been translated into the prescriptive power to impute needs for professional care by experts knowledgeable about invisible things.

5. *Need and Desire.* Desire is different from any of the sorts of need I have mentioned, and it resists reduction to a satisfiable need of any kind. Lacan particularly insisted on this difference. His concept of need is, however, unfortunately simplistic. We have needs, he thinks, because of a supposedly physical tendency of the organism to homeostasis, which state is Lacan's model for the satisfaction of a need.[11] Such needs are by definition satisfiable by discrete acts or objects (the need for drink and the water, the need to defecate and the act, and so on). Desire is genetically related to these eminently satisfiable needs, being induced in the infant as a by-product of the care that satisfies a vital, nonsexual need. Yet once awakened, desire becomes a source of demands that can be at odds with, indifferent, or even hostile to the satisfaction of mortal and telic needs.

According to Lacan, what is really at issue in distinguishing between need and desire is whether "the human *wish* [is] simply the lack inflicted on *need*," or whether "desire emerge[s] only out of frustration."[12] Unlike need, which is experienced as the negation of presence, desire is a primordial, original lack which is unsatisfiable in principle because it is the demand for a sign of the other's love, and because a sign can never be other than a sign and thus (for Saussure and Lacan) something deficient, secondary, lacking substance in reality.

> Something else is always going on in dealings between the need-driven subject and the other who may or may not provide satisfaction. A demand for love is being made. A divided subject, haunted by absence and

lack, looks to the other not simply to supply his needs but to pay him the compliment of an unconditional *yes* . . . But the paradox and the perversity to be found in any recourse to persons is that the other to whom the appeal is addressed is never in a position to answer it unconditionally. He is too divided and haunted, and his *yes*, however loudly it is proclaimed, can only ever be a *maybe*, or a *to some extent*, in disguise. Desire has its origin in this non-adequation between need and the demand for love, and in the equally grave discrepancy between the demand itself and the addressee's ability to deliver.[13]

One can respect Lacan's distinction between need and desire without accepting much else of his theory. There is a difference between any of the needs I have mentioned and the lack or wish that impels the idiomatic iterations of neurosis and romance, where there is no real question of "satisfaction," neither in the sense of homeostasis nor of telic needs fulfilled, because the want is practically infinite, a lack the lacking of which coincides with the impulsions of subjective life.

III

It used to be that people who could afford the luxury of a consultation chose physicians who suited them, judging the worth of a doctor's knowledge by their own sense of where their health was.[14] As in other liberal professions (for instance architecture and law), there was an element of mutuality, reciprocity, and free exchange. The physician did what personal knowledge, experience, and insight suggested, and ideally the patient recovered and happily paid. This older style of liberal professional makes recommendations, of course, but claims no disciplinary power of correction, serving the mortal and telic needs of clients who (unlike welfare "clients") are free to ignore the advice, and whose personal satisfaction alone justifies the professional's fee. Such professionals do not *impute* needs where they are unrecognized; they do not implant and cultivate hybrid needs or contemplate testing an entire population to identify those who, whether they know it or not, truly need their services.

Fewer and fewer physicians today are liberal professionals of the old school. The prescriptive power/knowledge of our physicians has grown at the expense of the power (or liberty) of clients to judge the worth of their work, being free to take it or leave it. Like the Christian priest, our disciplinary professionals have the power to impute (produce, identify, define) needs for which they alone have a legal power of prescription.

Wherever there is a profession there must be a clientele; wherever there is a disciplinary profession otherwise free or indifferent potential clients become a laity. What defines these new disciplinary professionals is their effective presumption "to define a person as a client, to determine that person's need, and to hand the person a prescription." Illich suggests that disciplinary professionals today exercise a triple authority: "the sapiential authority to advise, instruct, and direct; the moral authority that makes its acceptance not just useful but obligatory; and charismatic authority that allows the professional to appeal to some supreme interest of his client that not only outranks conscience but sometimes even the *raison d'état.*" Professional prescriptive knowledge claims to be self-disciplining, which in practice makes it self-certifying, leaving the discipline free to define the quality of its service in accordance with its own practitioners' satisfaction with the result. Unlike experimental knowledge, disciplinary prescriptions are simultaneously commodities and tutelary interventions; unlike the power of guilds and unions to control how and by whom work is done, caring professions claim the right to determine the reason why their services are needed, even when (as today) service professions often need their clients more than those clients need them.[15]

Under the present division of labor in the production of knowledge and the intensity of commodification in the provision of care, disciplinary inquiry reveals an unsuspected and paradoxical capacity for counterproductive effects. Knowledge can be disabling. This conclusion must be especially paradoxical to philosophers from Plato to Dewey who regard knowledge as an unmixed blessing. Dewey defined knowledge by its effectiveness in creative coping with novel problematic situations. By definition, choices governed by knowledge are ones whose outcome is adaptive, empowering, enervating, vital. "Knowing is a way of employing empirical occurrences with respect to increasing power to direct the consequences which flow from things . . . attaining the better and averting the worse."[16] But the pragmatist's wish to secure a practical difference between real knowledge and what is false, wrong, inappropriate, or otherwise unfit for the honor of knowledge by reference to intelligent creativity in the resolution of problematic situations comes to grief when the right to define better and worse passes from the client to the disciplinary provider of care. Organic metaphors of vitality and growth will no longer help to sort out real knowledge from its disabling counterparts (which merely pass for knowledge) so long as the disciplines have the right (or anyway the power) to say what is healthy, normal, exceptional, deficient, problematic, and so on, with pain and dissatisfaction interpreted in terms of the diagnostic categories of a commodified health-care service.

Dewey might argue that such effects, if real at all, are evidence of defective inquiry or the bad, inept, or inhumane use of tools. But they are not that, or not that alone. Instead, these are the counterproductive, disabling effects that we might have expected to accompany the introduction of an industrial division of labor into the conduct of inquiry.[17] Present-day professional disciplinary knowledge offers all too many examples of how knowledge can have the opposite, counterproductive effect, making us less well adapted, stupider, incapable of satisfaction. Among the disabling effects of prescriptive knowledge, three in particular may be mentioned:

(1) In order for it to continue to exist and provide a livelihood for its practitioners prescriptive knowledge must constantly translate mortal and telic needs (and desire) into professionally recognized deficiencies for which it can prescribe. Harlan Lane notes, "Behind the mask of benevolence is the professional engaged in the human-services market, staking out his particular claim in the fastest growing sector of our economy" (MB 77). They need a constantly increasing supply of deficiencies, for which sake we are *made* needy, or disabled, in ways we would not have been without their "help." The effect can be literally stupefying. Lane paints a disturbing picture of how deaf children have been condemned to vegetate some ten years in an environment in which learning is not possible for them because of the prohibition, sanctioned by disciplinary expertise, of manual language. Faced with the choice between permitting congenitally deaf children to accept their deafness with the enabling skills of manual language, and expanding disciplinary power/knowledge at the expense of those for whom they are supposed to care, experts prefer a typically intrusive, destructive, poorly tested, and practically useless, yet resource-intensive and (to hearing people) impressively high-tech solution like a cochlear implant, now licensed in the US for commercial use in children from the age of two years (MB 216–30).

(2) Professional remedial practice isolates individuals and shows them and the world their imputed needs as personal deficiencies. "By locating the source of the problem in the individual—the source of poor educational achievement in biological deficit, the source of criminality in psychiatric disorder, the source of deaf underemployment in cochlear malfunction—medical discourse mystifies; it screens the social origins of these problems" (MB 209). It also provides the reassuring aura of professional competence for disciplinary interventions and solutions. "The assumption is that I, the professionalized servicer, am the answer. You are not the answer. Your peers are not the answer. The political, social, and economic environment is not the answer. Nor is it possible that there is no answer. I, the professional, am the answer."[18]

Contemporary discourse on "disability" prides itself on its distinctions of *impairment, disability,* and *handicap.* The World Health Organization defines impairment as "disturbances in body structures or processes which are present at birth or result from later injury or disease"; disabilities are "any restriction or lack (resulting from an impairment) of ability to perform an activity in the manner or within the range considered normal for a human being"; while a handicap is "the social disadvantage individuals experience as a result of impairment or disability because persons with disabilities cannot or do not conform to the expectations of the social groups to which they belong." The strategy behind the distinctions is obvious. They rationalize the identification of people as "disabled" by postulating a speculative organic deficit which is the result not of the environment or the society or the perceptions of experts but a morally indifferent nature, *producing* subjects for the needs they invent and impute. Since these tendentious distinctions have been written into law and are relied upon for determining legitimate and proper claims to public assistance it seems hard to dispute Albrecht's conclusion that the major purpose of the clinical concept of impairment "is to assert and maintain physician control over the disability-determination process . . . expropriated by physicians who help government determine social policy."[19]

The organic "impairment" that is offered as the underlying physical cause of a so-called disability is *the artifact* of disciplinary knowledge and professional care. If, for instance, deaf people are "impaired" or "disabled" (most of them repudiate both labels), it is because hearing people demand them to live in an environment where their differences are magnified and mirrored back to them and the rest of society as clinical signs of need for special care. "Believing their deaf students to be intellectually handicapped, hearing teachers handicap them" (MB 176, 191–92).

(3) As tools and systems become more complex and specialized, it becomes increasingly plausible to assume that potential clients cannot understand whether they have a need, what the remedy is, the process that should satisfy it, or even whether the need has been satisfied at all unless experts express satisfaction at the outcome of their own interventions.[20] Such an arrogant presumption would be impossible apart from a docile laity prepared to accept that continuous specialization in the production of knowledge and the extension of care is a good thing, or that better tools must be more complicated ones and better solutions more resource-intensive.[21]

The disabling effects of knowledge include the production of counterpurposive imputed needs, which transform differences into impairments and motivates efforts to remake the bodies of those rich enough to demand professional care or too poor to say no. Nonprofessional, vernacular care is discredited if not actually made illegal, while the practical capacity and nondisciplinary knowledge required for self-care is laid to waste.

IV

We increasingly forget that no science can prescriptively define what is a normal or a healthy life. There are no "purely physical" facts about what bodily conditions are vital or normal, healthy or sick, nor even any independent, purely objective facts about the identity of our body's functional parts or their proper operation which can be established and known apart from attending to how ordinary people are accustomed to reacting, feeling, or being able to perform. It is true, of course, that by relying on clinical information and laboratory techniques physicians can sometimes see patients in people who do not feel sick. But, as Canguilhem points out,

> it is only because today's practitioners are the heirs to a medical culture transmitted to them by yesterday's practitioners that, in terms of clinical perspicacity, they overtake or outstrip their regular or occasional clients. There has always been a moment when, all things concluded, the practitioner's attention has been drawn to certain symptoms, even solely objective ones, by men who were complaining of not being normal—that is, of not being the same as they had been in the past—or of suffering. If, today, the physician's knowledge of disease can anticipate the sick man's experience of it, it is because at one time this experience gave rise to, summoned up, that knowledge. Hence medicine always exists *de jure*, if not *de facto*, because there are men who feel sick, not because there are doctors to tell men of their illnesses.[22]

This vital point is silently drifting into oblivion with the new legitimacy of what Illich calls an "iatrogenic body." Less and less is health defined by how we spontaneously feel; rather, how we feel, how healthy we feel we are, increasingly depends on how professional health-care providers tell us we are or should be feeling. Our very body itself—our sensations and corporeal wellness—is increasingly *iatrogenic*—physiciangenerated. We perceive ourselves and our bodies as physicians describe them. It cannot be enough to say, as Illich and others have, that medicine makes us sick, when how people feel and live with their bodies—the touchstone of "health"—is being redefined by medical gnosis. Hospitals and physicians still make people sick, but beyond this technical counterproductivity is the "symbolic fallout" of present-day medical technics: a docile body that feels its health or normality in accordance with the prescriptions of paid providers of care.

Historian Barbara Duden has witnessed the iatrogenic body under construction in a pregnancy clinic in Harlem. Referring to "the conceptual framework of a slum pregnancy in New York"—in other words, to the deployment of medical power/knowledge in an urban welfare system—she explains that she deliberately refrains from questioning "the medical and social effectiveness of these controls" because her interest is in their *symbolic* effects, "the symbolic result of the procedures." What do they do, not to women's bodies but to their understanding, their imagination, their subjective sense of their options, their liberty to choose and act? She finds that "as a system, in its mass application, I think it deeply undermines women's capacity to bear, in the literal sense." "The better the counselling, the more authoritatively convincing are certain modern ideas: that prenatal procedures are good, that pregnancies can be classified, imply risks, demand supervision, impose decisions, and require a large bureaucratic apparatus to arrange one's passage though the maze."[23]

Who says who is pregnant? Before the nineteenth century only the woman herself could establish the fact of her pregnancy, by letting it be known that she had quickened. Today a lab test tells. Quickening is scarcely a memory for women who, Duden feels, "can only stutter or keep silent in the face of the normative nomenclature of medical language" (DW 88).[24] The power to determine the fact of pregnancy is only the beginning of a regimen in which women's experience (either those rich enough to demand special care or too poor to say no) is translated into a series of precise medical events. Duden describes women who have forgotten what they used to feel, who fix instead on the fetus they are instructed to see in a digitalized (ultrasound) image. Disciplinary knowledge, epitomized in the sonogram, opens their once-gendered interior to a nongendered, anonymous gaze. The fetus which we think this technology lets us see is now a public fact, its image an icon of the times. By accepting this technoscientific image, with its presumption to offer her a peek at "the life" within her womb, a woman "not only disembodies her perceptions but forces [herself] into nine-month clientage in which her 'scientifically' defined needs for help and counsel are addressed by professionals" (DW 4).

One effect of the routine application of ultrasound technology is the docile assumption by the pregnant woman that its image is her baby.

Says Duden, "It is not." The ultrasound image "gives the appearance—when a woman sits in front of a real-time ultrasound scanner—that she sees the interior of her womb." But that is an illusion "because what they see is the electronic mapping of physically defined matter." I believe her point is that the image on the screen is not like the one Galileo formed when he turned his homemade *instrumentum* to the moon. Although nothing is said to disabuse women of this incorrect assumption, the ultrasound procedure does not literally enable an optical peek into their corporeal depths. Peering into the screen one does not see a pattern of light reflected from an inner surface. The image is not a "reflection" of anything except the assumptions built into the software that generates a digital image of what a theory says should be there. Yet what she sees may make a woman *think* she can see her unborn child. The purely artificial, theoretically constructed image may be more real to her than her own sensations. Some women, Duden says, demand "again and again to see it in order to know it's still there. It makes them dependent on this surveillance and it tells them something about the necessity to manage it" (HS 8).

I am not nostalgic for an innocent eye or an unmediated perception. But I think it is significant that the theory according to which the ultrasound image is constructed is not something that the woman who accepts the image as a true representation is invited or expected to understand. It is the privileged knowledge of a discipline which, in the name of health and care, translates the mortal and telic needs of the expectant mother into imputed and mimetic needs for its resource-intensive services. The effects are not only economic and political; there is also a symbolic effect, an effect upon the historical imagination, on what it is possible for us to understand. A woman for whom a computer-generated image is more real than her own sensations endows a carefully managed construct with the reality of her own body. She is carrying an iatrogenic pregnancy and living an iatrogenic body, a body *lived and felt* according to prescripts of medical gnosis.

It is a fallacy to believe that a more intensely medicalized pregnancy is healthier. A characteristic of our high-intensity market economy is the unsubtle demand to interpret any need in terms of a commodity, and any satisfaction in terms of the blandishments of the marketplace. To interpret one's own health in terms of the diagnostic categories of commodified medicine is only more of the same. An iatrogenic body is part of a historical translation of needing and the process of satisfaction from mortal and telic to predominantly imputed and mimetic needing, correlated with the intense commodification of health-care services and its disabling, counterproductive effects.

An iatrogenic body is a strategy of what Foucault calls bio-power. This term names the strategic tendency of relatively recent forms of power/knowledge to work toward the ever more comprehensive management of life—both individual life (mine, yours, the fetus's) and en masse, treating this abstraction "life" as the ultimate resource for which no sacrifice is too great. But the iatrogenic body is a strategy, not a fait accompli. As Foucault also emphasized, power does not exist apart from the multiple points of resistance upon which, in fact, the relation of power depends.[25] An interlocutor asks Duden, "Is there any way out?" "Yes, of course. You have to say *no*. I think women have to learn to say *no* to these procedures and that they basically should trust their own senses . . . I'm deeply convinced that the only way out is to say *no* to this and to argue from one's own senses" (HS 8–9).

> There is a lot of talk today about "reproductive choice" . . . [and] women *do* have a choice when they become pregnant. They can eschew the perception of pregnancy that has come into existence only in my lifetime but is now taken for granted. They can avoid giving embodied reality to managed constructs. As a society, we can learn to question the certainties that have led us into a corner where pregnancy is defined in terms of the modern fetus and then in terms of something called "life," for which we are all asked to take public responsibility. (DW 4)

Knowledge can be counterproductive; too much expertise makes us stupid, too much inquiry can imprison us in our discoveries, for instance of our true needs. It may be objected that I surely cannot mean that *knowledge* makes us stupid! Surely it would be pseudoknowledge passing for known or for true. But no. It is instead something we have only lately learned, something that the Greeks or the philosopher-scientists of the seventeenth century could not have expected, namely that knowledge does not have the unconditional value which philosophers from Plato to Dewey attributed to it. When its division becomes as reticulated and resource-dependent as elsewhere in our industrial economy, scientific inquiry turns out to produce its own form of pollution, a symbolic fallout which disables our imaginations and corrupts our capacities for autonomous coping. Professional advice and care may be good, but what makes them good is their sequel in somebody's life, and not the supposedly inherent value of "life itself." More generally, the good of knowledge depends on what happens when individuals act on it. It is not guaranteed to be good just because it is true, objective, or scientific—all qualities compatible with the production of disabling knowledge.

7

Natural Law and Sexual Morality

M.C. Dillon

Framework

Postmodern thinking reveals a binary opposition latent in the foundations of natural law theory.[1] The laws of nature can be regarded as descriptive and morally neutral (e.g., gravitation is a law of nature) or prescriptive and normative (e.g., natural law decrees that the organs of reproduction and excretion should be used exclusively for those purposes). Natural law theory in general—but particularly as it relates to sexual morality—depends upon an inference from the description of a fact to the prescription of a norm.

- The penis is an organ that fulfills the natural functions of reproduction and excretion (factual, descriptive).

Therefore

- It is contrary to nature to use the penis for other purposes (evaluative, prescriptive).

If it is proper to constitute description and prescription as binary opposites, as standing in a relation of mutual exclusion—description is not prescription, norms are not facts—then this inference is prima facie invalid. Yet, it is arguable that such mighty institutions as the United

States Constitution and Roman Catholic dogma rest in significant part on natural law theory, hence on some version of this inference.

What rationale might be supplied for the inference from description to prescription? The answer usually involves the related concepts of purpose (goal or *telos*) and design (form) which come together under the heading of function.

- Nature designed the penis to function in such a way as to fulfill the purposes of excretion and reproduction.

The concepts of purpose and design may be regarded as descriptive; but the fact described may also be regarded as pregnant with portent: if one can observe and describe some purpose fulfilled by a given design, one might find some warrant for conjecturing intent.

- Nature intends the penis to be used for excretion and reproduction.

Another premise is required to render this latent prescription explicitly normative. This is an exclusionary premise which limits the function to the purpose observable in the design.

- Nature intends the penis to be used exclusively for
  excretion
  and reproduction.

From this premise one can validly deduce that any other use is contrary to nature.

Three separate issues collide in this inference: (1) the exclusive disjunction of fact and value, description and prescription; (2) the constellation of design-purpose-intent which subsumes natural function under some teleological rubric; (3) the exclusionary premise which restricts function to a given end or set of ends. I shall take up each of these, but not in the order in which they were presented.

ı Teleology: Natural, Supernatural, Human

I begin with the second issue listed above: the constellation of design-purpose-intent which subsumes natural function under one of three teleological rubrics: the natural, the supernatural, and the human. The natural teleology relevant to love and sexuality falls in the domain of biology, the supernatural in the domain of onto-theology, and the human, as that which is preeminently in question, in the domain of politics and morality. These divisions are more than a little arbitrary: as I hope to show, the demarcating criteria break down under scrutiny.

To anticipate: the criteria at work in separating biological, onto-theological, and ethico-political teleology from one another center on the notion of final causality as a principle of explanation. I shall take Aristotle as spokesperson for natural teleology, but argue that his conception of the natural depends in essential ways on the supernatural and the human. The shift from Aristotle to Aquinas, my spokesperson for supernatural teleology, rearranges the priorities in the natural-supernatural-human triad, but, under my interpretation, still draws upon a principle of essential interdependency. Aristotle's empiricist approach to teleological explanation makes a somewhat reluctant appeal to supernatural grounds because in some ways and in some instances he saw the notion of *telos* as essentially related to that of finality or perfection. Aquinas's theistic approach is circumscribed by the regularities in nature which it seeks to explain, the explanation of nature being a defining goal of theology.

a Aristotle and natural teleology

I adopt here the interpretation of Aristotle's conception of natural law that regards it as derived from a biological paradigm.[2] Having repudiated the Platonic understanding of natural law as originating in the supernatural sphere of the eternal, immutable Forms, that is, in the sphere of the divine, Aristotle turns to nature in general and biology in particular to search for a ground and measure of lawfulness.[3] The science of biology, for Aristotle, is based on teleological explanation and, as such, is infused with values and norms.[4]

The issue of right-handedness provides an apt example. Consider the following passages from *De Incessu Animalum.*

> Human beings have their left limbs detached most of all the animals because they are according to nature (*kata phusin*) most of all the animals; now the right is by nature (*phusei*) better than the left, being separate from it, and so in human beings the right is most right [among all the animals]. (a18–22)[5]

We observe the predominance of right-handedness, but does the greater strength of the right hand, observable not universally but for the most part, ground a claim for the general superiority of the right? Aristotle's answer lies in a second passage from the same work.

> . . . Nature does nothing in vain, but always the best possible concerning each kind of animal with respect to its substance. Therefore, if one way is better (*beltion*) than another, that is also according to nature (*kata phusin*). (2.704b12–18)

The underlying premise is that "nature operates for the sake of the end, which is good, so that what is needed for the end is beneficial, and nature provides what is beneficial . . . or needed for the end or good of the organism, which in this instance is its continued existence."[6] Further support for the general superiority of the right can be found in Aristotelian arguments that associate the right with the origin of motion (which enjoys the superiority of the mover over the moved).

The teleological argument which explains the general predominance of the right hand over the left is based on the biological *telos* of serving the good of the organism, that is, what is beneficial or necessary for life. The reasoning just summarized proceeds from the empirically grounded premise asserting the predominance of right-handedness to the trans-empirical conclusion that asserts the general superiority of right-handedness. Bracketing the issue of its validity, the warrant offered in support of the inference is that "nature makes nothing in vain." This is clearly not an empirical assertion, but would traditionally fall under the general heading of metaphysics.[7]

To identify the assertion that nature makes nothing in vain as a metaphysical assertion is relatively uncontroversial, but when one attempts to analyze the import of that identification, one enters several debates. The debate of interest to me centers on the opposition between the postmodern categorization of metaphysics under the heading of onto-theology, on the one hand, and, on the other, the Aristotelian understanding of metaphysics as the endeavor to codify the organizing principles of scientific inquiry or reason at large. Postmodern thought characterizes Aristotelian metaphysics as onto-theological because Aristotle attributes intent to nature thereby betraying his essential dependence on a latent theology, a projection onto nature of cosmic intentionality modeled after the human but magnified to infinity. Further support for this characterization is found in the notion of the unmoved mover which informs Aristotle's physics.

Although I think it is mistaken to read Christian theology backward into Aristotelian metaphysics, I also think that Aristotelian ideas contributed to the development of Christian theology. At stake is the issue of teleological explanation and the constellation of design-purpose-intent informing Aristotle's understanding of nature. I see an ambivalence in Aristotle's standpoint: while it is true that his teleology depends on the attribution of intent-design-purpose to nature,[8] it is also true that he seeks to distance himself from the Platonic appeal to a supernatural domain of Forms as the source of natural organization or worldly meaning. I do not think Aristotle resolved this tension. I do think that this tension remains unresolved to this day. It remains unresolved because, following Aristotle, an opposition between the natural and the supernatural, the a-theological and the theological, has grown up to obscure the quest that defines Aristotelian natural philosophy, that is, the quest to find meaning and value in nature.

This quest drives Aristotelian teleological explanation. It also drives Aristotelian hylomorphism—where a related ambivalence, a similar tension may be found. Aristotle argues for the fundamental coincidence of form and matter in nature, but he also offers separate etiologies for the formal and the material elements and separates the two in his taxonomy of causes. If form and matter are distinct in origin and if equivalences are drawn between the material and the natural, on one side, and the formal and the supernatural, on the other, then nature degenerates into raw matter lacking meaning, and that meaning has to be attributed to a supernatural process of informing or organizing worldly matter.

To claim, as I have, that Aristotle's conception of the natural depends in essential ways on the supernatural, that the two domains cannot be separated if sense is to be made of his teleological model of explanation, is simply to stress that aspect of his philosophy that recoils against the disjunction of matter and form, nature and telic organization. It is not to deny the presence of proto-theological elements (unmoved mover, attribution of intent to nature) in Aristotle's thought. The project here is to follow the path of hylomorphism, the path of matter-pregnant-with-form or autochthonous organization,[9] opened by Aristotle, but left untended by Western philosophy as it pursued a divergent path at the fork created by Aristotle's ambivalence, the path of ontological dualism characterized by binary opposition between form and matter, supernatural and natural, fact and value, etc.

The teleology informing Aristotle's conception of natural law has a human component that must be considered in conjunction with the natural and the supernatural. Aristotle's assessment of competing political systems (i.e., differing constitutions and the bodies of legislation enacted in accordance with them) is based on the criterion of human teleology. The best system is the system that best serves the realization of the natural ends of humanity and attainment of the good life.[10]

To say, as Aristotle does in his *Politics*, that the state is a creation of nature, and that humans are by nature political animals (I.1253a2–3), is to ascribe to nature an intent in fashioning humans.

Nature makes nothing in vain, and human beings are the only animals endowed by nature with *logos* or speech. Human speech serves to reveal the advantageous and the harmful, and hence also the just . . . and the unjust. . . . Nature [also] endows humans with the desire to live together because life in political communities is necessary for their common advantage.[11]

Here, again, the teleological principle is invoked with the premise that nature makes nothing in vain. The human end of attaining the good life, which may be a matter of deliberate human intent, is inseparable from the natural inclination to be political which, in turn, is inseparable from the supernatural intent which dictates that nature make nothing in vain. I shall have more to say about the intertwining of the natural, supernatural, and human elements in natural law theory, but that will require a shift to a different level of interpretation, a critical reflection on the fact that natural law theory in particular and philosophy in general are, themselves, driven by human teleology in response to nature and what lies beyond it. This reflection takes us beyond Aristotle (although antecedents can be found in the Aristotelian thesis that all humans, by nature, desire knowledge).

Let me conclude this phase of the argument by anticipating its bearing on section II below (which follows a brief treatment of natural law in Aquinas). The constellation of design-purpose-intent drives Aristotelian natural law theory inasmuch as it allows Aristotle to draw inferences from what he observes to conclusions with normative weight. That is, Aristotle uses paradigms drawn from biology and metaphysics to generate criteria based on teleological explanation by means of which he can assess competitive normative theories and generate his own.[12] There are questions still to be raised regarding the validity of his reasoning and the soundness of his conclusions.

b Aquinas and supernatural teleology

I take up Aquinas to make two main points, one having to do with his standpoint, the other having to do with the posture I adopt with regard to it.

[i] The distinction between natural and supernatural teleology, although thematically operative in both, can no more be sustained as a binary opposition in Aquinas than it can in Aristotle. The difference between them has more to do with differences in the stance each takes with regard to the supernatural. They both use metaphysical paradigms to argue from empirical premises to trans-empirical[13] conclusions, but

Aristotle, preferring to retain firm footing in the empirical domain, designates his speculations about the unmoved mover as such, and distances himself from the Platonic tendency to ground ethics in onto-theology, whereas Aquinas operates from within the standpoint of faith and maintains that divine revelation provides a ground of certainty which is qualitatively different from and superior to natural reason.

For Aquinas, there is but one true ground of law and that is supernatural teleology. Nature is the creation of divinity and it fulfills the divine purpose. Extrapolations such as Aristotle's regarding the teleology apparent in nature set forth under the heading of natural law can discern the ends of humanity insofar as they are discoverable by finite human reason, but the understanding gained thereby is incomplete, and the life based on natural virtues designed to promote those ends cannot be satisfying precisely because humans were created for a supernatural end. Perfect beatitude requires faith as the fulfillment of the supernatural end and cannot be attained through the exercise of natural powers alone. Humans were created to attain perfect beatitude and given the power to do so by grace, but this end requires faith and cannot be known or attained through the exercise of human reason alone.

Since Aquinas regards natural law as a manifestation of supernatural law, there can be no real distinction between them: the relevant distinction is that drawn between the illumination of divine law provided by natural reason and that provided by faith.

[ii] I regard theology in general as founded on a metaphor that has outlived its credibility: god is the creation of humans rather than *vice versa* as supernatural law is an extrapolation from the scientific and political lawfulness derived from and applied to the finite domain of the human world. From my standpoint, infinitude is a name for the incomprehensible, apprehensible only in our awareness of our finitude, which serves the primary purpose of inducing humility and wonder, and is misused in the endeavor to substantiate positive cognitive claims.

The point I seek to draw from Aquinas here is that the ends apparent to natural reason point beyond themselves and are never completely satisfying. That is the reason for the human creation of the divine. The natural end of human life apparent to finite reason is decay and death. Faith regards death as the gateway to eternal happiness as reward for suffering the passion of finite life in the proper way. Finite reason finds the only source of happiness in the living of life, and anticipates death as the termination of the possibility of that happiness. Death brings complete satisfaction only through the extermination of desire, not its fulfillment. Finite satisfaction is therefore tainted by the realization of its own transience.[14]

II The Exclusive Disjunction of Fact and Value

Following Aquinas, the medieval tradition of Christian theology sedimented the subsumption of natural teleology under supernatural teleology so firmly that, with the Enlightenment, the discrediting of the latter led to the banishing of the former from the domain of orthodox science—until it became evident that orthodox biology could not do its job without the tool of natural teleology. Now, in the sphere of contemporary continental philosophy at least, the deconstruction of the onto-theological foundations of science in general and biology in particular is attempting, through a more reductive radicalism than was imaginable to Enlightenment thinkers, to complete the purge of final causality, not by separating science from religion, but rather by classifying science as religion, that is, as onto-theology, and suggesting that the pernicious effects of Western religion (e.g., phallocentrism and the host of evils that follow from it) are recapitulated within Western science and rendered all the more devastating by virtue of self-dissemblance, that is, for being much less obvious.

I maintain that this historical progression is regressive, that it begins with the mistake Plato made that Aristotle did not quite rectify—the mistake of conceiving the supernatural as ontologically disjunct from human pro-jection, that is, human teleology—that this mistake was compounded when Enlightenment thinkers decided to abandon teleological explanation rather than refine it, and that postmodern thinkers are inviting future thinkers to ignore their genuine insights by situating these insights in the context of an anti-science polemic against empiricism (conceived as a species of foundationalism) which further exacerbates the Enlightenment's overreaction to the Platonic mistake.

This mistake can also be described as the failure to distinguish between the finite ends of human teleology (becoming) and the infinite ends of divine perfection: human teleology is misconceived when understood as finality. Final causality is a misleading term for human and natural teleology. The logic of *tele* is properly conceived as open-ended. The positing of closure at infinity—i.e., perfection—is a way of misunderstanding both the human world and the natural world surrounding it. It is an instance of the onto-theological fallacy: a paradoxical reversal of thought which extrapolates cosmic intent from a finite human model . . . and then fashions a moral code based on the subsumption of human ends under divine finality.

The Platonic mistake which Aristotle perpetuates rather than corrects is contained in that use of the craftsmanship analogy[15] which attributes to nature the deliberate human intent manifest in human activities. In the first book of the *Nicomachean Ethics*, Aristotle establishes a teleological framework for his ethical theorizing: human activities are to be assessed on the basis of the end or good to which they are directed. Happiness is the name given to the final end, "that for whose sake everything else is done."[16] Happiness so conceived is described as "lacking in nothing," as "final and self-sufficient," and as "the end of action" (1.1097b15–22). To specify this end more concretely, Aristotle raises the question of the function of humanity. "Have the carpenter . . . and the tanner certain functions or activities, and has man none?" (1.1097b29–30) He then applies the craftsmanship analogy: just as the end of the craftsman is to attain "eminence in respect of goodness" in the performance of his function or craft, so is it the end of humanity, the "human good," to perform its function well. Just as the end or good of the craftsman is to perform his essential or defining function well, so is it the end or good of humanity to attain eminence in the performance of the unique function (or specific difference) constitutive of its essence or definition, in this case, "activity of soul which follows or implies a rational principle" or "activity of soul in accordance with virtue" (1.1098a8–18).

The analogy commits the onto-theological fallacy by reasoning from finite, circumscribed human functions to a function assigned to humans by nature. As shown above, Aristotle argues in the *Politics* that nature designs humans in such a way as to achieve the end of happiness. Here, in the *Nicomachean Ethics*, that end provides a measure for moral evaluation of human activities. The finality of that end is trans-finite: it is "self-sufficient" and "lacking in nothing." These terms belong in the domain of the causa sui, that which needs nothing in order to be; they have departed from the domain of human finitude where purpose and design are driven by lack and need.

The rectification of this mistake does not lie in abandoning teleology, but in delimiting teleology to the domain from which it was initially extrapolated. Guided in this manner, I would rephrase Aristotle's question. Is it the case that, as craftsmen, we are driven nonarbitrarily by certain intentions toward certain ends, but that, as humans, we have no intentions which incline us nonarbitrarily toward certain ends and away from others?

Happiness is as felicitous a term as any other to name the conceptual space which designates the harmonious fulfillment of human desires. It is the task of philosophy to work at the project of filling that space. It is the mistake of onto-theology to conceive that space as filled by a transfinite purpose which we must try to discover through nonempirical intuition or faith or interpretation of scripture guided by divine hands. But it is equally a mistake of deconstructionism to conceive nature and empirical circumstance as irrelevant to the task filling of that space or as cryptonyms for an antecedent onto-theological filling of that space. Nature is relevant to human teleology, to human intentions, needs, desires, and values: not nature as the book from which divine intent can be read, but nature as the source of organic life and all that sustains and delimits it.

The distinctions between the human, the natural, and the supernatural are human distinctions, to be sure, but they are drawn in response to a world that transcends humanity. Everything human is natural, but the converse does not hold. There are regularities in nature for which there are causes and ordering principles, but deliberate intent must be restricted to that domain of natural causality known as human: when intent is applied to nonhuman aspects of nature, one commits the onto-theological fallacy of conceiving the world as an artifact constructed by a cosmic artisan.[17]

The natural world includes the human world because we are natural entities, but it transcends the human world in space and time as it transcends our ability to understand it. Under this thesis, human culture is just as natural as the culture of an ant colony, and anything that takes place in human culture is just as natural as anything that happens in any other natural domain—whence follows de Sade's challenge to natural law morality that nothing that happens in nature is contrary to nature. The natural world also includes the supernatural world, if one accepts the thesis introduced at the end of the last section that the supernatural is an artifice of human culture. Given our natural needs, it is a nonarbitrary project to pro-ject a world yet to be contrived in which those needs are met. This ideal world projected as a future world is supernatural only if one commits the onto-theological fallacy; its transcendence is better conceived in terms of the no-longer and not-yet of natural or worldly time.

The inference from fact to value must be made—if one forsakes the absolutes of onto-theology, on one hand, and rejects the abject relativism to which anti-foundationalism commits itself, on the other—simply because there is no other ground for value. Traditional natural law theory correctly identifies the bridge between fact and value as intent, but errs in conceiving that intent as divine rather than human. The naturalistic fallacy is a fallacy only if the natural world we observe is devoid of value. The natural world we observe is devoid of value only if an antecedent commitment is made to separate facts from values and provide separate etiologies for their provenance.[18] Make that commitment and G.E. Moore's pronouncement that we must look beyond the natural world in order to ground our values follows inexorably. This I take to be a compelling reason not to make the commitment. The point here is that description is not value-neutral. Describe the penis as an organ of pleasure (as an erogenous zone pace Freud), and the argument which opened this paper would arrive at a conclusion which would conflict with the one restricting the uses of the penis to reproduction and excretion.

The truth of natural law theory is that natural entities (including the human body) lend themselves unequally to human goals. It is not contrary to natural intent to try to use the penis to pound nails—because nature has no intent in designing the penis as humans do in designing hammers—it is just stupid. The penis is ill-formed to be used prehensively (for using tools, grasping in general), therefore it is bad in some sense (stupid, awkward, insane) to try to use it for those purposes. Far better to use one's hands. One might use one's penis for ostention (i.e., to point in a given direction, toward some thing or other), but, here again, one's hands might do a better job. It is also stupid, but not unnatural, to insert an unprotected penis into an anus because the pleasure obtained is far exceeded by the risk. Perhaps it is even cruel if adequate preparation and consent are lacking. But the issue here is not a question of intent on the part of nature, it is rather the issue of natural limits or natural constraints upon human freedom.

III The Exclusionary Premise

We speak of natural organs or organisms as being designed for given purposes. We also speak of them as having evolved certain forms to fulfill certain natural needs within the constraints of natural circumstance. The difference here is properly conceived as the difference between the paradigms of onto-theological creationism and naturalistic evolution theory. Not unmindful of the problems attendant upon it, I shall simply acknowledge that I have adopted here a variant of the paradigm currently known as socio-biology: as should be evident by now, I regard it as human arrogance to construe our culture as supervenient upon the natural world rather than emergent from it. History cannot be reduced to biology, but it is inconceivable apart from biology.

Freud has been taken to task for arguing that anatomy is destiny—even though he contended that the destiny portended by gender differences is malleable and subject to the vicissitudes of racial and family history, cultural influence, and even personal decision. The laws of psychology are misconceived if they are taken as grounded in nature exclusive of culture or culture exclusive of nature for the two are inextricably intertwined. It is, I think, undeniable that the fact of being anatomical portends the inevitable destiny of death and the host of values that respond to that fact. One of the points I am attempting to make here is that the factual or biological aspect of the nature-culture continuum provides a basis for assessing the values that emerge in the human world. For example, I would claim that the values associated with the projection of a life after death are far less appropriate to the fact of death which limits finite human becoming—far less truthful—than the values associated with authentic acknowledgment that individual human lives are coterminous with the lives of individual human bodies: the values of the latter preclude the values that produced autos-da-fé during the Spanish Inquisition. To the extent that warriors are motivated by dreams of Valhalla, they are dupes of their priests and would be far better served to ponder their commitments to the causes they serve with full awareness that they will not be witness to the admiration to be earned in a brave and glorious death.

The thesis seeking to articulate itself here is that of a reversibility of nature and culture in which culture emerges from nature and returns to inform it. One reflects on death in order to choose among the options available in responding to it, the natural fact of death forecloses the option of immortality, but opens possibilities which range from martyrdom to health food addiction. When some options gain cultural supremacy and others are rejected, further limitations are placed upon human freedom: suttee is now illegal, but in former times it created serious restrictions upon Indian widows in responding to the deaths of their husbands. We are embodied natural entities. As such, we are constrained by biology and physics: we need food, water, air; we are held down by gravity. Culture responds to these constraints with various cuisines and technologies designed to distribute water to deserts and air to divers. Recently, we have learned to counteract gravity with surgical tucks. More to the point, we have learned to alter our cuisines and technologies to reflect what we have learned about the biological effects of fat in our diets and pollutants in our environment. The laws we enact in our cultures respond to the laws we find at work in nature and can be assessed in accordance with the measures provided by our own natural ends of health and happiness.

Nature, as we understand it, is constituted by our interests, that is, by our culture; but culture is constituted in response to the natural environment with which it has always had to contend. It is not accidental that we have always been interested in earth, air, fire, and water: we have no choice but to contend with these elements. How we contend with them is the issue. Fire heats our dwellings and also burns them down: there are natural constraints upon our uses of fire. This is the domain of the exclusionary premise.

Under traditional natural law theory, every natural element is conceived as fulfilling a purpose for which it was designed, and uses contrary to design are excluded, prohibited by taboo in human culture. There have always been places where fires may be lighted and other places where they may not. There are divinities for all the elements, and those divinities demand propitiation, obedience to their laws. The *Aufhebung* of the deities, which I advocate (on grounds that there are better ways to respect the elements), does not diminish the force of the laws they symbolized, it rather calls for greater degrees of delicacy and depth of understanding. My general point is that human teleology, based as it is on natural needs, commits us to respond to natural laws. But that response is grounded in our projects and designs rather than any deliberate intent attributable to nature or its putative creator.

The exclusionary premise restricts human behavior in accordance with human teleology, not divine teleology. The natural law of gravity does not tell us that it is contrary to nature for humans to fly, but it does set limits to the means and delivers brutal consequences when the means employed are inadequate to propitiate its demands: when the flight attendant says that we will be on the ground shortly, she or he is always telling the truth—it is a natural fact, a fact permeated with value.

Our natural needs generate nonarbitrary projects in the fulfillment of which we turn to nature. The exclusionary premise tells us what nature will and will not provide, and at what risk, what expenditure of time, labor, and ingenuity. What is contrary to nature is what we have not yet learned to coax from nature in ways that are consonant with our own desires and fears. We are always in the process of learning what is contrary to nature: it may, for example, be contrary to nature to have 7.1 million defecating human beings occupy the forty-eight-square-mile island of Manhattan. I suspect that it is, but tend to think that this is a matter of sanitation technology and its limits rather more than one of divine intent.

To argue, as I have here, for the reversibility of nature and culture is not to posit them as separate and discrete domains which interact or intersect, but neither is it to posit a homogenized and undifferentiable unity. The model I advocate is that of a spectrum delimited by bounds of possibility that stop short of pure nature on one end and pure culture on the other. The notion of a nature in itself apart from human cognition is a limiting point of human cognition—as is the notion of a symbolic domain with no ties to the sights and sounds of which symbols are made and through which they are communicated. But one can discriminate phenomena such as death and disease which have cultural significance but resist cultural manipulation from other phenomena such as art and morality which have ties to nature but are more susceptible to human contrivance. Gonococcus bacteria are resilient and persistent in their own quest to survive, but the social stigma attaching to gonorrhea infection has attenuated as our culture devises more effective ways to control the spread of the disease and alter the attitudes that have demonstrated their counterproductivity.

iv Natural Law and Sexual Morality

Aristotle struggled with the opposition between the universality imputed to natural law and the particularity or variance of culture-bound morality. The struggle continues. (And, I suspect, will go on indefinitely, due in part to Aristotle's efforts and notwithstanding my own.) The human body may be regarded as a natural constant across culture and history or as an artifact that varies with culture and epoch. In my view, it is wrong to set up the opposition, mistaken to polarize in either direction, and more accurate to say that biology constrains cultural variance, but does not univocally dictate a given praxis. No culture that I am aware of has left the human body unaltered and unadorned, but there is wide variance in the ways in which different cultures mutilate, pierce, paint, coif, and train their bodies. Different praxes produce different consequences. Romans may have learned too late that lead oxide whitens the face, but kills the body. Chinese aristocracy abandoned the practice of binding the feet of their infant daughters. Circumcision still appears to be salubrious, but I doubt that clitorectomy will survive into the twenty-first century. In any case, I hope it will not, as I hope the practice of incising the glans of the penis and embedding small sharp stones therein will rapidly fade. Eye shadow, however, is forever, and I fully suspect that men will adopt it as gracefully as we have taken to hair spray and cologne (and for much the same reasons). My point here is that there are natural limits which eventually delimit the range of practice. Cultural plurality and diversity may be regarded as a huge anthropological experiment to discover which sets of mores are more felicitous than others.

I am not asserting a categorical imperative which commands absolute respect for human bodies as Kant asserted his imperative based on the absolutization of reason. I am asserting an open-ended and emergent set of values which might be conceived as hypothetical imperatives. The antecedents are fuzzy in character and variable in force; they constellate around terms such as happiness, well-being, health, prosperity, and the like, all of which are multidetectable, but subject to natural constraint. If you (collectively or distributively) want to be happy or healthy or prosperous, etc., then you had better eat your vegetables, give up cigarettes, exercise regularly, use condoms, work hard, buy-low-sell-high, reduce your viewing time, recycle, and interview potential sex partners carefully and before the act. In short, I am adopting some classical Aristotelian virtues, such as *phronesis* and *sophrosyne*, as well as some newer ones, such as authenticity and nondemonic eros. The major change I propose is that of responding intelligently to what we know of natural regularity instead of exercising blind obedience to the gods that have been constructed to symbolize those laws. It is not an intent of nature that constrains us, it is our intent that is constrained by nature. If you look at the sun, you will go blind; if you want to observe the eclipse, use a filter.

As it is with one's eyes, so it is, I think, with one's genitals. Delightful though it might be to some tastes during some phases of life to maximize the number of sexual partners, the number of ways of generating frisson, and the frequency of that generation, this project, if carried out imprudently, is naturally bound to culminate in more pain than pleasure, more misery than happiness. We do not need a god to tell us that promiscuity is evil and threaten punishment. We need to know that sexual intercourse is the best way that nature has stumbled upon to transplant germs from one body to another. It is also a pretty good way to promote intimacy, pleasure, and affection—or alienation, pain, and rancor. Sexual mores have always been guided by the *telos* of happiness to minimize the threats to individual or collective well-being. These threats are grounded in both nature and culture, that is, under my model, they are grounded in some intertwining of nature and the response to nature on that part of nature which responds to itself.

I am advocating a morality predicated on the attempt to understand the biology of human sexuality and respond appropriately, that is, in accordance with the hypothetical imperatives devised to accommodate the natural constraints that delimit human behavior. It is a morality of consequences which depends on knowing how to produce the effects deemed desirable—and avoid those deemed undesirable—in that variant of human teleology which follows from one's own definition of happiness. As noted above, I do not take happiness to be a completely specifiable term, but neither do I regard it as empty: I think that pain, hunger, disease, oppression, poverty, ignorance, premature death, and so forth are, in general, threats to happiness.

Traditional natural law morality as applied to the sexual domain has based itself on such norms as the male-female reproductive dyad and male superiority as supernatural intentions discernible in nature. I have already repudiated the notion of supernatural intent, but the prudence I advocate prompts me to state explicitly that I regard perversity in sex just as I do perversity in other domains as practice contrary to human intent. I do not recognize any specifically sexual morality, but seek to subsume sexual behavior under the same precepts that govern other domains of human interaction. It is my intent to promote an environment in which consenting adults are free to do whatever they please with themselves and each other, subject only to self-imposed constraint based on knowledge of risk. Nor do I think that either gender—or any gender—enjoys general superiority over any other, although I do think that we are all constrained by genetic coding and bodily attributes.

Mystification is anathema to knowledge—which is why I repudiate traditional natural law morality. Mystification always entails separation of value from the grounding factuality. There is a paradox here. Divine intent is needed to bridge fact and value, to make natural circumstance relevant to human behavior—but the interposition of the bridge disguises a more intrinsic connection. It is better to avoid promiscuity because one knows it involves the risk of disease and unloved progeny than because one is obedient to a god whose motives are not to be questioned. What one does in the name of the father is not something one does on the basis of personal responsibility. Mystification and infantilization are traditional means of manipulation which have contributed to the neurosis and misery apparent in contemporary erotic praxis: we witness the purveyors of mystification poisoned by their own concoctions and know that the preachers of chastity illumine our lives by exemplifying true perversity.

In sum, we have many things to learn from nature that are relevant to the quality of our lives. One of them is that nature is not driven by intent. Another is that nature informs our intents. A third is that our intents are better served the better we understand the ways in which natural world constrains them. It is a frailty of postmodern thought that it resists this learning.

8

Reconstructing Rorty's Ethics: Styles, Languages, and Vocabularies of Moral Reflection

Evan Simpson and Mark Williams

R ichard Rorty's recent writings about the ethnocentricity of moral and cultural values are as frustrating as they are philosophically daring. Rorty's defiance of system makes his ideas difficult to appreciate and assess. However, it is not, we believe, inconsistent with his ethical pronouncements to develop a more formal statement of his views. We propose to reconstruct Rorty's ethics by constructing a typology of moral practice rooted in the terminology Rorty uses to distinguish diverse practices of moral deliberation.

The reconstruction we propose develops the following notions in a preliminary way. Rorty refers to "moral languages." This notion is explicated by Jeffrey Stout in *Ethics after Babel* and concerns those aspects of moral deliberation having to do with comprehending the meaning of moral utterances. Rorty also commonly uses the term "vocabulary," which may be used to describe the words and phrases characteristic of a practice of moral deliberation. However, Rorty also employs this term in another context. In the former usage, a 'moral vocabulary' refers to the rhetorical surface of a shared, social practice. A 'vocabulary of moral reflection,' by contrast, refers to the terminology an individual typically employs in making the moral discriminations central to their self-identity. Less explicit within Rorty's work is the idea of a 'style of moral reasoning.' With this notion, we are concerned to elaborate a further aspect of moral practice: the rules, norms, standards and the like, employed in justifying moral convictions. By laying out

some of the complex differences and relationships between these notions, we hope to accentuate the considerable merits of a reconstructed
Rortyan ethic.

Rorty's Ethnocentric Liberalism

To propose a reconstruction of Rorty's 'ethics' presupposes that he has
a 'moral philosophy' and this will depend on what one means by these
expressions. For reasons our account should make obvious, there is for
Rorty no interesting Hegelian distinction between an 'ethical life' lived
in accordance with human law and custom, and 'morality,' or the pure
insight "that calls to *every* consciousness: *be for yourselves* what you are *in
yourselves—reasonable*,"[1] even if for Hegel these at some point merge. As
Hegel noted, it is the former in which "the wisest men of antiquity . . .
declared that wisdom and virtue consist."[2] In Aristotle's analysis of ethos,
we find that the qualifications of sound judgment include contingent
attributes such as taste, cultivation and ethical habituation.[3] Whereas
modern moral theories typically assume that all human beings possess a
common faculty, reason, Aristotle was concerned to justify himself to his
fellow Greeks rather than to humanity-at-large. Along with most modern
philosophers, however, Aristotle supposed nonetheless that there is only
one way to the good life.

For Rorty, "moral reflection and sophistication" is a matter of "self-
creation rather than self-knowledge," a view which is a consequence of
seeing ourselves as "centerless, as random assemblages of contingent and
idiosyncratic needs rather than as more or less adequate exemplifications
of a common human essence."[4] Consistent with this view of the self as a
centerless web of beliefs, desires, and attitudes, Rorty asserts a form of
ethnocentrism, adding his voice as an advocate of liberalism. While he
distinguishes social from individual morality, social morality focusing on
"the effects of social practices and institutions on others" and individual
morality on "the effects of our private idiosyncrasies on others,"[5] both
in his view should be concerned with the alleviation of cruelty. Thus
his preferred social morality involves extending procedural justice to
marginalized social groups through the process of coming to see them
as "one of us," and individual morality properly struggles against the
inclination of aesthetes, or self-creative human beings, to be oblivious
to the pain and suffering their private obsessions may be causing others
(CIS, 190 & 141 ff.). In both cases, according to Rorty, human solidarity
is enhanced by expanding our sympathies, by "increasing our sensitivity

to the particular details of the pain and humiliation of other, unfamiliar sorts of people" (CIS, xvi). A commitment to solidarity thus works against tendencies to make invidious distinctions between the moral worth of different groups of human beings or to overhastily describe others without first making some attempt to understand them in their own terms. However, solidarity is not "a fact to be recognized" in virtue of a shared human essence, but "a goal to be achieved" (CIS, xvi). Thus, Rorty maintains, "the process of coming to see other human beings as 'one of us' rather than as 'them,' . . . is a task not for theory but for genres such as ethnography, the journalist's report, the comic book, the docudrama, and, especially, the novel" (CIS, xvi).

Rorty's positive ethical theses complement his ethnocentrism insofar as they are based on a set of agreements which distinguish our, broadly speaking, liberal point of view from less tolerant moral viewpoints. Rorty's ethnocentrism may thus leave us in no position to 'refute' hateful moral positions, but this fact need not undermine confidence in the moral superiority of our own, more tolerant viewpoint. Even if there are some moral viewpoints that liberals simply cannot take seriously, however, there is still a diversity of conflicting practices of moral deliberation within this broad liberal consensus. Each such practice has external competitors, some of which are attractive and must be reckoned with.

Rorty affirms the irreducible plurality of moral languages or vocabularies. If we are right, however, he makes his account unnecessarily obscure by glossing over differences between speaking and thinking, and sentences and reasons, in not distinguishing 'languages' and 'vocabularies' from what we refer to as 'styles of moral reasoning.' We do not deny the intimate association of thought and language but neither do we conflate them. We thus suggest that the plausibility of Rorty's account can be enhanced when one observes these distinctions.

Rorty often models the interaction of diverse moral viewpoints on Donald Davidson's account of translation between natural languages, and insofar as he treats ethics as a continuation of philosophy of language he arguably remains too attached to the linguistic turn in analytic philosophy. We do not dispute Davidson's claims that "beliefs are true or false, but they represent nothing. It is good to be rid of representations, and with them the correspondence theory of truth, for it is thinking that there are representations that engenders thoughts of relativism."[6] We shall touch on the issues of truth and representationalism insofar as they form the backdrop of Rorty's moral philosophy. However, although we are far from proposing a return to the idea of the mind as mirror of nature, we do argue that taking moral thinking as seriously as moral language makes possible a richer account of the diversity and competition of moral commitments.

Moral Theories and Moral Practices

Later, we shall distinguish 'styles of moral reasoning' from what Rorty refers to as moral 'languages' and 'vocabularies.' These notions are similar, however, insofar as they all concern diverse practices of moral discourse or deliberation in contrast to moral theories and the quest for a single set of standards which if stringently adhered to, or ethical principles which if punctiliously applied, promise to yield correct, universally binding, moral judgments. To search for such a set of standards or principles presumes that there are right answers to moral questions which all reasonable persons are obliged to accept. In resorting to philosophical conceptions of human nature or reason, most modernist ethical theories may thus be characterized as attempts to ground the domain and content of morality. Accordingly Stout describes the aim of these theories as the construction of a 'moral Esperanto'—"an artificial moral language invented in the (unrealistic) hope that everyone will want to speak it" or on the basis of the (vain) assumption that everyone ought to speak it.[7]

In place of theoretical attempts to limit the realm of the moral to a single 'language' or decision-procedure or to order varying moral practices hierarchically within a purportedly neutral, theoretical context, Rorty confides instead in a combination of liberal tolerance and "the ability of each of us to tailor a coherent self-image for ourselves and then use it to tinker with our behaviour" (EHO, 162). He approvingly quotes Michael Oakeshott, who suggests that

> a morality is neither a system of general principles nor a code of rules, but a vernacular language. General principles and even rules may be elicited from it, but like other languages it is not the creation of grammarians; it is made by speakers. . . . It is not a device for formulating judgments about conduct or for solving so-called moral problems, but a practice in terms of which to think, to choose, to act, and to utter. (CIS, 58)[8]

Oakeshott thus asserts what morality is and is not; it is not a device, a system of general principles, a code of rules or a creation of grammarians; it is a vernacular language, made by speakers and a practice in which we think, choose, act and utter. We see this emphasis on moral practices in contrast to systems of general principles as a useful corrective to philosophers who claim privileged epistemic status for certain grounds of morality. From a theoretical perspective, general principles based in human nature or reason are expected to govern practice. This knowledge contrasts with the 'know-how' required of participants in a practice.[9] Rorty spells out his conception of the relationship between principles and moral practices when he writes that

> Moral principles such as the categorical imperative and the utilitarian principle only have a point insofar as they incorporate tacit reference to a whole range of institutions, practices and vocabularies of moral and political deliberation. They are reminders of, abbreviations for, such practices, not justifications for such practices. (CIS, 58–59)

In Rorty's view, general moral principles cannot *take the place of* practices of moral deliberation except as pedagogical aids used primarily in the transmission of these practices from one generation to the next. Neither do principles justify participation in these practices. They do not flow from something common to all human beings—whether intuition, conscience, reason, intention, God's will, the Moral Law, or the logical structure of the language of morals—and thus seem not to be detachable from culturally specific practices of moral deliberation. At best they express a particularly central tenet of one among many ways of speaking to moral concerns.

Charles Taylor similarly relates general principles and moral practices. He notes that deontological theories rest upon at least the "insight" of the "universal attribution of moral personality" to all human beings.[10] His claim is that if 'formalist' ethical theories did not rest upon such insights, "they would not seem even plausible candidates as models of ethical reasoning" (DG, 224). In Taylor's view, however, these insights have no more persuasive foundation than that they go "almost unchallenged in modern society," so that the "claims of modernist ethical theories to firmer foundation are illusory" (DG, 234). Rather than laying foundations for morality, "what is really going on," he suggests, "is that some forms of ethical reasoning are being privileged over others because in our civilization they come less into dispute, or look easier to defend" (DG, 234). Yet Taylor's view is developed more subtly than Oakeshott's and Rorty's, for it lends itself to regarding principles as more interesting than summations of practices. All agree that principles do not provide good foundations for practices, but Taylor seems best prepared to recognize that principles, once clearly formulated, can motivate practical reform by clarifying and making more explicit accepted normative guidelines. Occasionally, what are theoretically informed principles in one generation may become the insights of educated common sense in the next.

Taylor also introduces the idea of a 'language of qualitative contrast' that will be useful to us later in reformulating Rorty's views. When philosophers treat compelling moral insights as formal principles, ethical theories offer "the hope of deciding ethical questions without having to determine which of a number of rival languages of moral virtue and vice, of the admirable and the contemptible, of unconditional versus conditional obligation, are valid" (DG, 224). Both deontological and utilitarian moral theories, according to Taylor, thus marginalize these languages of qualitative contrast or expunge them altogether. In Taylor's view, these languages are "central to our moral thinking and ineradicable from it" (DG, 227). The price of treating fundamental moral insights as universal principles has therefore been "a severe distortion of our understanding of moral thinking" in that the languages of qualitative contrast get "obscured by the epistemologically motivated reduction and homogenization of the moral" (DG, 226 & 227). Taylor does not deny the importance of such insights in moral thinking. Rather, his point is that there is a diversity of other goods which contend with these insights and that moral theories go wrong in excluding them.

To the extent that 'languages of qualitative contrast' are practices or aspects of practices, they are similar to 'moral languages,' 'styles of moral reasoning' and 'moral vocabularies.' In this respect, all of these notions are trying to get at the same thing. We have taken it as part of our purpose in this paper, however, to distinguish among them. In articulating one aspect of Rorty's moral philosophy, we draw upon Stout's account of moral languages. We focus on this account primarily because of details that support what Rorty has written about language and morality. We then supplement this approach with an account of the role of reasoning in moral practice.

Moral Languages

Stout notes that "there would be no point in asserting the plurality of moral languages without offering some notion of how moral languages, in the relevant sense, are to be individuated" (EAB, 67; cf. CIS, 7n.). To speak of a plurality of distinct moral languages is "philosophically interesting," he suggests, only if it can be distinguished from the familiar kind of moral diversity "displayed in disagreement over a proposition" (EAB, 67). According to Stout, distinct moral languages can be individuated "by reference to the sets of candidates for truth and falsehood they make available" (EAB, 68).

> [T]he language of human rights and the language of honor differ. How can we tell that they do? Because words are used in significantly different ways by the respective groups and this makes translation hard. What counts as a significant difference in the ways words are used? Any difference

that substantially alters what propositions are up for grabs as true-or-false. (EAB, 68)

The point might be illustrated by Taylor's characterization of formalist theories which marginalize or expunge languages of qualitative contrast. The claims made within these languages are then plausibly regarded as expressions of sentiment rather than as assertions that are true or false. To speak of actions as right or just may be taken as true, whereas to characterize them as virtuous or honorable is to express only a favorable attitude towards them. The different moral languages which Kantian and Aristotelian theories represent are thus made up of a different range of sentences that count as expressing moral truths or falsehoods.

To speak of sentences as up for grabs as true-or-false or as counting as moral truths makes Stout sound like a moral cognitivist. As he indeed affirms,

> I . . . believe that there are moral truths. For example, I hold that slavery . . . is evil. I accept the proposition that slavery is evil as true. We can share [Stanley] Hauerwas's doubts about appealing to the Moral Law, his emphasis on moral diversity, and his insistence that all justification depends on context without denying that moral propositions are capable of being true or false. (EAB, 21–22)

However, the position must be more complicated than this quotation suggests, for to count as true is not obviously the same as being true. Perceiving a conflation of these concepts, Taylor portrays Rorty's similar position as noncognitivist since, in Taylor's view, "a representation [or claim to truth] which is not made true by reality might just as well not be considered a candidate for truth at all."[11] Hence, as Rorty observes, "Taylor pictures me as saying . . . 'either true by correspondence to reality or not true at all, so moral judgments . . . can't be true.' "[12] Rorty, though, wants to drop the representationalist problematic altogether. (See ORT, 2ff.) He argues that "the difference between doing physics . . . and reflecting on one's moral character is not a matter of truth versus no truth, or of different kinds of truth. . . . Since no proposition is 'made' true by anything, and since no sentence is a representation of anything, all candidates for truth are on a par in respect of relation to an independent reality" (TT, 28n). In Rorty's view, once we give up on the theoretical idea that language or thought represents reality, "the only version of 'realism' one has left is the trivial, uninteresting and commonsensical one which says that all true beliefs are true because things are as they are" (TT, 29–30). In rejecting theoretical accounts in favor of a pragmatic view of moral truth, Rorty sets himself apart from both cognitivists and noncognitivists, purporting to have transcended a dispute which he regards as relying on untenable, representationalist assumptions.

Although Stout may disagree with Rorty as to whether cognitivism is still a live issue, on the Davidsonian view adopted by them both the meanings of words vary with the range of sentences held true or false in which those words appear. What may at first appear a simple disagreement—I hold that *p*, you hold that *not-p*—may turn out to be a difference in the meaning of a word that appears in *p*, a difference in meaning that results from the fact that we are using this word in significantly different ways, differences that substantially alter what propositions are up for grabs as true or false. So Rorty interprets Davidson as saying "you should not translate [or interpret] 'gavagai' as 'rabbit' nor '*Unheimlichkeit*' as 'homelessness' unless you are prepared to say that most of what you translate the natives as saying about rabbits, and most of what you translate the Germans as saying about homelessness is true" (ORT, 104). Rorty thus understands Davidson's holism as implying the view that "two groups are not talking about the same things if they talk about them very differently" (ORT, 103).

> [W]hen the natives' and our behaviour in response to certain situations is pretty much the same, we think of both of us as recognizing the plain facts of how things are. . . . But when these patterns of behaviour differ wildly, we shall say that we have different *Weltanschauungen*, or cultures, or theories, or that "we carve up the world differently." (ORT, 104)

Rather than following Thomas Kuhn in regarding these differences as indicating that we live in different worlds, or that we are employing incommensurable conceptual frameworks, Rorty chooses to think of these differences instead as particularly frustrating failures of communication. "[I]t would create fewer philosophical difficulties just to say that when these patterns differ, communication becomes harder and translation less helpful. Translation may become so awkwardly periphrastic, indeed, that it will save time to simply go bilingual" (ORT, 104).

Although on this view shared by Stout and Rorty, moral languages may be distinguished by the fact that people use words in significantly different ways, Stout observes that his point is not "to identify a moral language with the set of [truth-value] candidates it makes available, as if there were nothing to a moral language but that" (EAB, 68). Yet if moral languages are not just the sets of truth-value candidates they make available, it is unclear what else they are. Stout does not say directly, but his willingness to use such expressions as 'styles of moral reasoning' and 'moral vocabularies' is suggestive, pointing towards a more discriminating account that takes advantage of these additional concepts. We proceed by introducing these concepts in turn.

Styles of Moral Reasoning

Understanding what someone else is saying not only involves understanding what their words mean or the grammatical construction of their sentences. It also involves understanding the inferential interconnections between sentences and the order of moral concepts to which they typically appeal in terms of their relevance and importance. While Stout and Rorty focus primarily on the range of truth-value candidates that different moral languages make available in accounting for moral diversity, we propose to look as well at the different ways people go about justifying their moral judgments.

Carol Gilligan contrasts the justice- and care-perspectives in moral thinking.[13] These perspectives are ways of perceiving and handling moral problems. They reflect distinct patterns of inference and relevance and thus distinct sets of rules, norms, and standards employed in arriving at moral judgments. The rules of inference and relevance that are exhibited by these styles of moral reasoning define what legitimately counts as evidence, how much weight that evidence is to be given, the order in which norms are to be applied, what will count as a resolution to a problem, and so on. From the justice-perspective, judgments are arrived at by taking individual rights to be primary in moral deliberation, while from the care-perspective concern for and responsibility to others are basic. "Jake," seeing the question posed by "Heinz's Dilemma" in terms of competing rights to property and life, affirms that in the case in question life takes precedence over property. He thus concludes that stealing is justified in order to save a life. "Amy," thinking in terms of relationships, is not so sure that stealing is the appropriate response or even that the question is properly formulated. Concerned with consolidating the connections between the persons involved, she thinks that if they could only talk things out, they might be able to arrive at some compromise. While justice-thinking seeks an answer to the question in terms of an impersonal system of principles or laws, care-thinking seeks a response in the ongoing, dramatic particularity of the relationships between the persons involved.

If truth-value candidacy is the mark of distinctions between moral languages, then styles of moral reasoning should be distinguished from these languages. It is not that the solutions that the question as posed elicits are not all truth-value candidates for Amy, which her initial, apparent inability to deal with the question might suggest. Having been presented with the 'relevant' details of the case, Jake and Amy are asked whether 'Heinz' should steal so that his wife may not die. Taking a justice-perspective, Jake has a ready response. Amy, on the other hand, does not accept the either/or structure of the question. Her care-perspective does not permit a ready response because she is sensitive to the loss of connection that either option presents.

The difference between Jake and Amy is notable not for the difference in the meanings of the words they use, or in the grammatical construction of their utterances. What is instead remarkable is the thinking that led them to their judgments. Jake, in taking the rights of individuals as basic, treats caring and active responsibility for others as secondary to these rights. Amy maintains a different order of priority of concerns, and resists the examiner's desire to draw a straight line from the question posed to an answer. A satisfactory solution for Amy will require that she have more details about the lives of the people involved, details which go beyond the bounds of the case as presented. She is inclined, at least at first, to find some other solution to the problem. She may seem muddled to Jake, for whom the problem is perfectly clear. For her part, Amy may find it incomprehensible how Jake can reach his conclusion so confidently.

The incomprehension experienced when we witness someone employing an alternative style of moral reasoning is not simply that resulting from a misunderstanding of the words used but surprise or puzzlement or exasperation at the idea that 'this' is expected to follow from 'that,' or that 'this' is supposed to be more important than 'that.' A style of moral reasoning, in short, is not merely a set of truth-value candidates, but a set of rules of execution and operation, norms, standards, and so on—conventional arrangements that determine what counts as a good argument. Assessing the validity of moral judgments, then, depends on the variety of conventions characteristic of such a style of reasoning. The notion of a style of moral reasoning accepts that there is a diversity of frameworks within which it is possible to come to agreement on particular moral judgments but between which irresolvable questions may arise. (Of course, even within a shared framework disagreement may occur. Those who think predominantly from the perspective of caring, for example, may differ among themselves about which courses of action will satisfy the needs of relationships or even what constitutes 'caring.' These differences are not fundamental, however.)

Caring, it is worth noting, is more like feeling than talking. It reminds us that there may be nonlinguistic elements in our moral thinking.

This is more easily recognized while looking at styles of moral reasoning than when exploring moral languages alone. In considering the reasons that people employ in arriving at their tentative solutions to moral questions, it is possible to describe moral practices more fully than Rorty's explicitly stated views suggest. The notions complement one another in ways that may enhance the plausibility of his overall conception. So, too, for the notion of moral vocabularies to which we turn next.

Moral Vocabularies

Distinguishable from both moral languages and styles of moral reasoning is the idea of a 'moral vocabulary.' However, Rorty's notion of a 'vocabulary' needs to be approached with some care. Often when he uses this term, he is referring to what philosophers have traditionally called 'theories.' In practice at least, Hegel was, in Rorty's view, the first to treat philosophical theories as contingent, historical developments and, in this respect, as so many vocabularies (CIS, 78). He thereby humbles theories, depriving them of their pretensions to truth. While moral theories may seek to represent reality, vocabularies are neither true nor false and thus cannot provide foundations for intellectual and moral progress. To treat theories as vocabularies renders the former parochial and conventional, even arbitrary, just as the acoustical aspect of a sign is considered to be arbitrary with respect to what it signifies. Nevertheless, vocabularies in this sense are not simply lists of words. The relationship Rorty identifies between theories and vocabularies maintains the interconnections between the various terms that make up the vocabulary of, for example, psychoanalytic theory—Oedipal complex, father, mother, ego, unconscious, phallus. If one is unfamiliar with the practice of inquiry in which these items are interconnected, one will likely regard this list as random. The idea of a vocabulary thus assumes interconnections that are more explicit in the notions of moral languages and styles of moral reasoning. The notion of a moral language identifies holistic clusters of beliefs, where the meanings of words are a function of belonging to this whole. The notion of a style of moral reasoning concerns the clusters of rules, norms, standards of evidence, etc., that are used in justifying particular judgments. The connections assumed by a moral vocabulary, however, can best be articulated in terms of these additional aspects of a complicated practice which includes them all. It is thus not possible to adequately characterize a practice of moral deliberation by means of the notion of a 'moral vocabulary' without going on to talk about these other elements as well.

To identify a practice of moral deliberation with its rhetorical surface may obscure the differences and connections between languages,
styles, and vocabularies that we have been concerned to elaborate. At
worst, this may legitimate forms of argumentation that employ the rhetorical surface of a style of moral reasoning without regard for the established
conventions of right reasoning characteristic of a style. At best, given this
typology, Rorty appears guilty of conflating these various ideas when he
claims that

> To accept the claim that there is no standpoint outside the particular
> historically conditioned and temporary *vocabulary* we are presently using
> from which to judge this vocabulary is to give up on the idea that there
> can be *reasons* for using *languages* as well as reasons within languages for
> believing statements. This amounts to giving up the idea that intellectual
> or political progress is rational, in any sense of "rational" which is neutral
> between vocabularies. (CIS, 48, emphasis added.)

We suggest that his point can best be made in terms of styles of reasoning. Even if languages, styles of reasoning, and vocabularies cannot
be philosophically ranked, they may be usefully compared. The notion
of a style of reasoning complements Rorty's criticisms of the idea of a
neutral framework of rational arbitration. If reasons are bounded by
styles, however, then arbitrating conflicts between styles would apparently
be based on something other than reasons.

Most individuals in a pluralistic society conceivably employ a variety
of styles. Taylor has suggested that when faced with a diversity of goods
"many people find themselves drawn by more than one of these views,
and are faced with the job of making them compatible in their lives"
(DG, 229). In his view the "really important question" may thus not be
whether there is a single kind of demand that we should accept as moral
but "how we combine in our lives two or three or four difficult goals or
virtues, or standards, which we feel we cannot repudiate but which seem
to demand incompatible things of us" (DG, 229). Comparisons of the
words we use and those we avoid, the inferences we countenance and
reject, and the languages we prefer to others may be the basis of some
of our most important attempts at self-criticism and reform. In the case
of each of a variety of goals, virtues, or standards, we may give reasons
for pursuing or valuing them. When they come into conflict, however,
we are ostensibly confronted with reasons for pursuing some alternative
goal or standard. Reasons may play a significant role in persuading oneself
or others that a particular goal for this person in these circumstances is
higher than some other goal for which there are also compelling reasons.
Reasons may be drawn from a style in its own defense. Such reasons will

be decisive, however, only to the extent that a practice as a whole can be made to look comparatively attractive.

If we allow an analogy between intellectual and moral progress, another controversy between Taylor and Rorty bears upon this point. As Rorty interprets Taylor,

> Taylor criticizes me for saying that the world doesn't 'decide between' language-games, and for reinterpreting issues (e.g. between Aristotle and Newton) which 'have been quite conclusively decided rationally' as having been 'settled on pragmatic grounds'. What I meant by saying that the world doesn't decide is that we didn't have a criterion for choosing between Aristotle and Newton in the sense in which poker players have one for deciding who takes the pot. The former decision was taken in the same way that all large, complex, non–criterion-governed, rational decisions are taken—on pragmatic grounds. (TT, 29)

Styles of reasoning are akin to these 'language-games' in defining internal criteria of decidability. From this perspective, deliberation can only proceed according to reasons insofar as there is agreement on what would count as a resolution to the problem (even if this agreement is only tacitly present in regular employment). It is when these criteria are in dispute that styles come into question. A style of reasoning is a set of criteria that determine when reasons are decisive. In conflicts between styles, no neutral criteria exist. Holistic comparisons between particular practices in respect of particular contexts, however, may form a basis for rational persuasion. Such a view constitutes irrationalism only in allowing that occasionally such disputes will be, at least temporarily, irresolvable.[14]

Such concerns are relevant to another notion central to Rorty's postmodern conception of the self, the notion of a 'vocabulary of moral reflection' which may be usefully compared to the ideas already introduced.

Vocabularies of Moral Reflection

For Rorty, a 'vocabulary of moral reflection' is "a set of terms in which one compares oneself to other human beings" (EHO, 154). Such vocabularies contain terms like

> magnanimous, a true Christian, decent, cowardly, God-fearing, hypocritical, self-deceptive, epicene, self-destructive, cold, an antique

Roman, a saint, a Julien Sorel, a Becky Sharpe, a red-blooded American, a shy gazelle, a hyena, depressive, a Bloomsbury type, a man of respect, a grande dame." (EHO, 154)

In contrast to the abstract concepts of moral theory such as 'right,' 'ought,' and 'good,' such descriptively robust terms carry most of the burdens of actual moral discourse (CIS, 73; see also CIS, 77). "By summing up patterns of behavior," Rorty understands these terms as "tools for criticizing the character of others and for creating one's own" (EHO, 154–55).[15] One's moral identity, as one's self-identity more broadly, is focused by a description, and moral progress comes through the "continual redescription" that aims to "make the best selves for ourselves that we can" (CIS, 80). If one takes this view, "the availability of a richer vocabulary of moral deliberation" will be "what one chiefly has in mind when one says that we are, morally speaking, more sensitive and sophisticated than our ancestors or than our younger selves" (EHO, 155). Hence "the principal technique of self-enlargement will be Hegel's: the enrichment of language" (ORT, 154). From this perspective, "one will see the history of both the race and oneself as the development of fuller, richer ways of formulating one's desires and hopes, and thus making those desires and hopes themselves—and thereby oneself—richer and fuller" (EHO, 154). Leaving aside Hegel's teleology, moral progress is evolutionary, and so involves endless adaptations to an environment through constant tinkering with, not only that environment, but with ourselves.[16]

We do not dispute this view of moral progress as such, since we agree with Rorty that there is no single procedure or framework for bringing the self into alignment for purposes of action. When we compare this notion with the other ideas we have considered to this point, however, it becomes clear that while these other notions refer to practices or aspects of practices, with the notion of a vocabulary of moral reflection Rorty is describing not a practice but a model of contingent self-identity. A 'vocabulary of moral reflection' refers to the range of terms which individuals are inclined to use in describing themselves and others and in choosing how to act. Some of these terms may describe virtues— 'magnanimity' and 'decency,' for example—terms which would thus fall under Taylor's notion of a language of qualitative contrast. What such a list of terms seems to fail to describe are the clustered interconnections between some of these terms, precisely those captured in their different ways by the notions of moral languages, styles of moral reasoning and languages of qualitative contrast. In focusing on 'vocabularies of moral deliberation' rather than 'moral languages' or 'styles of moral reasoning,' certain lineaments of interesting moral diversity are obscured.

If, as Rorty's romantic liberalism seems to suggest to him,[17] there are potentially as many vocabularies of moral deliberation as there are individuals, then the clusters of beliefs and attitudes characteristic of moral languages or styles of moral reasoning become unrecognizable. A typical individual's vocabulary of moral reflection will instead look like an arbitrary mishmash. For agents to act with confidence and without regret, however, their beliefs, attitudes and desires cannot be merely a random assemblage but must possess some sort of coherence. One way in which these collections of terms come to cohere is when we rely on one of a number of moral languages or styles of moral reasoning. Since they are shared by many others, and are in a sense ready-made, we may often safely rely upon them.

By focusing on vocabularies of moral deliberation, Rorty distinguishes his view from those which posit a moral self, in Alasdair MacIntyre's words, "prior to and apart from all roles" (AV, 56).

> To say that the moral self exists apart from all roles means that it will remain the same no matter what situation it finds itself in, no matter what language it uses to create that self-image, no matter what its vocabulary of moral deliberation may be. That, in turn, means that the moral self has no need to work out a sensitive and sophisticated vocabulary as an instrument to create its character. For the only character that matters is the one it already has. (EHO, 157)

However, the alternative to such a character is not a sheer self-creator. Rorty admits that "there are no fully Nietzschean lives" in the sense that the self can create itself ex nihilo (CIS, 43). However, working out a sensitive and sophisticated vocabulary as an instrument to create one's character is not "necessarily private, unshared, unsuited to argument," since a lot of this working out is already done for us in the form of moral languages and prevailing styles of moral reasoning (CIS, xiv). Rorty's emphasis on self-creation needs to be balanced by an appreciation of the institutional nature of much of our moral reflection. The institutional nature of this thinking is perfectly consistent with the notion of a contingent self, since social practices are themselves historical contingencies. To see ourselves as having inherited moral practices is also consistent with emphasizing the creative aspects of how we come to think of ourselves in relation to others, and even with viewing moral change in terms of the production of new metaphors which, on Rorty's Davidsonian account, are by definition unsuited as media for argumentative exchange (CIS, xiv). To suggest that the primary modality of moral progress is private and unshared neglects the fact that vocabularies of moral reflection combine many shared, social elements. In a pluralistic society, however, the hatred of cruelty that Rorty's ethnocentrism commends becomes difficult to defend philosophically. We will attempt to draw out this point by considering the connection between vocabularies of moral reflection and Rorty's treatment of the moral significance of the novel.

The "Wisdom of the Novel"

As literary genres, philosophical theories are regarded by Rorty as subordinate to novels as vehicles of moral progress. For one thing, novels do not share philosophy's pretensions to truth. In proceeding directly to some sovereign concept such as "sincerity, or authenticity, or freedom," Iris Murdoch has argued, moral philosophy imposes an "unexamined and empty idea of unity" whereas "the most essential and fundamental aspect of our culture is the study of literature, since this is an education in how to picture and understand human situations" (quoted in EHO, 156). Accepting this judgment, Rorty can exploit one of the effects of Kant's moral philosophy, which was "to impoverish the vocabulary of moral philosophy and to turn the enrichment of our vocabulary of moral reflection over to novelists, poets, and dramatists" (EHO, 156).

Consistent with his notion of a vocabulary of moral reflection is his claim that "The most celebrated and memorable feature" of Dickens's novels is "the unsubsumable, uncategorizable idiosyncrasy of the characters" (EHO, 78). "In a moral world based on what Kundera calls 'the wisdom of the novel,'" Rorty claims "moral comparisons and judgments would be made with the help of proper names rather than general terms or general principles" (EHO, 78). Dickens's characters are interesting because they "resist being subsumed under moral typologies, being described as exhibiting these virtues and those vices. Instead the names of Dickens's characters *take the place* of moral principles and of lists of virtues and vices" (EHO, 78). Citing proper names and labels is a way of noticing particularity rather than focusing on what human beings have in common, and this may make possible a richer and fuller moral vocabulary. This approach does not, however, tell us much about how we actually proceed when wanting to justify our moral attitudes to others. Rorty's utopia is "carnivalesque, Dickensian, a crowd of eccentrics rejoicing in each other's idiosyncrasies" (EHO, 75). In the case of Dickensian idiosyncrasies the question of justification may not even arise.

Yet Dickens, according to Rorty, also spoke as " 'one of us'—as the voice of one who happened to notice something to which the rest of us could be counted upon to react with similar indignation as soon as we notice it" (EHO, 79). The cases which illustrate moral diversity are cases in which everyone cannot be counted upon to react in a similar way. Sources of indignation may differ from person to person or indignation may be misplaced. Dickens's power, though, resides in significant part in our sharing his 'generous anger' regarding Gradgrind's infliction of suffering upon others and Scrooge's insensitivity to the plight of the working poor. According to Rorty, this 'generous anger'—in Orwell's phrase—means "something like 'anger which is without malignity because it assumes that the fault is ignorance rather than malice, assumes that the evil has merely to be noticed to be remedied' " (EHO, 80). This presupposes not idiosyncrasy but a common standard.

This standard may be absent. As an empirical claim, Rorty acknowledges that the assumption that evil has merely to be noticed to be remedied "is often falsified" (EHO, 80). "As a moral attitude," however, "it marks the difference between people who tell stories and people who construct theories about that which lies beyond our present imagination, because beyond our present language" (EHO, 80). Unfortunately, this leaves us only with the generous but mistaken assumption that "people merely need to turn "their eyes toward the people who are getting hurt" and notice "the *details* of the pain being suffered, rather than needing to have their entire cognitive apparatus restructured" (EHO, 80). It is his willingness to stop the argument at this point that makes Rorty susceptible to accusations of relativism, but it is a problem that he visits upon himself unnecessarily. Were he to articulate his position in more analytical detail, it would be open to him to observe that there is available a nontheoretical sense of restructuring one's entire cognitive apparatus, after which the Dickensian assumption becomes valid. Adopting a style of reasoning that includes the relevance of suffering and cruelty constitutes such a restructuring. It marks a radical shift from the indifference to strangers that liberalisms often include. Yet in contrast to the acceptance of a theory as a statement of how things are, the adoption of this new style of reasoning is compatible with recognizing its contingency. The liberal style therefore can make no claim to unanimous agreement, but it enables those who share it to find the same details salient and permits them to advocate the same style to others, as Rorty has himself done to good effect. At the same time he makes good on his claim that moral progress depends more upon the novelist's ability to tell a compelling story than upon the theoretical philosopher's "essentialistic approach to human affairs" (EHO 154).

Conclusion

Styles of moral reasoning include prejudices the critique of which requires taking up an observer's or, we might say, a "philosophical" perspective in which for purposes of description we may temporarily withhold judgment. Rorty, tends to bypass this task, suspecting perhaps that distinctions of the kind we have articulated betray an attempt to uncover the 'deep' structure of moral discourse in contrast to the accessible rhetorical surface of moral vocabularies and vocabularies of moral reflection. He might also complain that in calling attention to more or less fixed rules and standards of moral reasoning, we must advocate 'proper' moral thinking rather than self-creation. The appropriate response to these concerns is to agree that even if contingency remains unavoidable and there is no standpoint from which to demonstrate the superiority of one style of reasoning or one vocabulary or one language over another, philosophical analysis is not limited to iconoclasm. When it comes to advocating a point of view, the philosopher's interest in detail is as justifiable as the novelist's.

9

Hermeneutical Ethical Theory

Paul Fairfield

Philosophers who renounce the foundationalist project in ethics, and who are inclined to emphasize the situated and hermeneutic character of social criticism, are faced with the following predicament. Having acquired a certain skepticism about an autonomous, a priori rationality, and having accepted the radically situated character of human existence, how is it possible for critical reflection to gain the perspective it needs in order to form judgments which can reasonably claim our assent? If the principal question facing moral philosophy is no longer how we can provide a firm metaphysical basis for social practices, but how these practices may become objects of critique, how is it possible, given the situatedness of moral reason within finite perspectives, to reflect critically upon the practices and traditions which constitute the social world to which we ourselves belong? If not from the standpoint of unconditioned objectivity, from what standpoint is social criticism of the ground on which we stand possible, and which—if any—of the methods, theories, or principles of moral philosophy are available to it? Must a hermeneutical ethics join the chorus of moral antitheorists, or can a conception of theory be articulated that would perform a task indispensable to moral philosophy while remaining invulnerable to the more telling objections levelled against traditional foundationalist attempts at theory construction?

While there can be little doubt that critical reflection is indeed possible without moral theorizing, I shall argue that the scope and force of such reflection is limited—sufficiently limited to motivate us to continue the task of theory construction with the aim of formulating a conception of universal right. Acknowledging the situated character of reflection does not preclude the possibility of constructing a universalistic conception of justice. Abandoning totalizing perspectives entails renouncing only certain forms of moral theorizing. It precludes all attempts by philosophers both to privilege a particular conception of the good life and to eliminate the need for practical judgment through the construction of formal decision procedures. The task of ethical theory on this account is not to prescribe particular courses of action or to provide a grounding for social practices, but to assist our efforts at critical reflection by identifying principles of universal right.

After reviewing the case against theory construction in ethics—entertaining arguments presented by Jean-François Lyotard, Richard Rorty, and certain recent hermeneutical philosophers—I shall outline and defend a universalistic conception of justice which takes its bearings from the liberal tradition while incorporating arguments from both Hans-Georg Gadamer's philosophical hermeneutics and Jürgen Habermas's communicative ethics. A historically conscious universalism, I maintain, may furnish critical reflection with principles instrumental in protecting the autonomy and inviolability of the human being. Hermeneutical ethical theory establishes constraints on local practices and norms by rendering thematic the normative dimension already inherent to the practice of communicative understanding.

The Primacy of Practice and the Case against Theory

The predominant aim in modern moral philosophy has been to identify those principles that have a legitimate claim to universality and whose status is foundational in the justification of particular judgments and practices. Principles were to provide the moral theorist with a decision procedure capable of solving problems generated by conflicting norms and preferences, and in general with a method for deciding what is to be done in any given case of moral action. The traditional view had it that the task of theory construction in ethics was to provide an objective grounding for normative appraisal, thus rendering our evaluations invulnerable to the arguments of the moral skeptic (such arguments being viewed as a cause for anxiety by an epistemology-centered conception of philosophy).

In recent years, this view of moral philosophy's basic aims has been called into question by a variety of nonfoundationalist thinkers. Opponents of moral theory argue that once we dispense with foundational

metaphors we shall no longer feel the need to ground normative judgments in something transcending social practices, contingent though the
latter be. Antitheorists contend that the search for a philosophical basis
of our moral lives ought to be abandoned along with the foundationalist's
quest for certainty in epistemology. The suspicion that we are not going
to uncover a common source of all legitimate moral standards, or gain a
universal theoretical perspective on local norms of behavior, has gained
some currency. This suspicion is owing in part not only to the decline
of foundationalist epistemology but equally to a rising skepticism about
the possibility of a metaphysics of human nature or of the moral law,
traditional candidates for the role of foundation of ethical life. In directing attention away from foundations, decision procedures, and universal
principles, antitheorists defend the view that evaluative judgments are
not in need of constraints beyond local consensus, and that the modern
thesis concerning the primacy of theoretical reason should be replaced
with a conception of rationality in which local practices are paramount.
Moral argumentation need appeal to nothing transcending—nothing
more "basic" than—the historically contingent behavioral and discursive
practices that have taken hold in our culture. Being already reflective,
such practices do not require philosophical grounding.

This opposition to normative theorizing is a prominent theme
in the writings of Jean-François Lyotard. The conception of justice defended by this postmodernist is formulated largely as a response to certain metaphors and themes characteristic of political modernity. Truth,
consensus, convergence, universality, finality, and other touchstones of
modern political thought are replaced by Lyotard with divergence, multiplicity, contestation, novelty, and opinion. Political discourse is conceived
as aiming not at consensus or convergence upon the truth, but at a
perpetual invention of novel and contesting claims. Justice, so conceived,
belongs to the order of opinion and not to the order of knowledge
or truth. Following the sophists in this respect, Lyotard also follows
Aristotle in asserting the priority of practical judgment over method
and theoretical frameworks. In matters of politics and ethics, he argues,
we form evaluative judgments without the aid of criteria or categories
of any kind. Judgments are neither regulated by criteria, nor educated
by training and habit, nor guided by common sense, but are instead
essentially decisionistic. "One is without criteria, yet one must decide."[1]
All talk of criteria in postmodernity, Lyotard supposes, is illegitimate since

> the idea of criteria comes from the discourse of truth and supposes
> a referent or a 'reality' and, by dint of this, it does not belong to the
> discourse of justice. This is very important. It must be understood that

if one wants criteria in the discourse of justice one is tolerating de facto the encroachment of the discourse of justice by the discourse of truth. (JG 98)

We are faced on Lyotard's account with two fundamentally incompatible conceptions of political discourse. We may either seek a science of politics—a method of grounding evaluative judgments in theoretical statements pertaining either to the nature of reason, human nature, natural law, or something of the kind—or we may form judgments on a case by case basis without the assistance of theory, principles, or criteria of any kind. Preferring the latter over the former, Lyotard contends that a politics of judgment must forswear all theoretical "metanarratives" and reinstate the rights of small and local narratives. The proper function of the moral or political philosopher is to hazard opinions for general discussion, rather than to devise theories or learned discourses concerning the nature of justice.

Perhaps the most noted opponent of normative theory on this side of the Atlantic is Richard Rorty. Following in the tradition of American pragmatism, Rorty urges us to give up all talk of philosophical foundations and of grounding our practices and political commitments in anything outside of, or transcending, those practices and commitments. It is, on Rorty's view, no more necessary (nor are we able) to step outside of our local ethical and political commitments by means of theoretical reason than it is to somehow step outside of our language to verify its resemblance to a reality which obtains objectively. The criteria that are available to critical reflection are in no sense axiomatic, but are instead "never more than the platitudes which contextually define the terms of a final vocabulary currently in use."[2] The only constraints on moral action, as well as on what comes to pass for truth and justice, are conversational ones. They are not universal principles deduced from foundational premises, but local and historically contingent commitments that have managed to generate some degree of consensus within a particular culture at a particular time.

The thesis defended in one form or another by these and other opponents of ethical theory concerning the primacy of practice—the thesis, that is, that social practices are already sufficiently reflective that they do not require the kind of philosophical grounding that a variety of normative theories were intended to provide—is by now a familiar one in nonfoundationalist, hermeneutical, and postmodern circles. That thesis will not be contested here. It will be asserted neither that social practices are in need of grounding upon some metaphysical conception of how things stand with the world, nor that our judgments must proceed from a common source (such as the utilitarian maxim or contractarian methodology). The foundationalist project in ethics has been ably deconstructed by a variety of thinkers, not all of whose arguments can be rehearsed here. However, does our assent to the view that normative rationality must take its bearings from the realm of practice commit us to abandoning theory construction? There is a temptation here to simply reverse the usual depreciation of practice relative to theory, to abandon one pole of this and other traditional philosophical dichotomies for the other. Time and again we are told that we must choose between a science of politics or a politics of judgment, a theoretical grounding of ethical life or a socialized decisionism, a priori principles of reason or a final vocabulary, knowledge or opinion, theoretical reason or practical reason. In each case, we are urged to abandon the former in favor of the latter, a move usually accompanied by an expression of skepticism or exasperation with the former alternative. Those of us who share Nietzsche's distrust of philosophical dichotomies, however, are more inclined to challenge the dichotomies themselves than to abandon one pole for the other, since the latter move often renders one vulnerable to much the same difficulties as those to which one is responding (or, at any rate, this kind of move normally creates as many problems as it solves).

The problems that are generated by renouncing theory for practice, principles for judgment, and so on, begin to emerge at those places where a transition of sorts is made from skeptical argumentation about the need for, or possibility of, objective grounding for practices and evaluations (argumentation that is frequently compelling) to passages in which some particular set of values or norms is advocated. We are told, for instance, not only that we must be on the lookout for forced consensus and bad metaphysics, but that we must defend the rights of local narratives, live with and celebrate difference, plurality, otherness, and so on. Without offering a detailed ethical or political program, there is an unmistakeable normative thrust in the writings of Lyotard, Rorty, and numerous other contemporary antitheorists—one which celebrates the liberal virtues, recognition, respect, civility, freedom, equality, diversity, and democratic communication. The sentiments expressed in the following passages from Rorty and Lyotard (respectively) are representative of this (partial) convergence of moral and political commitments:

> I want to see freely arrived at agreement as agreement on how to accomplish common purposes (e.g., prediction and control of the behavior of atoms or people, equalizing life-chances, decreasing cruelty), but I want to see these common purposes against the background of an increasing sense of the radical diversity of private purposes, of the radically poetic character of individual lives, and of the merely poetic foundations

of the 'we-consciousness' which lies behind our social institutions. (CIS 67–68)

And the idea that I think we need today in order to make decisions in political matters cannot be the idea of the totality, or of the unity, of a body. It can only be the idea of a multiplicity or of a diversity. (JG 94)

Difficulties arise when we begin to ask—as we inevitably shall in moral philosophy, whether we be foundationalists or not: What is the philosophical justification of this particular constellation of values? Abandoning the foundationalist's quest for objective grounds and methodological rigor does not relieve philosophers of the responsibility of giving an account—a rationale of some description—of why they maintain the moral commitments that they do. Were we to accept that dichotomies of the kind mentioned above (theory or practice, knowledge or opinion, principles or judgment) inevitably confront us whenever we begin to reflect upon moral questions, then it would seem that the only possible response to questions of justification is of the kind presented by Rorty. That is, we must not expect to justify our moral commitments from a transcendental perspective or on the basis of a metaphysical foundation. We must not allow the epistemologist's or skeptic's "why" questions to become a cause for anxiety, tempting us thereby into making a foundationalist move of one kind or another. Instead, we ought to admit that "we are just the historical moment that we are,"[3] that justification need appeal to nothing beyond the sphere of local convictions, practices, and institutions that defines our way of life. Such a response would have to suffice if the only alternative to it were the kind of objective grounding sought by traditional forms of moral theorizing. But is this a dichotomy that we ought to accept? Is our only alternative to the quest for foundations, decision procedures, and moral certainty, the kind of appeal made in one form or another to the local, the ethnocentric, the historically contingent? I shall argue in the following section that these are not the only alternatives available to us, and that the numerous dichotomies that have recently taken hold in moral philosophy (owing in part to such thinkers as Rorty and Lyotard) need not be accepted.

While justifying the moral commitments that we make through appeals to local narratives and solidarities has a certain degree of persuasiveness (in the case, at least, of questions of the good),[4] such appeals encounter difficulties when questions of justice arise. It is not an uncommon occurrence for the norms which take hold in a community to harden into dogma or to become corrupted in one manner or another.

Communities are not immune from dogmatism and intolerance in their most ominous forms. The members and representatives of a community may (and frequently do) become so enamored with what comes to pass within their borders, or on their membership lists, for the truth that their concern for justice and human well being may well take a back seat to furthering an agenda, clinging to an outmoded belief system, or retaining power. Basing moral claims upon local consensus, as any number of historical examples would illustrate, faces serious difficulties when an appeal to consensus becomes a crude majoritarianism or a strategy for excluding unwelcome opinions. Settled convictions must be occasionally unsettled, yet attempts to challenge such convictions may be undermined by unreflective appeals to "community standards" or "the American way." While critical reflection may always be possible, even within very unreflective communities, the limits of reflection become a cause for concern when not only our judgments but the standards used in adjudicating these begin to deteriorate or are dubious from the start. Local solidarities may be infected with false beliefs and abhorrent attitudes (typically, but not exclusively, directed against those who are "not of our kind"). When the self-understanding that underlies a community's moral beliefs is itself based upon dubious metaphysical schemes, the difficulty in critically assessing moral convictions is especially pronounced.

Difficulties arise not only when we ask for a justification of our moral commitments, but also when the objects of critical reflection are elements of foreign cultures and traditions. Rorty assures us that there can be no noncircular justification of a final vocabulary. The adoption of a vocabulary is a matter of social decision, not philosophical argumentation. At most, we can defend our settled convictions by showing how they favorably compare with those of foreign cultures. A pragmatic justification takes the form of inter-societal comparisons in which one demonstrates the practical advantages of our own norms and institutions over various alternatives.[5] However, a problem arises here concerning the degree of force that critical reflection "by our lights" can claim for itself when it takes foreign institutions and practices as its object. When we take exception, for example, to the treatment in certain cultures of "heretics" or "counterrevolutionaries" by pointing out how such treatment violates certain norms of behavior which we in our tradition consider important, it is unclear why anyone who stands outside of our tradition should regard this as a forceful criticism—or indeed as a criticism at all (as opposed, that is, to a mere announcement that we happen to hold a different view). What is absent from such a critique is a reason why anyone who does not share our final vocabulary ought to adopt our moral beliefs. A difficulty in criticizing even the most extreme acts of oppression in cultures different from our own is that often such acts are all too easily justifiable within the final vocabulary of that culture. For every inquisition or religious crusade there is an ancient tradition of belief, a moral vocabulary, a set of well-established institutions and social norms. For every massacre of political dissidents there is a tradition of social hierarchies, a consensus on the importance of authority and of knowing one's place within the society. As local solidarities legitimate themselves, so too may they legitimate (what become very difficult to recognize as) forms of oppression.

A further difficulty arises concerning the notion of a pragmatic justification. Rorty tells us that a way in which we lend support to our final vocabulary is by showing how it favorably compares with others in terms of practical advantages. Yet this overlooks that what is regarded as a practical advantage is intelligible only in light of a set of prior values and interests, which in turn is a function of the final vocabulary one has already adopted. If, as a consequence of the tradition to which one belongs, one views as advantageous, for instance, preserving the party's grip on power, enlightening the infidel, or creating the divine kingdom on earth, then inter-societal comparisons of the kind Rorty describes are most likely merely to confirm the prejudices one already holds. The circularity of pragmatic justifications and ethnocentric appeals, in short, severely limits the force of critical reflection and provides little reason for those who do not already share our vocabulary and think as we do to reform their practices and institutions.

Recent contributions from hermeneutical philosophers to the debate over foundationalism and ethical theory[6] have taken as their point of departure an array of premises and problematics similar to that shared by Rorty and Lyotard, while taking up positions distinct from both. While not renouncing ethical theory, these authors are inclined to emphasize the situated and practical character of moral reasoning. Taking Gadamer's philosophical hermeneutics as their primary inspiration, P. Christopher Smith and Georgia Warnke[7] attempt in different ways to draw out some of the normative implications of Gadamer's thought. With Rorty and Lyotard, these authors share an opposition to modes of theorizing that seek grounds external to local practices and traditions from which to form an objective appraisal of these. Principles are not generated through acts of abstract autonomous reasoning, but are inherited from the cultural and linguistic tradition within which we are situated.[8] The legitimacy of moral principles is a function of the ways in which a community understands itself and recounts its history. On such a view, the task of a hermeneutical ethical theory is to recover principles from tradition and to clarify the meaning of local norms and institutions. Its task is, in Warnke's words,

> to uncover and articulate the principles already embedded in or implied
> by a community's practices, institutions and norms of action. The theory
> of justice becomes an attempt to understand what a society's actions,
> practices and norms mean, to elucidate for a culture what its shared
> understandings are so that it can agree on the principles of justice that
> make sense to it and for it. (JI 5)

Warnke argues that a hermeneutical conception of justice must proceed
from an understanding of a society's norms and political traditions.
The latter are thus taken as text analogues, the significance of which
is contested by conflicting (and often equally legitimate) interpretations.

Hermeneutical conceptions of ethics focus not on justifying abstract
and universal principles but on the centrality of dialogue and the need
to promote open communication in matters of public policy. Because
ethical theorizing is an interpretive exercise in clarifying the meaning
of local practices and traditions, and because for hermeneutical philosophers no interpretations can ever be said to be uniquely and supremely
authoritative, this creates the necessity of continually reinterpreting social phenomena without philosophical methods of adjudicating between
conflicting understandings of social meaning. In lieu of such procedures,
moral theorists must remain open to the possibility of learning from
opposed viewpoints, just as traditions may gain something of value in
encountering other traditions. So conceived, the justification of social
customs and moral claims is a matter of hermeneutic conversation. What
such conversation requires is not methodological rigor but the intellectual virtue of open-mindedness—a willingness to listen to the claims of
other speakers with an eye to their possible truth value. An enriched
understanding is gained through an open exchange of viewpoints. While
this may or may not lead to consensus on the meaning or relative importance of our behavioral norms, these open communicative exchanges are
the medium in which the one-sidedness of our private interpretations is
overcome and insight is gained. As Warnke expresses it in the following
text, hermeneutical ethics gives rise to a commitment to interpretive
pluralism and to democratic forms of decision making in a free and open
public sphere:

> The idea behind the notion of hermeneutic conversation is the idea that
> an interpretive pluralism can be educational for all the parties involved. If
> we are to be educated by interpretations other than our own, however, we
> must both encourage the articulation of those alternative interpretations
> and help to make them as compelling as they can be. And how can we do
> this except by assuring the fairness of the conversation and working to give

all possible voices equal access? If we are to learn from our hermeneutic
efforts, then no voice can retain a monopoly on interpretation and
no voice can try to limit in advance what we might learn from others.
Democracy thus turns out to be the condition for the possibility of an
enriching exchange of insight. Democratic conditions act against the
entrenchment of bigoted interpretations by offering others a fair fight
as equals and hermeneutic conversation itself acts against the reduction
of diversity by allowing that more than one rational interpretation might
'win.' (JI 157)

Democracy, openness, pluralism and so on are presented here not as
universal principles of right but as central elements of a conception of
justice that makes sense for us given our cultural heritage and political
traditions.

Notwithstanding the many important differences that separate the
authors mentioned above (as well as numerous other thinkers who are
proponents of a variety of related positions variously termed communi-
tarian, hermeneutical, neo-Aristotelian, pragmatic, and postmodern), a
degree of consensus has emerged between them with respect not only to
their shared opposition to foundationalist moral and political theories,
but also to their conceiving of moral justification as a demonstration of
coherence between moral beliefs on the one hand and local forms of
self-understanding, settled convictions, social practices, tradition, or a
final vocabulary on the other. As I have argued above, this conception
of justification faces serious difficulties. These pertain primarily to the
degree of force critical reflection can claim both when it takes as its object
institutions or practices which fall outside the "boundary," so to speak, of
local culture, and when local solidarities harden into dogma. To this, we
may add further difficulties that arise most notably for hermeneutical
philosophers following in the wake of Gadamer.[9] When questions of
justification arise, such authors frequently speak to a different issue.
The question of what philosophical reasons can be offered in defense
of a moral belief is typically transformed into the issue of where such
beliefs have their historical roots: "Why ought one to believe X?" becomes
"Where does the belief in X come from?" When the answer to the latter
question is that the belief in X has been appropriated from tradition, one
is given to conclude that such a belief warrants our assent. Typically, this
sort of answer is accompanied with an expression of skepticism about
an autonomous a priori rationality—which, it is maintained, must be
presupposed should we wish to distinguish these two questions. However,
to collapse these questions runs the risk of making tradition into a ground
of proof for moral claims. For hermeneutical philosophers interested in

spelling out the ethical implications of Gadamer's thought, it should be noted that Gadamer has been careful in his rehabilitation of tradition to avoid making appeals to tradition into philosophical justifications or proofs of any kind. His thesis that tradition is a source of understanding (one source among others) is never collapsed into the view that tradition is a basis of justification for those beliefs and judgments that are in need of such justification.[10]

While it is unlikely that we could ever formulate a set of necessary and sufficient conditions under which it is necessary to seek a philosophical justification for our traditional moral beliefs, there undoubtedly are circumstances in which we are forced to question our commitment to traditions. We may come to believe that certain pivotal elements of the belief system which has been handed down to us deserve to be rejected—perhaps as a result of our participating in more than one tradition. It is not an uncommon phenomenon, particularly within contemporary Western culture, for one to belong within several traditions—moral, political, religious, or what have you—which produce conflicting demands upon us.[11] Experiencing conflicting demands for our loyalties in virtue of the different traditions within which we stand is a sufficiently commonplace phenomenon that it can be said without exaggeration to represent the normal course of experience for any moderately reflective person today. Under such conditions, questions of justification will inevitably arise. What we shall need to know is which tradition most deserves our continued loyalty, and which ought to be modified or abandoned.

Similar difficulties arise when we justify moral claims by appealing to our social practices. It is well known that lifeworld practices frequently produce conflicting demands upon persons in the course of their experience, while in many other cases such demands are ambiguous or lacking entirely. There are periods in history (such as the present) in which entire communities face stresses and strains that habitual practices have more than a little difficulty dealing with. Either a sense of direction is absent in our moral lives or there are too many conflicting directions with which to cope. One of the difficulties we encounter today is precisely that we face a plethora of social norms and demands for our loyalties, each arising from a particular practice or tradition, and each a product of some measure of consensus. While it would not be reasonable to expect from moral philosophy a method of producing definitive solutions to all ethical conflicts, there are numerous questions that those of us who wish to view the realm of practice as paramount will need to take seriously: In cases of conflict, which social practices merit priority over which others, and for what reasons? Which local practices warrant our continued respect? Which require modification, and how may such modification be undertaken? Which practices ought to be abandoned entirely, and for what sorts of reasons? Above all, to what could the philosopher interested in adjudicating conflicts between various local practices and traditions appeal, except to other local practices and traditions which may themselves deserve to be put in abeyance? Even when we recognize the limits imposed upon reflection by our historicity, we are still left with the need to participate in debates of this kind. It would be odd if moral philosophy had nothing more to contribute to such debates beyond pointing out the limits of our reflective capacities and directing attention to habitual practices and traditions when such a move only raises a further series of questions that we should very much like philosophers to address.

What this line of argument points out is not the need to renounce all justificatory appeals to local consensus and tradition, nor the necessity of providing an objective grounding for ethical life, but the need for moral philosophy to place constraints upon agreements generated within communities as these pertain to just forms of interaction. These constraints may be found within a conception of universal right. A universal theory of justice may enable critical reflection to adjudicate certain kinds of moral conflict by establishing constraints upon local solidarities. Without reintroducing totalizing perspectives, a hermeneutical theory of justice can circumscribe those practices, norms, and expectations that may reasonably claim our assent. Principles of universal right are instrumental in enabling the critic not merely to interpret the meaning of our practices and settled convictions, but to decide under what conditions these should be considered unacceptable. While sometimes the differences of principle that separate moral or political philosophers can be analyzed as interpretive differences concerning the meaning of social norms or the coherence of these with traditional modes of self-understanding, sometimes they cannot. Often these differences pertain not to what forms of interaction are befitting us as inheritors of modern Western culture, but what forms of interaction are befitting us as human beings.

Between Gadamer and Habermas

Does a hermeneutical ethics—one that adopts a skeptical view of totalizing perspectives and philosophical foundations—logically commit itself to an anti-theoretical and/or anti-universalist position? Must we come to a full stop once we have pointed out that critique proceeds from where we are, and not from some transcendental or objective vantage point? Renouncing theory construction, or restricting its role to interpreting traditional norms and self-understandings, generates problems that motivate us to inquire whether it is possible to articulate a universal theory of justice which will solve some of the problems pointed out in the previous section. This is what I propose to undertake in the present section. I shall argue that while moral theory cannot resolve all of the conflicts that are generated in our discourse about the good and the right, it can perform a function which is indispensable to critical reflection. It can provide a philosophical justification for universal principles of right, principles that establish universal constraints upon local norms and solidarities. Accordingly, it is my view that acknowledging the primacy of practice need not entail abandoning theory. Moral theorizing must take its bearings not from an autonomous a priori rationality, but from the realm of practice itself, and it must have as its aim the explicit comprehension, cultivation, and reform of social practices.

The theory of justice that I shall formulate, while liberal in orientation, incorporates key elements in the thought of both Gadamer and Habermas. I shall argue that the liberal virtues of universal freedom, mutual recognition, openness, and respect can be justified as practical entailments of hermeneutic experience. When we thematize the normative dimension already inherent to the practice of dialogue oriented toward mutual understanding, what are generated thereby are liberal principles of right. The argument to be developed takes as its point of departure Gadamer's analysis of hermeneutic experience while bearing a close methodological resemblance to Habermas's communicative ethics. The conclusions reached by this line of argument will lead us to take up a position likewise congenial to philosophical hermeneutics and communicative ethics—a position, as it were, between Gadamer and Habermas.[12]

Before formulating this argument, it is worth making some distinctions to indicate what may and may not be expected from a hermeneutical ethical theory. As opponents of theory have persuasively argued, some (at any rate) of the traditional expectations philosophers have had of moral theory ought to be discarded, as is entailed by renouncing the foundationalist project generally. In particular, it will not be asserted here that ethical theorizing must produce formal procedures for prescribing the correct course of behavior to be followed in any given case of moral action. The rationalist dream of constructing general decision procedures for solving all moral problems in a rule governed manner would best be forgotten. This manner of theorizing, best represented by utilitarians and contractarians, presupposes an abstract and autonomous rationality which has no place outside of a foundationalist, epistemology-centered conception of philosophy. If theory cannot supply procedures for resolving all moral conflicts and issues, neither can it eliminate the need for practical judgment. Moral knowledge has a concrete specificity which can never be successfully mapped out within the terms of a theory. Specific conceptions of how one ought to conduct oneself in life—how to prioritize different values and interests, what occupations to pursue, how to manage one's personal affairs—call for practical judgment and not formal methodology. Neither can moral theory prescribe a particular conception of the good. The classical Greek view of ethics as an attempt to discover a general answer to Socrates's question, "How should one live?," an answer that would provide a philosophically compelling conception of the good and a rational direction in life for each individual to follow, was an overly ambitious view of what moral philosophy could achieve. There is no rational method for adjudicating conflicting notions of the good life since these notions stem from conflicting and philosophically undecidable self-understandings and ego ideals, and are closely bound up with personal and nonuniversalizable beliefs about the meaning that our lives have for us—beliefs that are not suitable objects of moral theorizing.

If moral theory cannot single out a particular conception of the good as uniquely worthy of our assent, this does not entail that it must also renounce a universal conception of right. Justice considerations are best viewed as having their basis not in the settled convictions or final vocabulary of a particular community, but in a universal conception of humanity, the meaning of which will be spelled out as we proceed. A theory of justice establishes constraints within which local norms can be generated, agreements can be reached concerning institutions and forms of government, and competing conceptions of the good can be legitimately pursued. What can be expected from a moral theory, then, are principles of right, the legitimacy of which is not tied to a particular tradition or final vocabulary, and which place limits upon our practices and modes of interaction. Such a theory would constitute an historically conscious universalism, one which recognizes at once that morality always remains tied in some measure to tradition—that universality and particularity can never be unproblematically severed—and the need for critical perspective in assessing particular elements of cultural traditions.

A historically conscious universalism must take up residence between the poles of the following dichotomy: it must occupy a position distinct both from the localism of a Rorty or a Lyotard, and from the abstract rationalism of a Plato, a Kant, or a Hobbes (to name but a few). A nonfoundationalist and hermeneutical theory must forswear an autonomous a priori rationality together with the quest for moral certainty, but with equal importance it must oppose conceptions of morality that so closely link questions of justification to locality that the perspective available for critical reflection is inadequate. Subverting dichotomies of this kind—rationalism or localism, foundations or social decision, principles or judgment—means recognizing the limits of our reflective capacities and the situatedness of theoretical rationality while maintaining a commitment to universality. It entails a rejection of the traditional subordination of practice to theory, and a recognition of the primacy of practice.

Moral theorizing that does not pretend to be unconditioned and transcendental must begin from some identifiable vantage point. Theoretical reflection must begin from the point of view of practice. The traditional view in moral philosophy that in order to judge social practices the theorist must occupy a perspective that transcends the realm of practice altogether (an a priori, scientific, or presocial perspective) would best be discarded and replaced with a conception of theory that arises from within the realm of practice itself. This would be a theoretical rationality that is subsequent to practice in the sense that it recognizes the reflective character of social practices and does not assert the need to provide any kind of grounding for these. It claims neither to provide foundations for social practices nor to proceed from a standpoint transcending such practices. It represents a practice-immanent mode of moral theorizing. Rather than subordinating practice (conceived since Plato as defective, contingent, unreflective, and merely empirical) to theory (conceived since Plato as unconditioned, pristine, and transcendental), the practice-immanent view takes the region of our social and discursive practices as its contingent starting point.

The aim of a theory which is immanent to practice is twofold. It assists critical reflection, first, by achieving a thematic understanding of practices and, second, by directing or redirecting action in light of an explicit comprehension of such practices. On the first point: it may be granted that to be a human agent is already to have a certain involvement with a wide variety of practices, including everything from language use to commerce, education, and so on. Our involvement in practice is never without a certain degree of understanding of what the practice aims to achieve, of what kinds of action are appropriate to it, and of ways and means of competent performance. This kind of understanding is frequently prereflective and consists primarily of practical know-how. The first service that theory can provide is to thematize this practical know-how. It endeavors to gain an explicit comprehension of what we are doing when we are engaged in a practice—what actions characterize its performance, what aims are in view, what rules and principles are always already operative within the practice, and so forth. Theorizing at this stage is a purely phenomenological enterprise, focusing solely upon gaining a thematic or comprehensive grasp of what the practice is about.[13] The second aim of theories of this kind is to gain critical perspective on the conduct of our practices. In light of a thematic understanding of a practice, the objective of theoretical rationality is to formulate principles and/or methods for directing or redirecting action. It supplements the know-how that we already have with principles for assessing performance and (sometimes) methods for successfully attaining particular ends. As well, theoretical knowledge often allows us to challenge our common sense know-how by demonstrating how it may actually fail to bring about the ends that the practice aims to achieve. In articulating the rules and principles already operative (prereflectively) within practices, theorizing makes it possible to reorient, or even radically overhaul, the manner in which practices are conducted.[14] Practice-immanent theorizing, then, aids critical reflection by gaining as comprehensive an understanding of a practice as is possible,[15] and by formulating principles for the direction or assessment of our actions. As an immanent mode of theorizing, it views a practice as it were from "within," analyzing its internal make-up and the actions and principles that constitute it as a practice.

Theoretical understanding is especially mindful of what we may describe as the teleological structure of practices. A practice may be understood as a complex of action types displaying a variety of interrelations and an important element of sociality. To engage in a practice is to participate in certain social relationships and to observe particular rules of interaction and constraints on our conduct. These actions, relationships, and constraints have a common orientation toward the realization of specific ends—ends that are defined by the kind of practice that it is. Just as individual actions are oriented toward the realization of goals, practices have a teleological structure which it is the task of theorizing to describe. Practices circumscribe a sphere of activities oriented toward the realization of what Alasdair MacIntyre has called "internal goods."[16] As MacIntyre points out, one properly engages in a practice in order to realize the goods that are internal to that practice.[17] It is in light of the teleological structure of practices that a theory which is immanent to practice is able to formulate principles for critical reflection. Given an understanding of the ends toward which a practice is phenomenologically oriented, the theorist may articulate critical principles which have their basis in, and are a reflective expression of, the ends that belong to that practice. This mode of theorizing thus appeals to the principles that are already inherent to, or performatively operative within, the practices themselves. The conduct of these is judged under the assistance of practice-immanent principles.

After identifying the teleological dimension of practices, then, the aim of theoretical reflection is to generate principles for critically assessing the manner in which practices are conducted. In addition to posing questions about ways and means by which individuals pursue the ends that are inherent to practices, this mode of theoretical reflection can often bring to light the ways in which extraneous considerations and goals can enter into the conduct of a practice, and how these may corrupt the practice itself. The introduction of extraneous factors into social practices can produce a kind of distortion. Education, the arts, competitive sports, and so on, can all be distorted when extraneous factors such as the personal desires or political agendum of individuals supplant the internal goods of these practices.

This practice-immanent mode of theorizing thus recognizes the reflective character of the complex of activities that it takes as its object of reflection. It recognizes that neither social practices nor the ends to which they are oriented are in need of philosophical justification—that they are ends in themselves, as it were, and central to the manner in which we both understand and orient ourselves within social reality. Practice-immanent theories are not foundational justifications but aids to critical reflection which attempt to describe and assess the manner in which practices are pursued. The question which arises at this point, however, is the role that moral considerations play in assessing social practices. As is well known, the ends that are internal to practices may be pursued in ways that we would wish to characterize as unjust: corporations may pursue profits in ways that are harmful to their customers, employees, or to the environment; teachers may employ certain forms of corporal punishment as a method of educating students in proper behavior; and politicians may pursue their particular vision of the public good in ways that involve flagrant violations of liberty. Examples of this kind can be readily multiplied. What they all point out is that the manner in which one participates in a practice may be considered objectionable not only for the reason that it fails to attain the proper ends or replaces these with extraneous goals, but on the grounds that such actions constitute violations of justice.[18] Accordingly, our question becomes whether it is possible to formulate a theory of justice that is at once practice-immanent and universalistic. Can a mode of theorizing that takes the domain of social and discursive practices as its point of departure, and that forswears autonomous, unconditioned rationality, generate universally warranted principles of justice?

I propose to answer these questions in the affirmative. The objective of a theory of universal right is to provide critical reflection with a set of principles to act as constraints on our practices, norms, and local solidarities—principles that give expression to a notion of our common humanity. Justice may be conceived as a reflective and practical recognition of our common humanity, not in the sense of a recognition of the other as sharing the same metaphysical core as oneself (another noumenal self), but as a recognition of the other as truly other. The point of departure in constructing a hermeneutical ethical theory—a historically conscious universalism—is once again the realm of practice, and the method to be employed is an incorporation of Gadamerian and Habermasian arguments.

If theorizing arises from within the realm of practice, which practice(s) in particular shall we take as our point of departure in constructing a moral theory? A practice-immanent theory of justice must have an identifiable methodological starting point within the region of human practices. I propose that this methodological starting point may be found within the universal human practice of communicative or dialogical understanding. To explain why, let us recall the ontological turn taken by hermeneutics in the twentieth century, beginning with Heidegger's *Being and Time* and extending through Gadamer's *Truth and Method.*

In *Being and Time,* Heidegger initiated the transformation of hermeneutics from a discipline that viewed understanding solely as a methodological problem within the humanities and social sciences to one that conceived of understanding as the fundamental mode of being of human existence. Understanding for Heidegger is not merely what we do, but what we "are." It represents the basic mode in which the human being orients itself and finds its way about in the world. It belongs to the very constitution of human subjectivity and of the world in which we live. Along similar lines, Gadamer speaks of interpretive and dialogical understanding as belonging to the ontological condition of human beings. It is through the practice of dialogical understanding that human beings reflectively cope with our experience of the world in general. As linguistic beings, our manner of gaining familiarity with, and orienting ourselves within, the world involves articulating it in language. While human experience is never without a certain prereflective comprehension of the world, of itself, and of its possibilities, the "universal human task" (as Gadamer describes it) is to bring to speech the phenomena that confront us—to find the words that allow us to reflectively understand and speak of what confronts us in the world, in dialogue with others. Gadamer, in speaking of "the conversation that we ourselves are,"[19] recommends that we regard the practice of dialogue oriented toward intersubjective understanding as, in a sense, constitutive of our humanity. Not merely a form of behavior one voluntarily undertakes, dialogical understanding is a practice the scope of which is universal, and the import of which is best described as ontological.

What distinguishes communicative understanding within the domain of practices is that it is this complex of interrelated actions—speaking and listening, persuading and convincing, making truth claims and giving reasons, justifying and criticizing, projecting possibilities of interpretation and achieving self-understanding—that is constitutive of our humanity. Phenomenologically speaking (and without having recourse to a metaphysics of human nature), what appears to universally characterize human forms of community is the presence of this complex of related actions. While it has been traditional since the Greeks for philosophers to view our capacity for thinking and reasoning—our sharing in the logos—as the distinguishing attribute of human beings, it is significant that the term logos, as Gadamer has noted[20], carries a meaning that is more fundamental than thought or reason—namely language. As linguistic and social beings, our efforts to find our way about in the world and to develop lasting forms of community are never without this important dimension of dialogical understanding. It is in this sense that we may speak of communicative understanding not merely as what we do, but as what we are. It is this universality of scope and ontological import that gives understanding a special place in the realm of human practices. It is, accordingly, to this practice that we may look in identifying a starting point for moral theorizing.

Habermas also takes the practice of communication oriented toward mutual understanding as a point of departure in developing his theory of justice. On Habermas's view, it is language that constitutes the distinguishing feature of human life, and the analysis that he undertakes into the different modes of human interaction and language use concentrates upon that mode which warrants a type of priority over the others—namely communicative action, or linguistic interaction the implicit telos of which is mutual understanding. Without going into the details of this investigation, Habermas's analysis leads him to the conclusion that communicative action has a kind of primacy relative to strategic action since the latter is derivative from, or parasitic upon, the former.

If we wish to develop a theory of justice which is both practice-immanent and universalistic, it must take as its point of departure a practice that is universal in scope. With Habermas, I contend that the practice of communicative understanding represents an appropriate point of departure. Having identified our starting point, then, our task is to investigate the teleological structure that this practice displays. If it belongs to the structure of a practice that it contain an implicit telos, what constitutes the teleological dimension of communicative understanding? What are the ends that belong to this practice, and what principles are implicitly operative in its performance? By investigating these questions, we may see that the communicative process contains an important normative dimension. Our method, then, will be to render explicit the normative dimension of communicative understanding and to demonstrate its implications for ethical critique. An observation of David Ingram's will prove useful in this regard. Ingram has claimed to identify a teleological dimension operative within Gadamer's analysis of hermeneutic understanding. Ingram writes:

> [T]he very *modus operandi* of human understanding is teleologically oriented toward a recognition of the 'thou' as one whose individuality merits an equal right to be respected and understood. Though such an attitude no doubt informs any search for new meaning, it is especially definitive of communicative understanding. Indeed, Gadamer regards reciprocity as in some sense a transcendental condition for the very possibility of human communication as such.[21]

This reading of *Truth and Method* arises from a section of that text in which Gadamer undertakes an analysis of historically effected consciousness. Gadamer distinguishes three modes of hermeneutic experience—three ways in which an interpreter can approach a text or tradition—and correlates each of these with a corresponding mode of interpersonal experience. For Gadamer, the I-Thou relation may be taken as paradigmatic of communicative understanding generally, and by investigating this relation it may be possible to uncover a teleological dimension operative within all hermeneutic experience, or within the practice of dialogical understanding.

The first mode of interpersonal experience which Gadamer identifies is dominated by an objectivating attitude toward the other. This is a manner of encountering the other along the lines of a research subject: one seeks a knowledge of behavioral regularities as a means of predicting the other's future actions. Its correlative within hermeneutic experience involves a similar objectivating attitude toward tradition or the text. The interpreter investigates tradition in the detached and objective manner of the scientist, and is given to believing that by applying the appropriate methods, one may extricate oneself from one's own historicity and gain a neutral perspective. This objectivistic manner of encountering tradition, as Gadamer puts it, "flattens out the nature of hermeneutical experience" (TM 359). In overestimating the objectivity of its methods and forgetting the limits of reflection, this mode of hermeneutic experience overlooks the claims that tradition or the text makes upon the interpreter. The second I-Thou relation Gadamer describes includes a recognition of the other as a human being (rather than a mere object of scientific investigation), but it is a form of recognition that is without the important elements of reciprocity and openness. Here one purports to know the other in an unconditioned fashion. The claims that are advanced by the other are encountered not as truth claims, but "reflectively" and from a distanced perspective. Because one is already in full possession of the truth, the claims of the other inevitably meet with an authoritative reply. This relation between I and Thou is thus dominated by the self-certainty of the I. Its correlative within hermeneutic experience includes an interest in the claims of tradition that is primarily antiquarian. One knows of the past in its otherness and uniqueness, but in a manner that keeps it at a distance and forbids us from learning something that we did not already know. Being without prejudice, the interpreter need rely only upon the exactitude of his methods and not consider the possible truth value of the claims of tradition.

It is only in the third relation between I and Thou that the teleological dimension of communicative understanding becomes visible. Characterizing this as the "highest" form of interpersonal and hermeneutic experience, Gadamer here describes a relation of openness, reciprocity, and mutual recognition. Here the other is encountered in a manner befitting human beings: unlike the first two, this relation is not dominated by an objectivating attitude or a dogmatic self-certainty, but involves a condition of openness to the claims of the other and a recognition of the possibility of learning from the Thou. In a passage with unmistakeable ethical connotations, Gadamer writes:

> In human relations the important thing is, as we have seen, to experience the Thou truly as a Thou—i.e., not to overlook his claim but to let him really say something to us. Here is where openness belongs. But ultimately this openness does not exist only for the person who speaks; rather, anyone who listens is fundamentally open. Without such openness to one another there is no genuine human bond. Belonging together always also means being able to listen to one another. When two people understand each other, this does not mean that one person 'understands' the other. Similarly, 'to hear and obey someone' does not mean simply that we do blindly what the other desires. We call such a person slavish. Openness to the other, then, involves recognizing that I myself must accept some things that are against me, even though no one else forces me to do so. (TM 361)

This is a relation in which the I allows itself to be called into question by the Thou. The conversational virtues of open-mindedness and mutuality—a willingness to listen to the claims of the other with an eye to their possible validity, and to allow oneself to be led by the dynamic back and forth movement of the dialogue rather than dominate it in the monological fashion of the expert—are here fully manifest. Correspondingly, within hermeneutic experience understanding culminates in what Gadamer calls historically effected consciousness. Recognizing the historical contingency of its own perspective, this mode of hermeneutic consciousness resists all dogmatic privileging of one's own knowledge and remains open to further inquiry and questioning. In allowing its own perspective to be called into question, historically effected consciousness never culminates in final determinations or methodological self-certainty, but in an openness to further experience and dialogue.

It is here that the teleological and normative dimension of communicative understanding becomes apparent. "[T]he process of interpretation 'which we are,'" as Ingram writes, "is itself teleologically oriented toward a state of openness and mutual recognition" (39). Participation in the communicative process involves more than merely demonstrating the truth value of our hypotheses. It is to have an implicit orientation to a condition of openness and reciprocity, a condition in which neither I nor Thou asserts for itself special authority within the conversation, but remains open to the possibility of learning from opposed perspectives. Inherent to the communicative process is a common orientation to the meaning or truth of the subject matter, a meaning or truth that is brought to light only in the dialectical movement of question and answer, assertion and reply, and is not the sole possession of the I or the Thou. Within the back and forth movement of understanding, participants in dialogue are drawn into a common endeavor to uncover the truth about the subject matter, a process that presupposes a recognition of, an openness toward, and a willingness to be called into question by, the other. The practice of dialogical understanding, then, contains and presupposes not only an orientation to uncovering the truth of the text, but an important normative dimension as well. This normative dimension constitutes at once a condition of the possibility of communicative understanding as well as its implicit telos. It is the common orientation without which our speaking and listening would not belong to the practice of dialogue, and without which dialogue would not be the practice that it is.[22]

The practice of communicative understanding, then, contains an implicit orientation toward mutual recognition. Herein lies the normative core of a universalistic conception of justice: universal principles of justice represent constraints upon local practices, norms, and institutions which give expression to a notion of our common humanity. Justice may be viewed as an ethical, institutional, and legal application of this notion of reciprocal recognition. It is a practical mode of recognizing the individual as such, and this means as a free and autonomous human being. Recognizing the other as an other entails, in Kantian language, respect for persons as ends in themselves and an obligation to refrain from reducing the latter to a mere means for one's own ends. Principles of universal right give content to the idea of treating others as human beings—as beings capable of understanding, communication, and argumentation with others.

Habermas also conceives of communicative action as teleologically oriented toward a state of mutual recognition and respect for persons. Like Gadamer's analysis of hermeneutic experience and the I-Thou relation, communicative ethics may be viewed as an elaboration and application of the Hegelian themes of recognition and alterity as well as of the Kantian notion of respect. There is, accordingly, an important area of common ground between a theory of justice inspired by philosophical hermeneutics and the communicative ethics of Habermas: both may be read in light of, or as practical applications of, these Hegelian and Kantian themes; both identify the practice of communicative understanding as the appropriate point of departure for generating a theory of universal right; and both adopt the methodology of rendering explicit the normative dimension or pragmatic presuppositions of the communicative process.

Communicative ethics endeavors to reconstruct the presuppositions and principles that are always already operative in the practice of communicative interaction oriented toward understanding. Habermas proposes that communicative action contains within itself unavoidable pragmatic presuppositions which have normative import. Our capacity to engage in discourse—our "communicative competence"—possesses a universal core of presuppositions and rules, some of which function as indispensable normative conditions of discourse aimed at reaching consensus. Anyone who engages in the practice of communicative understanding has, Habermas maintains, always already presupposed and accepted certain normative principles of argumentation, principles that no speaker may contradict without falling into a performative contradiction. Habermas writes:

> Briefly, the thesis that discourse ethics puts forth . . . is that anyone who seriously undertakes to participate in argumentation implicitly accepts by that very undertaking general pragmatic presuppositions that have a normative content. The moral principle can then be derived from the content of these presuppositions of argumentation.[23]

Moral principles are generated through an analysis of the structure of communicative action. This analysis brings to light substantive moral principles which are already performatively at play within that practice, and which are necessarily accepted by all speakers by virtue of their participation in it.[24] If communicative action is a search for the truth rather than an exercise in strategic action, speakers must presuppose the conversational virtues of respect, recognition, tolerance, and open-mindedness, as well as the principles of freedom of expression and equal access to the conversation.[25] These substantive normative commitments, Habermas contends, underlie the communicative process and make it the kind of practice that it is. It is these that constitute the core of a universalistic conception of justice.

It is the communicative process that underlies and makes possible all humane forms of community and just modes of interaction, and it is these principles that constitute the teleological and normative dimension of this universal practice. Accordingly, the set of principles that this method of theorizing generates—reciprocal recognition, respect for persons, freedom, equality, difference, alterity, plurality, solidarity, civility, and personal autonomy—is best regarded not merely as an accidental feature of our particular time and place, but as inherent to the universal human practice of persons coming together in solidarity to discuss, debate, and understand the world in which they live. These principles are constitutive of a conception of justice centered around the integrity of the human being, a theme that is at the heart of the liberal tradition. It is within this tradition that justice is conceived in terms of the conversational virtues, and that social interaction is governed in principle by a respect for persons as individual ends in themselves. In liberalism the other has a status that is identical to the I: self and other are moral equals as well as equals before the law. The liberal conception of justice is dominated by an ideal of human beings freely choosing and pursuing their own values within a system of constraints based upon recognition of, and respect for, others as equals. Within this tradition, identifying the limits of what I or we may do in relation to the other—the extent to which our actions may legitimately influence, govern, or interfere with another's freedom—represents what John Stuart Mill properly calls "the principal question in human affairs."[26] The principal questions for a liberal view of justice pertain to the limits of the legitimate exercise of power in relations between persons as well as between citizens and the state: Within what limits may one impose duties upon another or otherwise restrict their range of options? To what extent may prevailing social norms reasonably govern the actions and life plans of the individual? Under what conditions may the state properly override the decisions of individuals to act in the manner of their own choosing? Liberalism answers these questions by delimiting (in however imprecise and approximate a fashion) a sphere of activity within which one is at liberty to pursue goals of one's own choosing without interference from others or from the state. The limits imposed on human action by justice considerations are such that the liberty of persons to fashion their lives in the manner of their choosing is respected in a way that is compatible with respecting the identical liberties of others. The liberal virtues of universal freedom, respect, equality and so on thus give rise to an ideal of moral interaction as maximizing the integrity and autonomy of the individual human being within the limits of respecting the integrity and autonomy of others.

Moral theorizing may thus provide an invaluable service to critical reflection in generating universal principles of right. It serves the important function of placing constraints upon what may reasonably pass for justice in our practices and social relations. Finally, a theory of justice that is both universalistic and immanent to the domain of human practices represents an important area of common ground between hermeneutics and critical theory. A theory of justice that proceeds methodologically by analyzing the normative presuppositions of hermeneutic dialogue or communicative action constitutes an important—if limited—point of convergence between these two frequently antagonistic schools of thought.

10

Phenomenology and Communicative Ethics: Husserl, Sartre, and Merleau-Ponty

Thomas W. Busch

Phenomenological ethics is usually identified with the discourse of values, while communicative ethics is assigned to the hybrid tradition of Marxism and the social sciences. However, there exists an incipient communicative ethic in the work of Husserl, Sartre, and Merleau-Ponty as well as instructive lessons to be learned on the direction of such an ethic in the differences that obtain among them.

On those occasions when Husserl reflects on the phenomenological project, he never fails to mention its practical consequences. In *Philosophy As A Rigorous Science*[1] he identifies phenomenology with the movement of Western scientific philosophy which "satisfies the loftiest theoretical needs and renders possible from an ethico-religious point of view a life regulated by pure rational norms" (PRS 71). Indeed, "the highest interests of human culture demand" the development of a rigorously scientific philosophy, so that he sees philosophy's "vocation" as that of carrying on "the eternal work of humanity." Husserl locates the heart of phenomenology's rigor in essences: "I would say that it is the phenomenological theory of essence alone that is capable of providing a foundation for a philosophy of the spirit. . . . Phenomenological investigation is essence investigation and is thus a priori in the authentic sense" (PRS 129; 121). Essence delivers one from "point of view" and "interpretation" into "supratemporal universality" (PRS 135), "absolute timeless values" (PRS 136), "intersubjective validities" (PRS 134). Essence, in turn, is achieved by "direct intuition," free of "the pressure of prejudice." The ground inhabited by such a vision is that of "origins." This differentiates phenomenology from naturalistic and cultural (historicist and *Weltan-schauung*) views, which are saturated with naive assumptions.

The universality, timelessness, and intersubjective validity of essences lead Husserl to his references about "humanity as an eternal idea" (PRS 138). This is, he says, "an ethical ideal" for which one has "ethical responsibilities" (PRS 138). Husserl is formulating a sort of communicative ethic around the idea of science and essence. If through science one escapes point of view and interpretation (differences), one can achieve essence (identity), "definitive" concepts and their fixed, univocal expressions. The resulting "humanity" would be a homogeneous and supposedly peaceful society bound by the same vision or vision of the same. However, at the time Husserl is writing, science has not achieved its ideal destiny. What is required is a "critique of reason" (phenomenology) which will put it on its true track.

In the 1930's, after the shocking experience of the First World War and on the eve of the Second, Husserl wrote *The Crisis of the European Sciences and Transcendental Phenomenology.*[2] At a time when so many thinkers were seriously questioning the idea of rationality itself, Husserl is adamant: "The reason for the failure of a rational culture . . . lies not in the essence of rationalism itself . . ." (C 299). Reason, he argues, ought not to be identified with its reductionistic, positivistic, and instrumental deformations. Reason's failure is only "apparent." Once again he calls for a critique of reason, in the form of transcendental phenomenology, which will rehabilitate reason. This time, however, there is a noticeable urgency in his appeal: "There are only two escapes from the crisis of European existence: the downfall of Europe in its estrangement from its own rational sense of life, its fall into hostility toward the spirit and into barbarity; or the rebirth of Europe from the spirit of philosophy through a heroism of reason" (C 299).

Husserl dramatically identifies science as the *telos* of history, with its origins in the Greeks. While all peoples live within the horizons of a life-world, it was the Greeks who introduced a new, theoretical attitude toward the world, one which distinguished the "represented" world from the "actual" world.

> In this attitude, man views first of all the multiplicity of nations, his own and others, each with its own surrounding world which is valid for it, is taken for granted, with its traditions, its gods, its demons, its mythical powers, simply as the actual world. Through this astonishing contrast there appears the distinction between world-representation and actual world, and the question of truth arises: not the tradition-bound, everyday truth,

but an identical truth which is valid for all who are no longer blinded by traditions, a truth-in-itself. (C 285–86)

The philosopher "becomes a nonparticipating spectator, surveyer of the world" (C 285), and is not "bound to the soil of a national tradition." Thus, there arises the idea of a "supranationality" of a Europe which would be no longer "a conglomeration of different nations influencing one another only through commerce and power struggles" (C 289). This "new man," "new humanity," "new culture," "new community," is based upon a "communicative understanding," itself based upon ideas which "belong to all identically," wherein truth is "common property" (C 287). Philosophy finds its vocation, mission, and responsibility within this telos.

The basic ideas expressed in the "Vienna" lecture of *The Crisis* recapitulate those of *Philosophy As A Rigorous Science*. What *The Crisis* adds, of course, is the move to incorporate his views within a theory of history. It is this problematic of history, which is featured most notably in *The Origin of Geometry*, that has led to so much speculation on whether Husserl had changed his mind about the nature of phenomenology as rigorous science. Has Husserl, for example, abandoned the intuition of essences, the longstanding foundation of his phenomenology and of his previous ideal of "humanity"? The question comes to settle on his view of language, on the relation between ideality and language. In discussing the origin of geometry, Husserl recognizes the reality and significance of linguistic communities. A linguistic community is based upon the "written document," which "makes communications possible without immediate or mediate personal address" (C 360–61). Science itself is such a community with its distinctive tradition. However, language is dangerous, for it can lead to deformations between "original formations" and "sedimented meanings" (C 371). This, in fact, has happened to science, according to Husserl, with the result of a deformed naturalistic and positivistic reason. However, the deformations can always be corrected by returning to original insights. "The reader," he claims, can make it self-evident again, can reactivate the self-evidence" (C 361). Thus, Husserl has not abandoned his intuitionism. In fact, his own claims regarding the eidetic structures of any life-world whatever (and even the eidos of history itself as science) are based upon eidetic intuition: "we have the capacity of complete freedom to transform, in thought and phantasy, our human historical existence and what is there exposed as its life-world. And precisely in this activity of free variation, and in running through the conceivable possibilities for the life-world, there arises, with apodictic self-evidence, an essentially general set of elements going through all the variants . . ." (C 374–75). Indeed, running consistently throughout Husserl's work is the reduction to a core stratum, intuitable eidetically, and expressible univocally. The method of free, imaginative variation discovers the limits of the identifiably same while disengaging difference and multiplicity of perspective. It is not surprising then, that his community based upon "communicative understanding" is both homogeneous and exclusive. In *The Crisis* he rejects non-Western thinking as unphilosophical and bankrupt. Of Westerners he writes:

> There is something unique here that is recognized in us by all other human groups, . . . something that, quite apart from all considerations of utility, becomes a motive for them to Europeanize themselves even in their unbroken will to spiritual self-preservation; whereas we, if we understand ourselves properly, would never Indianize ourselves, for example. (C 275)

Husserl's communicative rationality is an appeal for the European nations to rise above their national boundaries and differences in order to recognize their supranational identity as Europeans.

Ironically, Husserl is rejecting insular traditionalisms in favor of a "Western" tradition that, being scientific, rejects the prejudices and assumptions characteristic of traditions. For his phenomenology there exists a cultural "epoche," whereby traditional assumptions are thematized, scrutinized, rejected or approved by virtue of scientific legitimation. Western people, living on the level of theoria, are, for Husserl, on a different level of being from those peoples who live on the mythical/religious level of life. Western peoples are a "new humanity." The responsibility of the Western philosopher toward non-Western peoples is to be teacher and leader.

Husserl's *Crisis* contests itself in a tension between the continued discourse of strict science and its cluster of notions—timeless essences, origins, intuition, transcendence of perspective—and his newly acquired interest in language, history, and tradition. By identifying the universal as a supratemporal essence accessed by intuition, Husserl opens himself to the posssibility of confusing the particular with the universal, a relatively benign problem in science, but much more serious in ethics and politics.

Sartre had concluded his first philosophical work, *The Transcendence of the Ego*,[3] his existentialist theory of consciousness, by proclaiming that his discoveries formed the way for a "positive ethics and politics." His concluding remarks in *Being and Nothingness*[4] reiterated his resolve to formulate an ethics. There is no doubt that Sartre's aim was ethical, and later, political. Over the years, he can be seen trying, in several different ways, to work out an ethics. One of his earliest and most overlooked forays in this direction was *What is Literature?*.[5] Here, in the midst of defining literature as communicative art, Sartre discovers communicative ethics: "Although literature is one thing and morality a quite different one, at the heart of the aesthetic imperative we discern the moral imperative" (WIL 56).

Investigating literature compelled Sartre to take a stand in regard to language. In his brief comments on language in *Being and Nothingness*, Sartre had treated language as a tool, a technique, the meaning of which depends upon human meaning-giving. Words are, physically, marks on paper and must be animated by consciousness for them to have meaning. Like Husserl, Sartre was a philosopher of consciousness who held that language was constituted by consciousness. He approached literature with this view, but was constrained to nuance it in sorting out literature from other arts and, in particular, distinguishing the literary arts of poetry and prose from one another. For Sartre, words normally function as signs, employed to designate objects. The word, he holds, is "transparent" in its functioning, that is, it designates by melting into its communicative function. Prose engages language in its designative or "utilitarian" function. The prose writer "is a *speaker*; he designates, demonstrates, orders, refuses, interpolates, begs, insults, persuades, insinuates" (WIL 13–14). This radically separates the prose writer from the poet in Sartre's eyes. In poetry, words are not simply designators. Words are things, drawing attention to themselves, their look and sound. Poets intercept the transparency of words. Words are used by the poet as colors are used by painters and sounds by composers. For Sartre, between prose and poetry "there is nothing in common . . . except the movement of the hand that traces the letters" (WIL 13). Words are objects for the poet, not signs, but the stuff of images. Poetry is a magical substitution for the world, whereas the prose writer reveals the world.

For Sartre the prose writer, in revealing the lived world, raises it to the thematic level where it is presented to others for their response. Literature is a dialectic between writer and reader, wherein each recognizes the freedom of the other. As Sartre depicts the writer/reader dialectic we see a relationship presented which differs considerably from the sort of inauthentic and deadend relationships depicted in *Being and Nothingness*. Literature's essence is expressive and communicative and this implies an ideal community. Literature is not a reflection of the master/slave dialectic, but involves a collaborative relationship, "the conjoint effort of author and reader. . . . the writer appeals to the reader's freedom to collaborate in the production of his work" (WIL 37; 40). The writer, in addressing his work to readers, assumes their freedom, their powers to reproduce the work as aesthetic object. Readers, in picking up an author's work, implicitly recognize the author's power of creation. Literature is "co-creation," a shared responsibility for bringing the aesthetic object into being.

This aesthetic community in which freedoms recognize each other as ends implies the ethical "city of ends."

> Let us bear in mind that the man who reads strips himself in some way of his empirical personality and escapes from his resentments, his fears, and his lusts in order to put himself at the peak of his freedom. This freedom takes the literary work and, through it, mankind, for absolute ends. It sets itself up as an unconditioned exigence in relationship to itself, to the author, and to possible readers. It can therefore be identified with Kantian *good will* which, in every circumstance, treats man as an end and not as a means. Thus, by his very exigence, the reader attains that chorus of good wills which Kant has called the City of Ends, which thousands of readers all over the world who do not know each other are, at every moment, helping to maintain. (WIL 265)

Reading, according to Sartre, is "directed creation." The reader puts him/herself, in the act of reading, at the disposal of the writer's intentions, loans his/her imaginative capacity to the bringing about of the author's meaning. This gift of oneself is identified as Kantian good will. If the community of ends which Sartre depicts here is the very condition of possibility of literature then, he concludes, "it would be inconceivable that this unleashing of generosity provoked by the writer could be used to authorize an injustice, and that the reader could enjoy his freedom while reading a work which approves or accepts or simply abstains from condemning the subjection of man by man" (WIL 57). The aesthetic, dealing as it does in Sartre's view with unreality, nevertheless depends upon real freedoms. Aesthetic communication, at least in the form of prose, demonstrates how positive human relationships, those implying mutual respect, are possible. This communicative fraternity becomess the paradigm of the ethical and political: it must be *realized* in historical circumstances. This requires fulfillment of two conditions. One must transform one's identity as reader by the concrete intuition of one's real social presence with others. And there must be an attempt to historicize "abstract good wills" into "material and timely demands" (WIL 265). Otherwise, "lacking the wherewithal, the city of ends lasts for each of us only while we are reading; on passing from the imaginary life to real life we forget this abstract, implicit community" (WIL 265). The ethical "appeal" of communicative understanding is that of assuming responsibility for the "real" world and of shaping it to meet the demands of freedom, the very condition of communication itself. The ethical demand of communicative understanding is inseparable in Sartre's mind from the social and political demand for democracy. Here, once more, his argument begins with literary communication and is then transposed to the real world.

Sartre claims a distinction between an actual and virtual audience for a literary work. The virtual audience consists of all who can read and respond to the work. The actual audience consists of those who, under specific historical conditions, know how to read, have access to books, or might have a particular interest in reading a particular book. Sartre spends a good bit of time in *What is Literature?* discussing literary life and communication from the Middle Ages through the nineteenth century, pointing out how class structure defined the actual communication taking place. This constitutes in his eyes an alienated (distorted?) literature and communication.

> The examples we have chosen have served only to *situate* the freedom of the writer in different ages, to illuminate by the limits of the demands made upon him the limits of his appeal, to show by the idea of his role which the public fashions for itself the necessary boundaries of the idea he invents of literature. And if it is true that the essence of the literary work is freedom totally disclosing and willing itself as an appeal to the freedom of men, it is also true that the diffferent forms of oppression, by hiding from men the fact that they were free, have screened this all or part of this essence from authors. (WIL 145)

Sartre's conclusion is that there is only one political way of life which is compatible with the essence of literature: "In short, *actual* literature can only realize its full *essence* in a classless society" (WIL 150). There is, according to Sartre's reasoning, an implication, an inherent telos, in communicative understanding which passes through the Kantian imperative to treat others as unconditioned ends to the Marxist imperative to change the world by eliminating classes. Sartre thought that in the really true free society, the realization of "the reign of human freedom," human relationships would be "transparent" because there would be no distortion. And only Marxism could bring this about. His utopianism called for "total freedom" (WIL 272), which he defines as "the freedom of changing everything; which means, besides suppression of classes, abolition of all dictatorship, constant renewal of frameworks, and the continuous overthrowing of order once it tends to congeal" (WIL 153). This perhaps explains Sartre's impatience with, and willingness to impose violence against, an inertia in human affairs that he believed in no way inevitable.[6]

Claude Lefort informs us that Merleau-Ponty was profoundly impressed with *What is Literature?* and that he wrote a "substantial resume" of it, along with a critical commentary, in 1948.[7] At the end of the unpublished commentary, Merleau-Ponty wrote: "I must do a sort of *What is Literature?* with a longer section on the sign and prose . . ." Many of the ideas sketched out in these unpublished notes find their way into *The Prose of the World* and, first articulated in that book culminate in the essay later published in *Signs*[8] "Indirect Language and the Voices of Silence." At the same time as he was writing this essay in its finished form, he was recommencing his dialogue, begun many years earlier, with Husserl. This time language, institutions, values and culture formed the focus of major essays in *Signs*, and Husserl's *Crisis* was a continuous reference.

At the beginning of "Indirect Language . . .", Merleau-Ponty challenges Sartre's and Husserl's views on language. "Language is much more like a sort of being than a means" (S 43). This is an admission, against Sartre, of the thickness as opposed to the transparency of language and has the effect of putting literature and the other arts on a similar footing. "Indirect Language . . ." both is and is not about painting as expression and communication. Painting "echoes" all expressive modalities. Historical phenomena, for Merleau-Ponty, find their paradigm in "the model of language and the arts." Thus, as Sartre attempted to connect the aesthetic and moral imperatives, Merleau-Ponty, at an important juncture in this essay, will claim that "political thought itself is of this order," that is, the order of the life of expression and communication. In addition, and in opposition to Husserl, Merleau-Ponty holds that "author himself has no text to which he can compare his writing, and no language prior to language" (S 43). This is a denial of the constitution of language by consciousness and a reiteration of the thesis of *Phenomenology of Perception*[9] that there is no thought without expression. Merleau-Ponty's analysis of painting shows it to be a form of "indirect" communication, antithetical to the notion of a mastery and control of meaning by consciousness. Constitution (the heart of the views on language of Husserl and Sartre) is replaced by his notion of institution or tradition. By institution, Merleau-Ponty tells us in his course lecture notes, he means "those events in experience which endow it with durable dimensions" and are "the invitation to a sequel" (10). Time, within the context of institution, is the "fecundity" of a present, a concrete nexus of possibilities in the products of culture which "open a field of investigations" (S 59). Merleau-Ponty's instituted subject is a hermeneutic subject, grounded in a tradition with others in a communicative life. Indeed, for him, as for Husserl and Sartre, this communicative life implies an ethics and politics. But Merleau-Ponty's understanding of the processes of expression and communication differs from theirs, as we have noted. When he claims that "ideal existence is based upon the document" (S 96), he is not repeating Husserl's view of writing in *The Origin of Geometry*. For Husserl, writing is the external clothing for meanings and the source of their alienation and distortion. For Merleau-Ponty the meaning is the text and every text *exceeds* authorial intention for a number of reasons. Ambiguity and plurivocity are unavoidable and one cannot clear them up by returning to "origins" as Husserl had suggested. Understanding is situational. Every reading is an "intentional transgression" in which certain possibilities of the text are actualized. Since the point of communication is not to reach a definitive meaning rooted in mental intentionality, its point becomes that of bringing about common understanding: "Words, even in the art of prose, carry the speaker and the hearer into a common universe by drawing both toward a new signification through their power to designate in excess of their accepted definition . . ." (S 75) The "universal" is no longer the supratemporal essence, eidetically intuited, univocally defined, and expressed by clothing it with an empirical language. The universal is always hammered out and provisional. Merleau-Ponty calls this the "lateral universal which we acquire through ethnological experience and its incessant testing of the self through the other person and the other person through the self" (S 120). In contrast to Husserl's understanding of ideal being in supratemporal essence, Merleau-Ponty proclaims a "new idea of truth" founded upon finitude and the inability to escape time.

> . . . it is up to us to understand that whatever truth we may have is to be gotten not in spite of but through our historical inherence. Superficially considered, our inherence destroys all truth; considered radically, it founds a new idea of truth. As long as I cling to the ideal of an absolute spectator, of knowledge with no point of view, I can see my situation as nothing but a source of error. But if I have once recognized that through it I am grafted onto every action and all knowledge that can have a meaning for me, and that step by step it contains everything which can *exist* for me, then my contact with the social in the finitude of my situation is revealed to me as the point of origin of all truth. (S 109)

Truth, like rationality, is made. The idea of Greek rationality, Merleau-Ponty claims, commenting on Husserl's theme in *The Crisis*, must "prove" itself "by the knowledge and action it makes possible" (S 111), and must get itself recognized. Truth and rationality are social and come about through incessant testing. In *Signs*, Merleau-Ponty warns about reducing philosophy "to the rank of . . . a propagandist in the service of objective knowledge" (S 113). (Was he thinking of Husserl here and his view of the "mission" of the West?) Philosophy as a participant in communicative life, is, rather, for Merleau-Ponty, "co-existence," and "adds to my obligations as a solitary person the obligation to understand situations other than my own and to create a path between my life and others . . ." (S 75). Communicative life, as understood by Merleau-Ponty, "prohibits the philosopher from arrogating to himself an immediate access to the universal" (S 109). The methodology of an eidetic intuition based upon imaginative variation is insufficient. At one point he asks how it would be possible for "a German, born in the nineteenth century" to know by imaginative variation the different possibilities of humanity as instantiated by primitives. In contrast to Husserl's attitude toward non-Western thought (non-Westerns must learn from us, but "we would never Indianize ourselves"), Merleau-Ponty claims that "Western philosophy can learn from them to rediscover the relationship to being and the initial option which gave it birth, and to estimate the possibilities we have shut ourselves off from in becoming 'Westerners' and perhaps reopen them" (S 139).

Merleau-Ponty, as with Sartre, sees an ethics of mutual recognition and respect in the communicative situation. "At the moment of expression the other to whom I address myself and I who express myself are incontestably linked together"(S 73). The others I address "are worth exactly what I am worth, and all the powers I give them I give simultaneously to myself. I submit myself to the judgment of another *who is himself worthy of that which I have attempted,* that is to say, in the last analysis, to the judgment of a peer . . ." (S 73). The call or appeal of expression to the other is a "recognition" of the other, and as I open myself to the others, their taking up of my expression is a recognition of me. We are "peers." What Merleau-Ponty resists in the communicative ethics of *What is Literature?* is its utopianism, and this is due to Merleau-Ponty's differing view of language. Because Sartre thinks that language is transparent, he sees no reason why human relationships cannot be transparent. Sartre claims that "the literary object, though realized *through* language, is never given in language" (WIL 38). This is because the literary object, for him, exists in consciousness. Language is the means of conduction of objects or meanings from one consciousness to another. If language is transparent there can be perfect communication. In an interview many years after the publication of *What is Literature?* Sartre continued in this utopianism: "I think transparency should always be substituted for secrecy. I can imagine the day when two men will no longer have secrets from each other, because no one will have any more secrets from anyone, because subjective life, as well as objective life, will be completely offered up, given. . . . A man's existence must be entirely visible to his neighbor, whose own existence must be entirely visible in turn, before true social harmony can be established" (11). Sartre sees only two alternatives, tranparency or secrecy. He sees no thickness, ambiguity, plurivocity, excess, interpretivity of an inevitable sort in language itself. He would in fact, remove all "order once it tends to congeal" (S 153). Ideally, there must be "the freedom of changing everything." Lyotard calls this "the arrogance of the for-itself." Merleau-Ponty sees it as a reflection of the constituting subject of phenomenology, which must be replaced by a more humble, instituting or hermeneutical subject. Such a subject, truly finite, accepts the inevitability of ambiguity, or instituted meaning, traditions, democratic structures, compromises. There is no utopian end of history for Merleau-Ponty. That is a dangerous idea, one that represses finitude and leads to demands to remake human beings. There are no final solutions. Ethics and politics take place "only in the relative and the probable" (12).

With Husserl and later with his appropriators, Sartre and Merleau-Ponty, phenomenology necessarily implied a communicative ethic. Their particular notions of ethics and politics (although barely sketched out) differed according to their respective understandings of truth, language, expression and communication, as evident in Husserl's views on geometry, Sartre's on literature, and Merleau-Ponty's on painting. Of the three, Merleau-Ponty offers an understanding of communication which is the most faithful to finitude, to the linguisticality, sociality, historicality of rationality and truth. While he cannot be said to have developed fully a communicative ethic, he did point it in its rightful conversational and nonutopian directions.

11

The Ethics and Politics
of the Flesh

G. B. Madison

> De même que le moteur de la langue est la volonté de
> communiquer ("nous sommes jetés dans le language et par
> lui engagés dans un processus d'explication rationnelle avec
> autrui"), de même ce qui meut tout le développement historique,
> c'est la *situation commune* des hommes, leur volonté de coexister
> et de se reconnaître.
>
> —*Maurice Merleau-Ponty, "La conscience et l'acquisition du language"*

M idway through his tragically short career, Merleau-Ponty wrote, in an assessment of his work:

> The study of perception could only teach us a "bad ambiguity," a mixture of finitude and universality, of interiority and exteriority. But there is a "good ambiguity" in the phenomenon of expression, a spontaneity which accomplishes what appeared to be impossible when we observed only the separate elements, a spontaneity which gathers together the plurality of monads, the past and the present, nature and culture into a single whole [*un seul tissu*]. To establish this wonder [*La constatation de cette merveille*] would be metaphysics itself and would at the same time give us the principle of an ethics.[1]

The document in which the text just cited occurs is one Merleau-Ponty prepared in the early 1950s when he was establishing his candidacy for the Collège de France; it was thus a survey of what he believed he had accomplished up until then and an outline of future research. Things did not turn out as planned. Merleau-Ponty never did produce an ethics, and by 1959 he had (due to Heidegger's influence?) ceased speaking of doing "metaphysics." In the first of the "Working Notes" that Claude Lefort appended to his edition of Merleau-Ponty's last, unfinished work, *The Visible and the Invisible,* Merleau-Ponty proclaimed instead the "Necessity of a return to ontology."[2] This ontology would focus on, among other things, "the subject-object question" and "the question of inter-subjectivity." It is an ontology which would, thanks to the notion of the "flesh," seek to probe subjectivity—a key concept in his earlier, phenomenological work—to its depths. It is the thesis of this paper that, in undertaking this "hyper-reflexive," archeological exploration of the roots of subjectivity, Merleau-Ponty did in fact give us, his readers, "the principle of an ethics."

To say exactly what an "ethics of the flesh," fully worked out in theory, would look like is no easy matter, given the inchoate nature of Merleau-Ponty's later work. Any attempt at spelling out the chief traits of such an ethics would necessarily be highly reconstructive, amounting to what might even be called an "active interpretation." Given, however, Merleau-Ponty's lifelong concern with language and communication, it is safe to say, I think, that a Merleau-Pontyan ethics would focus on the communicative process and would indeed be concerned with "*un processus d'explication rationnelle avec autrui.*" Given also Merleau-Ponty's abiding concern to defend the traditional philosophical notions of reason and universality (albeit in a strictly nonfoundational way), one could also legitimately surmise that a full-fledged ethics of the flesh would be a rational ethics laying claim to universality. With contemporary discussions in mind, I would be tempted to label an ethics such as this an ethics of communicative rationality.

Lest one be inclined at this point to accuse me of reading Habermas back into Merleau-Ponty and, accordingly, of obscuring what is original and noteworthy in Merleau-Ponty's own thought,[3] let me hasten to add that, as I see it, a "reconstructed" Merleau-Pontyan ethics of communicative rationality would possess certain features that would make it philosophically preferable to Habermas's "discourse ethics." Merleau-Ponty's notion of the flesh, I submit, provides an *ontological,* and therefore a truly philosophical, grounding for the communicative ethics that Habermas for his part seeks to justify in a more abstract as well as a more limited way by appealing to analytic speech act theory and theories of psychological development (of, moveover, a highly speculative nature), on the one hand, and, on the other, the transcendental, counterfactual, and altogether utopian notion of an ideal speech community.[4] Merleau-Ponty's exposition and defense of communicative rationality is, in short, much less "theory-laden" than is Habermas's. Let us therefore consider in more detail how the notion of the flesh, this "*fondamental*," furnishes the principle of a philosophical ethics and how, in addition, this principle is able to generate an ethics of communicative rationality having universal scope.

If, as Merleau-Ponty suggested, the "study of perception [i.e., the *Phenomenology of Perception*] could only teach us a 'bad ambiguity,' a mixture of finitude and universality, of interiority and exteriority," his later explorations of "the flesh of the sensible" were such as to enable him to uncover a "good ambiguity." The flesh is indeed a "spontaneity" which, unlike what he called "experience" or "existence" in the *Phenomenology*, expresses not simply a *mixture* of "finitude and universality" and of "interiority and exteriority" but constitutes rather "a single whole," "*un seul tissu*," in which are gathered together, in a single but complex, chiasmic intertwining nature and culture, subject and object, self and other. Merleau-Ponty's notion of the flesh enables one to argue that while the imperatives of ethical theory are indeed rational, and thus universal (escaping in this way the debilitating relativism so prevalent in present-day ethical thinking), this theory is nevertheless, for all that, not a form of metaphysical absolutism but is fully anchored or embodied in the human lifeworld, and thus is in no need of a theoretical recourse to empiricistic-transcendental arguments of a Habermasian sort—a noteworthy gain in itself.

The "ground" (*principium*) of Merleau-Ponty's universalist ethics is that most remarkable feature of the flesh (which in fact serves to define it) that he referred to as "reversibility" and which he called "the ultimate truth" (VI, 155). What reversibility means is that the flesh, in its dehiscence and its coiling over upon itself, is neither subject nor object, in the traditional philosophical sense of the terms, but is both subject and object, both sensing and sensible at one and the same time. Between the two "leaves" (*feuillets*) of the flesh there is an *écart* or spacing that is both proximity and distance, a kind of identity in difference. I could never, as a perceiving subject, touch (know) anything, if my hand that touches, which is to say, were I myself not, as it were, touchable by things, and thus object as well as subject. As Merleau-Ponty says:

> This can happen only if my hand, while it is felt from within, is also accessible from without, itself tangible, for my other hand, for example, if it takes its place among the things it touches, is in a sense one of them, opens finally upon a tangible being of which it is also a part. Through this crisscrossing [*recroisement*] within it of the touching and the tangible, its own movements incorporate themselves into the universe they interrogate, are recorded on the same map as it; the two systems are applied upon one another, as the two halves of an orange. VI, 133

The same is true, Merleau-Ponty immediately goes on to say, of vision. Just as touching occurs in "the midst of the world," of things, so likewise does vision. Between myself as seeing subject and the world as seen there exists an "encroachment" or "infringement." This means not only that "he who looks must not himself be foreign to the world that he looks at," it means—even more importantly for our purposes—that I could not see were I not, *as* a seer, capable of being seen seeing *by another seer*. As Merleau-Ponty states: "As soon as I see, it is necessary that the vision . . . be doubled with a complementary vision or with another vision: myself seen from without, such as another would see me, installed in the midst of the visible, occupied in considering it from a certain spot" (VI, 134).

The ontology of the flesh that Merleau-Ponty sketches out in this last chapter of his unfinished manuscript, "The Intertwining—The Chiasm," has extremely significant implications for any eventual ethics. For, as the text just cited indicates, what the reversibility of the flesh means is that the self, in its innermost self, is an *other* of its own self. *Alterity* does not confront the sensing subject from the outside but is inscribed in the very heart of *ipseity* itself.[5] Intersubjectivity is as primordial as subjectivity itself, for subjectivity is, at its roots, an *intercorporeity*, as Merleau-Ponty makes explicit a few pages further on: If "there is a relation of the visible with itself that traverses me and constitutes me as a seer," the field is open, he says, for an "intercorporeity." "If my left hand can touch my right hand while it palpates the tangibles, can touch it touching, can turn its palpation back upon it, why, when touching the hand of another, would I not touch in it the same power to espouse the things that I have touched in my own?" (VI, 140–41). If the sensible body is "synergic," why, Merleau-Ponty asks, "would not the synergy exist among different organisms, if it is possible within each?" (VI, 142). "The handshake too is reversible," as he says.

The basic point should now be evident. The principle of an ethics is here firmly established in the *Urphänomenon* of the flesh, in that the constitution of myself as subject is not only contemporaneous with the constitution of the other as subject but is in fact fully "reversible" with it. Self and other coexist symbioticly, reciprocally confirming each other in their own being, as the following text suggests:

> There is a circle of the touched and the touching, the touched takes hold of the touching; there is a circle of the visible and the seeing, the seeing is not without visible existence; there is even an inscription of the touching in the visible, of the seeing in the tangible—and the converse; there is finally a propagation of these exchanges to all the bodies of the same type and of the same style which I see and touch—and this by virtue

of the fundamental fission or segregation of the sentient and the sensible which, laterally, makes the organs of my body communicate and founds transitivity from one body to another. (VI, 143)

Just as there is a lateral or transversal relationship between the different powers of my own body, which constitutes it as a synergic body, as a subjectivity, so likewise, between that body which I call my own and other bodies "of the same type and of the same style," there is a relationship of "transitivity" as well, another form of synergy which constitutes the phenomenon of intersubjectivity. The phenomenon Merleau-Ponty is describing here could be illustrated with the aid of a Möbius strip. A figure of this sort is indeed a single, yet complex, chiasmic intertwining. Let the notion of a Möbius strip function therefore as a metaphor for the sentient body; the metaphor is productive. Fashion, for example, a Möbius strip out of paper; cut it lengthwise—and what do you get? Not two new, separate strips, but rather an even more complex and crisscrossing strip. Cut it again, and again, and again—and you get ever more complex, interlocking strips. What, in short, you get is a metaphor for the way in which any number of sentient bodies intertwine in the flesh of the world.

What we have here in the reversibility that defines the flesh is indeed the *principle* of an ethics, inasmuch as the question of ethics is the question as to what kind of selves we are to make of ourselves in our reciprocal dealings with other selves. As David Michael Levin points out, reversibility "names an experience that can serve as our ground for the cultivation of those reciprocities so necessary for ethical life."[6] The ethics that appears here in germ could perhaps most appropriately be labelled an ethics of reciprocity or an ethics of recognition.

As was mentioned above, speech and communication constitute the focal point of Merleau-Ponty's incipient ethics, as they do in Habermas's own "discourse ethics." But once again the crucial difference between these two thinkers is apparent in that Merleau-Ponty "grounds" language and the communicative process directly—phenomenologically—in the synergic dynamics of the flesh. After depicting the reversibility of the flesh in the way we have just seen, Merleau-Ponty goes on to note that corporeity is not "all there is to the body" (VI, 144). Indeed, the most prominent phenomenological fact about the human body (one which had greatly occupied Merleau-Ponty's attention in the *Phenomenology*) is that it is a gesturing and *speaking body*. For Merleau-Ponty speech traces directly to the dynamics of reversibility. Among the movements of the body there are, Merleau-Ponty points out, "those strange movements of the throat and mouth that form the cry and the voice." Moreover, when

I am close enough to another speaking body, "I almost witness, in him as in myself, the awesome birth of vociferation."

What accounts for this phenomenon of "vociferation"? Why should the sensing body be irresistibly impelled to make of itself a speaking body? The answer is: *desire*. As Merleau-Ponty had learned from Hegel (thanks to Kojève), consciousness is the desire of the desire of another consciousness. This is exactly what the reversibility of the flesh means; already in the depths of the sensible, our being is communication and desire. Speech, Merleau-Ponty says, "takes flight from where it rolls in the wave of speechless communication."[7] And it is desire that "pushes two 'thoughts' out toward that line of fire between them, that blazing surface where they seek a fulfillment which will be identically the same for the two of them, as the sensible world is for everyone." The sensing subject must inevitably deploy powers of expression "which are a secret to him" since, as we have seen, the subject is for itself an other, and thus cannot properly exist (cannot exist *en propre*, in its own right) until it receives back an echo of its own being from its own other, an echo that confirms it in its being. Since this is naturally true of the other as well, the relation between two or more embodiments of the flesh is that of *reciprocity*. The desire to be—to be *is* to desire to be, as the Medievals had already said—is the desire to be oneself, which is to say, to know (*connaître*) oneself, and, given the dynamics of reversibility, one cannot know who one is until one is recognized (*reconnu*) as such—by one's own other. An ethics of the flesh is necessarily an ethics of recognition, in the proper Heglian sense of the term (*Anerkennung*).

In order better to delineate Merleau-Ponty's ethics of recognition, let us attempt to take explicit note of the ethical implications that subtend Merleau-Ponty's view of the communicative process. The first thing to be noted in this regard is that, for all his interest in the structuralist approach to language, Merleau-Ponty always took *speech* to be the paradigmatic instance of language, not *la langue*, in the Sausurian sense of the term. Like Gadamer after him, Merleau-Ponty rejected the view that words are mere signs and that language itself is essentially nothing more than a semiotic code; unlike Derrida, Merleau-Ponty was never a "semioticist."[8] For him language was not a disembodied realm of free-floating signifiers but was essentially the means by which one incarnate, speaking subject communicates with another, bringing into existence thereby a common cultural and historical world, an "inter-world," a *logos* of the sensible world.[9] For Merleau-Ponty, language was the very flesh of what we call the "world."

To express the matter ever more forcefully, Merleau-Ponty, like Gadamer, took the essence of language to be *dialogue*. As Tom Busch has very appropriately observed: "The dialogical relation is at the heart of Merleau-Ponty's thought."[10] Consider, for instance, the following text from the *Phenomenology*:

> In the experience of dialogue, there is constituted between the other person and myself a common ground; my thought and his are interwoven into a single fabric, my words and those of my interlocutor are called forth by the state of the discussion, and they are inserted into a shared operation of which neither is the creator [cf. Gadamer's notion of "play"]. We have here a dual being where the Other is no longer for me a bit of behavior in my transcendental field, no I in his. We are collaborators in a consummate reciprocity. Our perspectives merge into each other [cf. Gadamer's notion of a "fusion of horizons"], and we coexist through a common world. In the present dialogue, I am freed from myself, for the other person's thoughts are certainly his; they are not of my own making, though I do grasp them the moment they come into being, or even anticipate them. And indeed, the objection which my interlocutor raises to what I say draws from me thoughts which I had no idea I possessed, so that at the same time that I lend him thoughts, he reciprocates by making me think too.[11]

In short, in the "consummate reciprocity" of dialogue, the other frees me to be myself—just as I likewise free the other to be him or herself.[12]

Let us further note that what Merleau-Ponty means by *rationality* is nothing other than the dialogical or communicative process itself; indeed, for him "rationality" and "communication" were synonymous.[13] By "reason" Merleau-Ponty did not understand some sort of metaphysical "faculty" by means of which we are able to form epistemologically correct "representations" of the "objective" world. Approaching the issue in a thoroughly postfoundationalist way, Merleau-Ponty viewed reason or rationality as essentially an *appeal to the other*, a dialogical attempt to arrive at a mutual understanding. Consider, for instance, the following text:

> Language leads us to a thought which is no longer ours alone, to a thought which is presumptively universal, though this is never the universality of a pure concept which would be identical for every mind. It is rather the call [*appel*, appeal] which a situated thought addresses to other thoughts, equally situated, and each one responds to the call with its own resources. (P 8)

In addition to pointing out that all communication is an appeal to the other, a solicitation of recognition and agreement, Merleau-Ponty is here also underscoring the *universalist* character of communication. There exists, Merleau-Ponty said, "a universality which men affirm or imply by the mere fact of their being" (SNS 70). "Our life is essentially universal" (P 10). It is, of course, the phenomenon of reversibility that accounts for this appeal to universal agreement; one hand always desires another hand. Let it be noted, however, that the universalism Merleau-Ponty is here defending is not of a metaphysical or "Kantian" sort; the universality of common understandings arrived at through communication, such as a simple handshake, is always only "presumptive," as Merleau-Ponty so aptly says. Unlike the more deconstructive postmoderns who came after him, Merleau-Ponty does not deny the "principle of universalizability" (to say that a truth-claim is rational means that it is, in principle, universalizable), but he does seek to conceptualize it in a nonmetaphysical or nonfoundational way. "The universality of knowledge," he insists, "is no longer guaranteed in each of us by that stronghold of absolute consciousness in which the Kantian 'I think' . . . was assured a priori of being identical to every other possible 'I think.'" The "germ of universality," he says, lies instead "in the dialogue into which our experience of other people throws us by means of a movement not all of whose sources are known to us" (SNS 93).

To communicate is always to communicate *"dans la risque"*; it is to place one's own being at risk. Unlike Kant, Merleau-Ponty did not attempt to justify his commitment to universalism by appealing to "a secret mechanism of Nature." There are no metaphysical guarantees enabling us to overcome the adversity and contingency of existence; all attempts to achieve universality are inherently fragile and must always remain only presumptive.[14] And yet, we can no more avoid an appeal to universality than we can avoid an appeal to the other—indeed the existential basis of universality is this appeal itself. Human life is essentially universal, since it is essentially dialogical.

Since, as Merleau-Ponty says, all appeals to the other, to, at the limit, the universal, are *situated*, since we can never transcend, metaphysics-wise, our own historical and cultural situations in such a way as to attain to a suprahistorical absolute, perhaps a better (postmetaphysical) term than universal would be *transversal*.[15] For, unlike some of today's ethnocentric "incommensurablists" who deny outright the possibility of transcultural rationality, Merleau-Ponty never abandoned his faith in (the universalist notion of) humanity, i.e., his belief that, in spite of all the obstacles and difficulties that lay in their way, people can, with sufficient good will, always communicate and arrive at understandings which have some legitimate claim to universality, however tentative and "presumptive" such claims might be. It was precisely with "the problem of philosophical universality" and the question of alien cultures in mind that Merleau-Ponty sought to defend what he called "a sort of oblique universality."

Believing that were we to view the ideas or practices of a foreign culture in their own setting, "we would find in them a variant of man's relationships to being which would clarify our understanding of ourselves," Merleau-Ponty believed also in "the unity of the human spirit." "It already exists," he said, "in each culture's lateral relationships to the others, in the echoes one awakes in the other" (S 139).

Being an ethics of "transversal reciprocity" for which the relation between the self and the other is a two-way lateral or horizontal relation (rooted in the flesh), Merleau-Ponty's ethics contrasts with an ethics of a Heideggerian or Levinasian sort. An ethics of the latter type is characterized by a fundamental asymmetry, and by verticality rather than horizontality. Let us call this sort of ethics an "ethics of obligation." Like a kind of ontologized Kantianism, it centers not on the *call* that one desiring, embodied subjectivity makes to another, and vice versa, but rather on the unconditioned *demand* that some sort of capital-O Other (Being, God, . . .) makes, from the outside, on the self ("man"). For Merleau-Ponty the "other" is not some sort of transcendent, deus ex machina Other (*Sein als Solche, le visage de Dieu*) but is rather my equal, my "double," my "twin."[16] Herein lies the reason why, as I shall suggest in the following section of this paper, Merleau-Ponty's ethics provides the basis for a politics of democratic, egalitarian praxis (in contrast, we know what kind of politics followed from Heidegger's antihumanistic ethics of obligation to Being).

Although Merleau-Ponty did not, as a matter of fact, ever formulate an ethics in the proper sense of the term, i.e., an ethical theory, I hope I have nevertheless succeeded in showing that the principle of an ethics is latent in his later philosophy of the flesh (conceived of as reversibility). And I hope I have also shown (or at least suggested) that the key elements of a full-fledged ethical theory can be found in Merleau-Ponty's philosophy of language and the communicative process. When suitably reconstructed, it becomes apparent that a Merleau-Pontyan ethics is an ethics of communicative rationality (with striking affinities to a hermeneutical ethics),[17] whose core notions are reciprocity and recognition. As such, it is a rational (or philosophical) ethics based on the principle of universalizability (contrasting in this regard with much of contemporary thought which tends to reduce ethics to *ethos*, universality to particularity).

It goes without saying that ethics has to do with values and that any particular ethics (philosophical or other) privileges certain values; indeed, to the degree that an ethics is philosophical or theoretical, it is structured coherently around a particular core value. What, it may be asked, is the value at the heart of Merleau-Ponty's ethics of communicative rationality? The answer is self-evident, given a moment's reflection. Any ethics of recognition (such as Merleau-Ponty's or Hegel's) must privilege above all the value of *freedom*. Richard Bernstein has made this perfectly clear; he writes:

> Recognition for Hegel is not "mere" recognition, not simply an abstract cognitive awareness. Recognition comes to mean encountering and fully experiencing the other itself as a free, independent being. And this requires that the other self-consciousness that we confront *become* free and independent. We achieve and recognize our freedom in the fully realized freedom of other self-consciousnesses. Politically this means that our freedom is *mutually* bound up with the concrete realization of the freedom of others—indeed with the freedom of all "individual self-consciousnesses." All projects to achieve individual freedom that do not foster the universal freedom of all self-consciousnesses is doomed to failure.[18]

It is surely no accident that in the *Phenomenology of Perception* Merleau-Ponty maintained that the essence of (human) existence is freedom and that in his lectures at the Sorbonne he stated that "the perception of other people is the perception of a freedom that appears though a situation."[19] Although Merleau-Ponty had, and continued to have to the end, a number of serious philosophical differences (or *differends*) with Sartre and with Sartre's rather absolutist conception of freedom, he could never have disagreed with Sartre's assertion: "In wanting [*voulant*, willing] freedom, we discover that it depends entirely on the freedom of others, and that the freedom of others depends on our own."[20] There is perhaps something of an irony here. While a good many efforts have been made to legitimate philosophically Sartre's off-the-cuff remark in terms of his own thought-system (none of which are terribly persuasive), the statement itself could stand as a fine summation of Merleau-Ponty's own position, grounded as it is in the phenomenon of reversibility. What the philosophy of the flesh tells us is that no one can be free by himself, just as no one can be rational by himself. Just as rationality is dialogical, so likewise is freedom universal ("presumptively"). No one who desires recognition—which is to say, everyone—can be oblivious to the unfreedom of others. This is indeed the principle not only of a universalist ethics but of a universalist politics as well. Borrowing a term from Hans-Georg Gadamer, we could call it *solidarity*. In our carnal desire for freedom and recognition, we stand in a relation of solidarity with all other such desiring beings.

Just as there is a synergy in the *corps propre*, so also there is a synergy in the *corps social*. The name for this sort of synergy, having to do with the "body politick," is *politics*. Merleau-Ponty's politics—which followed directly from his largely understated ethics—was a politics of freedom, *une politique de la liberté* (as Tocqueville might have said). To be sure, in his early days Merleau-Ponty (like any self-respecting young French intellectual at that time) bent over backwards to try to accommodate the marxist theory of revolution in his own belief in freedom, the freedom of all.[21] However, unlike most of his fellow travelers, and in conjunction with such exceptional individuals as Albert Camus and Raymond Aron, Merleau-Ponty, early on, resolutely renounced all forms of revolutionism and reaffirmed the abiding validity of traditional liberal theory.[22] Unlike his erstwhile friend and colleague Sartre, who, up to the very end, was never able to read the handwriting on the wall, Merleau-Ponty was an early critic of totalitarianism (something which only became fashionable in France in the 1970s, some twenty years later) and of the socialist regimes of Eastern Europe. While one can obviously only speculate on the matter, it is, I think, fair to assume that had Merleau-Ponty lived to respond to new developments on the political scene in the 1970s and, above all, the 1980s, his politics would probably have been very much like the politics pursued throughout this period by his student and colleague, Claude Lefort, which is to say that it would have been a politics based squarely on the notion of *universal human rights*. Merleau-Ponty's politics would almost certainly have amounted to a theoretical defense of democratic praxis, and, as Lefort clearly perceived, the notion of universal human rights is the most effective instrument, in both theory and practice, for instituting and safeguarding democracy (a fact that the poststructuralists, who disparaged the notion of human rights as a form of metaphysical "humanism," only began to wake up to after the 1989 liberal revolutions in Eastern Europe).[23]

The raison d'être of human rights is that they are the principal means whereby a politics based upon the idea of the mutual recognition of the freedom of all can be articulated and defended. A politics of freedom and democracy based on universal human rights is in fact the most ethical of all forms of politics; it is, in other words, a politics which is at the same time an ethics. It contrasts in this regard with all forms of Realpolitik, mere opportunistic politics based on nothing more than "national interest" and amoral *raison d'état*, as well as with all forms of utopian politics appealing to such apparently noble goals as the "liberation" of humankind from the "reign of necessity" (the marxist politics of revolutionary violence was, as we now know, the most unethical and immoral of all politics).[24] Merleau-Ponty's politics of mutual recognition and solidarity was in fact the direct anticipation of the politics of civility championed in our times by Vaclav Havel.

One of the most interesting things about Merleau-Ponty's politics (as he himself had the occasion to articulate it and as we might quite legitimately surmise he would have continued to articulate it had he lived longer) is its, so to speak, remarkable *contemporaneity*. As I have suggested, Merleau-Ponty's politics directly anticipates Havel's politics, which is itself a decidedly postmodern politics (as Havel himself so labels it).[25] A Merleau-Pontyan politics is the politics most appropriate to a "post-1989" world, to, that is to say, the freedom and democracy movement sweeping the world today. In this it contrasts sharply with the more recent (and already outdated) politics of the "philosophers of '68," as Luc Ferry and Alain Renaut have so aptly dubbed them.[26] Obsessed as they were with the ersatz "revolution" of "mai '68" and with the antihumanism popularized by Heidegger (at no time a friend of democracy), the writings of the philosophers of '68 had, in spite of their claims to the contrary, either very little political relevance to the actual world (Derrida being a case in point) or, to the degree that they did, this relevance was "irrelevant" in that, ignoring the all-important question of human rights, the philosophers of '68 were sublimely oblivious to the actual course of world history.

Moreover, antitotalitarian though the philosophers of '68 were and ardent supporters of freedom though they claimed to be (cf. Foucault), the notion of freedom they entertained tended to verge on utter vacuity, amounting to little more than an amorphous kind of anti-institutionalist libertarianism. In line with the antinomian follies of the "revolutionaries" of '68, the kind of freedom they advocated (to the degree that one can piece it out) tended to reduce to one or another variety of *carnivalesque* freedom ("liberation of the libido!"), a "wild liberty," *une liberté sauvage* (Lyotard being a case in point). In contrast, Merleau-Ponty had clearly perceived that freedom (like human rights themselves) can be real only if it is given the appropriate institutions, which is to say, institutions as defined by classical liberal theory. As Merleau-Ponty stated ten years earlier, in 1958: "The problem is to find institutions which implant this practice of freedom in our customs [*moeurs*]" (S 348). If there is any acceptable solution to social problems, Merleau-Ponty said, "it is a liberal one." In short, real freedom, Merleau-Ponty insisted, speaking in a distinctly Hegelian tone of voice, "requires something substantial; it requires a State, which bears it and which it gives life to" (S 349). In his political thought (itself informed by clear ethical imperatives), Merleau-Ponty was decidedly in advance of his poststructuralist successors. And in this respect the events of 1989 amounted to nothing less than a vindication of Merleau-Ponty's own earlier thought (as the Czech revolutionaries delighted in pointing out, '89 is '68 turned upside down).[27]

If the philosophers of '68 were out of sync with their times—and increasingly so—Merleau-Ponty's own contemporary Sartre was a retrograde, pure and simple, a political dinosaur and, to the day he died, a living (albeit somewhat fossilized) relic of the darkest days of the Cold War. As late as 1960, in his *Critique de la raison dialectique*, Sartre was still insisting that marxism is "the unsurpassable philosophy of our time." He even went so far as to call it *le Savoir*, Knowledge itself.

The term Merleau-Ponty used in *The Adventures of the Dialectic* a half a decade earlier to refer to Sartre's political thought (for which he was never forgiven) was most appropriate: "ultra-Bolshevism." Whereas Merleau-Ponty had already realized by the early to mid-fifties that "Marxist culture" was utterly decadent and that the notion of "proletarian power, direct democracy, and the withering away of the State" was a worn-out myth, just as the idea of "the revolution which recreate history" was but a pipe dream,[28] Sartre never tired of defending the Soviet Union ("the homeland [*patrie*] of the revolution") against all hostile Western criticism of a liberal nature. The Soviet Union may not be perfect, he admitted, and it may still have some way to go in bringing about a proletarian paradise on earth, but it is still mankind's best hope (he in effect said) and for this reason should never be subjected to unkind criticism. Extremely revealing in this regard are some of the remarks of Merleau-Ponty and Sartre, respectively, at an encounter of Eastern and Western intellectuals that occurred in Venice in 1956 during a brief lull in the Cold War.

The overall message that Merleau-Ponty sought to convey in his remarks at this conference was that the "thaw that brings us together here" should be the occasion for a renewed dialogue between East and West, in which there should be a place for mutual and friendly criticism, in the light of certain universal, humanistic values. "Current events," he said, "call into question what I would call the intellectual formula for the Cold War, according to which intellectual life is not a dialogue, but a battle." And as he directly went on to say: "Universalism . . . is always implied in the will to dialogue."[29] Against the (so to speak) ultra-Bolsheviks, Merleau-Ponty sought to point out (rather mildly) that the marxist East does not have a monopoly on truth and that it is actually possible for people in the capitalist West to be in the truth, even if this be not the "truth" of marxism. He referred to this state of affairs as "a new kind of universalism," of which he said:

> This is no longer the universalism criticized under the name of "bourgeois philosophy," that is to say, an abstract reason that imagined one could, on the basis of principles truly common to all human beings and independent of all situations, pronounce truths and discover values. This is no longer

that kind of universalism, but there will be within it the seed of a new universalism; that is, a universalism encompassing the idea that if we place ourselves on the level of what men *live*, it is possible, in a non-Communist country, that living men will freely express what they live, and that they will find themselves going beyond the boundaries of their class or society. It would be the case for someone who was more than his or her class, given that we place ourselves on the level of what we live, and not on the level of abstract principles by which we are largely depersonalized and through which we are in much less contact with the social totality we live in. (*TD*, p. 29)

Picking up on a buzz-word at this conference, Merleau-Ponty criticized that way of conceiving of "engagement" (between East and West) which would preclude non-Marxist Westerners from criticizing the East and which, accordingly, would oblige Western intellectuals to behave in a "Manichean" fashion, one which would "lead them to lie or, what amounts to the same thing, not to say what they know or not to express themselves fully" (*TD*, p. 30). It is as if Merleau-Ponty were here referring to Sartre (I am inclined to believe that he in fact was). For his part, Merleau-Ponty preferred not to mince words; he stated that there can be a genuine thaw in the Cold War and there can be a new universalism only if the Soviet regime underwent "a very profound and substantial change" (*TD*, p. 35). (When in 1988 Gorbachev came out with his "New Thinking" [based on a recognition of human rights], it is as if the Eastern marxists were finally, some thirty years later, responding to Merleau-Ponty's earlier calls for dialogue and for the creation of a "new universalism.")

Remarks of this sort would obviously have been anathema to Sartre, the ultra-Bolshevik par excellence, and, accordingly, at one turn in the conversation, he began to get his digs in at Merleau-Ponty—furnishing, in the process, a perfect illustration of Merleau-Ponty's opening observation that for some intellectuals life is indeed a battle and not a dialogue. What provoked Sartre's ire was obviously Merleau-Ponty's defense of universalism. Reacting to this, Sartre dragged out all the old Marxist clichés:

[C]ultures are also ideologies. This is what we in the West do not take into account, and in this respect I see proof that we Westerners have not thawed out [Note how Sartre is here placing all the entire blame for a lack of "engagement" on the West]. We are not aware that we live in a period of bourgeois ideology, that our ideas, in one way or another, are conditioned by bourgeois ideology. . . . In the West, "diversity" is the hallmark of bourgeois ideology. (*TD*, p. 39)

Poor Merleau-Ponty! How do you respond to ideological nonsense such as this? Throughout the discussions, Merleau-Ponty was obliged to say in response to no end of ideological misinterpretations on the part of *bien-pensant* Western Marxists of what he had said: "I did not say that." Defending in particular his appeal to universality, Merleau-Ponty said in response to Sartre:

> I used the word "universality" because, after all, it is a matter of universality. And Sartre is within universalism when he speaks this way because if he reasons from the notion of ideology, what does our meeting represent, then, from the ideological point of view? It is obviously a superstructure of Western bourgeoisie. Yet is all that can be done here to be condemned by this fact? (*TD*, p. 36)

To which Sartre could do no better (ideologically speaking) than to respond: "No, because we also have among us some representatives from the other side." [!!!!] Doing his very best to hold to the ethical imperatives of communicative rationality and to the civility they demand, Merleau-Ponty responded in turn:

> But they haven't spoken up to this point. And even if they don't speak, I do not count the time as lost because from the moment we begin discussing as we are now, we necessarily transcend the concept of ideologies. The latter, if I employ it while speaking to others, consists in telling them that I cannot intrinsically consider anything they utter, because it belongs to a specific social formation, and that everything I utter has no truth value, because I myself am also only the expression of another social class. From the moment we engage in discussion as we are doing right now, we transcend the concept of ideologies.

A bit further on in the discussion (which eventually simply broke off), and in response to Sartre's wild assertion that it is possible to reappropriate any truth (such as that of American sociology) only "if it is situated within marxism," Merleau-Ponty replied, as if in utter desperation: "My point is precisely that all this is possible in conversation."[30]

Like the (in)famous discussion between Gadamer and Derrida in Paris in 1981,[31] this particular discussion between Merleau-Ponty and Sartre went nowhere. Let us therefore leave it at this point, taking note as we so do of how well it illustrates (albeit *a contrario*) the meaning and significance of Merleau-Ponty's own universalist ethics and politics of communicative rationality.

It is time to conclude. I shall do so by citing the very last lines of Merleau-Ponty's *Adventures of the Dialectic,* since they seem to sum up nicely the basic impetus behind his universalist ethics of mutual recognition and communicative rationality, centered around the ideal of the equal liberty of all:

> Happy we would be if we could inspire a few—or many—to uphold their freedom, not to exchange it at a loss. For it is not only their thing, their secret, their pleasure, their salvation, it concerns everyone else [*tous les autres*]. (313)

This message to his peers was as pertinent when he uttered it in 1954 as it was in 1968 (though there were few at that time who were prepared to hear it) as it is now in a post-1989 world. Perhaps today, finally, we have acquired the ears with which to appreciatively hear it. Mutually recognized freedom is indeed the supreme human value, and the sole legitimating principle of a universalist ethics. It can, however, exist as a reality only when it is everywhere recognized for the value it is. For, as we have come to realize thanks to the phenomenon of globalization, the freedom of each is inseparable from the freedom of all. Postmodernity and postmodern globalism have given us a new beginning and have freed us from many of the avatars of our past. Let us hope, as Merleau-Ponty would surely have, that there is some unshakable truth to Hegel's belief that human history is, in the last resort, the history of the progress of the consciousness of freedom.

Like it or not, we are all integral parts of the flesh of the world seeking its own destiny. In contrast to today's communitarians who tend to view people as if they were plants, forever rooted in the soil of their origin ("localism"), Merleau-Ponty reminded us as far back as 1958, that "this great feverish and overwhelming arrangement of what is called developed humanity" cannot seriously be considered an evil. For it is "what will one day enable all men on earth to eat." More important, Merleau-Ponty said, it has "made them exist in one another's eyes, instead of each proliferating in his country like trees." Whatever attitude one might wish to take to the emerging global civilization, it cannot be denied that, as Merleau-Ponty pointed out, "we are all embarked together and it is no small matter to have begun this game [*d'avoir engagé cette partie*]" (S 336). As these remarks indicate, the core concept in Merleau-Ponty's ethical vision was that of *humanity*—a humanity which in the course of history comes to know itself as such and to construct for itself a humane social world, premised on the priority of dialogue over violence. As Merleau-Ponty stated in the document from which I quoted at the outset of this paper:

[T]here is a history of humanity or, more simply *a* humanity . . . [I]n other words, granting all the periods of stagnation and backtracking, human relations are capable of growing, of turning their avatars into lessons, of gathering together the truth of their past in their present, of eliminating certain secrets which render them opaque and thereby making themselves more transparent. (P 10)

Such then was the position taken up by Merleau-Ponty in regard to ethics. What this philosophical stance represents for us today is an appeal to us from another era to pursue in our own postmodern times the elaboration and implementation of a universalist ethics of global solidarity, solidarity in a freedom which by its very nature is synergetic—in whatever way we can and in each and every one of our own local situations.

12

Metaphor and Metamorphosis: Luce Irigaray and an Erotics of Ethics and Hermeneutics

Morny Joy

We must always already have a horizon in order to be able
to place ourselves in a situation. For what do we mean by
"placing ourselves" in a situation? Certainly not just disregarding
ourselves. This is necessary, of course, in that we must imagine
the other situation. But into this other situation we must
also bring ourselves. Only this fulfils the meaning of "placing
ourselves." If we place ourselves in the situation of someone else,
for example, then we shall understand him, i.e. become aware of
the otherness, the indissoluble individuality of the other person,
by placing ourselves in his position.

—Hans-Georg Gadamer, *Truth and Method*

A revolution in thought and ethics is needed if the work of sexual
difference is to take place. We need to reinterpret everything
concerning the relations between the subject and discourse,
the subject and the world, the subject and the cosmic, the
microcosmic and the macrocosmic. Everything, beginning with
the way in which the subject has always been written in the
masculine form, as *man*, even when it claimed to be universal or
neutral.

—Luce Irigaray, *An Ethics of Sexual Differnece*

Introduction

Apart from certain female theorists in religious studies who have adapted Paul Ricoeur's "hermeneutics of suspicion" when dealing with a feminist approach to biblical interpretation within a modernist framework, the topic of hermeneutics has not figured as a term or an approach in feminist studies.[1] For many feminist theorists, this is because hermeneutics and its (con)-textual significations/representations are regarded as presupposing outdated modernist or irrelevant metaphysical assumptions. The role of metaphor in hermeneutics, in particular, is viewed as simply one tool among many of patriarchal privilege, with either the Derridean critique of it as either signifying presence or the Lacanian view as denoting lexical substitution prevailing[2]. My task in this essay is to attempt a recuperation of metaphor (against the backdrop of a philosophy of the imagination) with the prospect that it may make a contribution to the discussion regarding the play of sexual difference and its representation, specifically in the field of ethics and hermeneutics. The work of Hans-Georg Gadamer, Luce Irigaray, and Paul Ricoeur will be central to the discussion. More specifically, however, I intend to focus on the productive and practical implications of Luce Irigaray's work, especially with reference to *An Ethics of Sexual Difference*, and her more recent text *I Love to You*.[3] In these texts I believe she employs metaphor as a key device among other innovative strategies. Whether her approach still should be named hermeneutics is also a moot point.

Irigaray is one of the most radical and controversial figures on the contemporary philosophical scene, and her work would not seem to have an affinity with hermeneutics as it is traditionally conceived. In her initial works, *Speculum of the Other Woman* and *This Sex Which is Not One*,[4] Irigaray sought to investigate and displace the barriers to women's formation of an autonomous identity or subjectivity. In a later work, *An Ethics of Sexual Difference*, Irigaray attempts to map the ideas which would begin to alter the (ir)-regular arrangements that have existed between the sexes. The traditional obliteration of woman as the sacrificial maternal-feminine can only be corrected by an ethics that allows women a distinct identity, an otherness that cannot be manipulated into conformity with masculine needs. In this context, meaning can never be predetermined according to the requirements of a method: "The circuit is open. Meaning does not function like the circularity of something already given and received. It is still in the process of making itself" (ESD 178).

In reading Irigaray's depiction of a recast form of communication (that is the basis of her ethical mediation), I recognized familiar ideas. In many ways, there is a strong resemblance to the ideals that have been promoted as the basis of the hermeneutic enterprise. This becomes especially evident when a comparison is made between Irigaray's approach and the dialogical orientation of Hans-Georg Gadamer. In her book *Sexual Subversions* (1989), Elizabeth Grosz formulates Irigaray's model of interaction as one which seeks:

> [An] interlocution, a reciprocal and reversible relation between addressee and addressor, where neither position is reducible to or occupied by the other . . . neither addressee nor addressor has primacy nor control over the dialogue, for this is the product only of their mutual interaction.[5]

This can be compared to Gadamer's notion of dialogue as play which, though he initially develops it with reference to art, is seen as characteristic of all hermeneutic undertakings. For Gadamer, play has no distinct end, but involves a dynamic whereby the "real subject of the game . . . is not the player, but instead the game itself."[6] As such:

> When one enters into dialogue with another person and then is carried along further by the dialogue, it is no longer the will of the individual person, holding itself back or exposing itself, that is determinative. Rather, the law of the subject matter is at issue in the dialogue and elicits statement and counterstatement and in the end plays them into each other.[7]

In this context, knowledge is in the mode of becoming, where "truth" is understood more in terms of existential reverberation, rather than of ultimate ideals or formulas.[8]

It would thus appear that Irigaray holds certain notions in common with this mode of hermeneutics, particularly with regard to the refusal to define knowledge according to a personal agenda or the requirements of a method. Yet, in her emphasis on the conditions necessary to allow women to explore and name their notions of identity and responsibility that would involve a non-hierarchical relationship between the sexes, Irigaray's model radically puts into question the interplay of equals presumed in Gadamer's hermeneutic exercises. This essay will explore some of the crucial areas where Irigaray's program undermines the ethics of equivalence endorsed by contemporary male hermeneutic theorists. At first glance, it would appear that Irigaray is adamant in her rejection of hermeneutics, and of the linchpin of its *modus operandi,* metaphor. On closer examination, however, it could be that some elements of hermeneutics—especially the role of metaphor—when revised with a sensitivity to gender, could be of help to Irigaray in formulating an ethically viable exchange between men and women.

Historicality

For Gadamer, hermeneutical reflection is inevitably conditioned by its historical context.[9] The extent of this influence is at the center of a heated debate concerning Gadamer's work. Given the inextricable grounding of a human being within a specific cultural and historical milieu, to what extent can he/she recognize its influences and take account of its effects? This would be a crucial issue for Irigaray, who maintains that the Western tradition, as it has been implemented, has been confined to the male register. Regarding this feature, Irigaray could be hypothesized as evaluating Gadamer's notion of historicality in a manner similar to Jürgen Habermas.[10] This is that hermeneutics is simply an apologia for traditional practices with their embedded machinations of power and exclusion.

In her book on Gadamer, Georgia Warnke discusses this seemingly conservative impulse on Gadamer's part with specific reference to women:

> In focusing on truth, however, does he [Gadamer] ignore the ideological function certain perspectives may have in maintaining a repressive status quo and uneven distribution of power? The example of the traditional consensus on women's needs and interests may help clarify the problem here. One could argue that too many women took the possible truth of this consensus too seriously for too long since it served to mask a hierarchical power structure.[11]

As Warnke depicts it, the problem resides in the fact that any such admittance of the inevitability of tradition does not address the vested interests of certain privileged individuals, with their class and race affiliations, have in maintaining such a system. Obviously, in a hermeneutic exercise, there is no timeless absolute by which to evaluate the various inequities involved, but it does seem somewhat disingenuous on the part of Gadamer to raise the specter of anarchy, or the irrevocable supersession of one ideology by another, to bolster his defence of the intrinsically stabilizing effect of tradition. Critique would seem to be a necessary element of any procedure that no longer presumes autocratic standards of rationality. Yet, such a critique, with its built-in frame of suspicion of magisterial moves, need not imply the inevitable dogmatic or ideological replacements that Gadamer fears. Appropriate reflexive awareness is, in fact, what Paul Ricoeur has endeavored to do by introducing "a hermeneutics of suspicion."[12]

Such a move, however, produces another question. Is it enough to take to task the cultural and economic forces at work in a society (as Habermas does) so as to allow women to emerge as self-contained creatures who can now enter the public realm (including the rational disciplines) on their own terms? Irigaray is highly critical of those who believe that simply addressing the material situation is sufficient.[13] And it is in this connection that she presents her own idiosyncratic approach by which she hopes to illuminate two things: 1) the sexual indifference that has permeated Western philosophy, and 2) the distinct nature of difference that woman embodies that has revolutionary implications for sexual and textual relations.

An Ethics of Difference

In *An Ethics of Sexual Difference*, Irigaray outlines the basic parameters of her task as a virtual reformation of the Western orientation.

> [I]n order for an ethics of sexual difference to come into being, we must constitute a possible place for each sex, body, and flesh to inhabit. Which presupposes a memory of the past, a hope for the future, memory bridging the present and disconcerting the mirror-symmetry that annihilates the difference of identity. (ESD 14–15, 18)

For Irigaray, the quality and tone of this sexual difference has an emphatically carnal aspect. And this carnality finds its ultimate expression in the act of love which becomes for Irigaray the exemplar of a passionate encounter where there is no exploitation of the other partner—but a recognition and enhancement of difference. Such an insistence also introduces a revitalized, even amatory element to the professed achievement of a creative hermeneutic undertaking—the production of new insight and awareness that results from "the fusion of horizons" (TM 273–74, 337–41).

To quote Irigaray:

> Sexual difference would constitute the horizon of worlds more fecund than anything known to date—at least in the west—and without reducing fecundity to the reproduction of bodies and flesh. For loving partners this would be a fecundity of birth and regeneration, but also the production of a new age of thought, art, poetry and language: the creation of a new *poetics*. (ESD 5)[14]

If this is hermeneutics, even in its most lyrical guise, it is a revolutionary interpretation of hermeneutics that moves beyond conventional perceptions of poetics and its assumed lack of sexual distinctions. It could perhaps be characterized as an amorous playful hermeneutics that has a chiasmus rather than a circle as its focal image—so that there is no mirror imaging or refraction of the same, but rather a commensurate impetus to a more abundant awareness. And perhaps what Irigaray is advocating in all her experiments is the realization of "one's ownmost possibilities,"[15] which is expanded to incorporate the flesh. In this regard, it is immediately obvious that Irigaray has been influenced by both Heidegger and Merleau-Ponty—of whom she herself has undertaken amorous explorations,[16] but her own route from these two thinkers to a revised understanding of hermeneutics and ethics of difference that incorporates women is by way of Derrida, Lacan, and Levinas, rather than Gadamer and Ricoeur. Nevertheless, Irigaray will engage also with Derrida, Lacan, and Levinas in ways that interrogate their particular appropriations of otherness and of desire, for Irigaray still views them all as operating according to the presumptions of a male-referential system, where desire, as need, distorts the other.

> [T]he *Other* often stands . . . for *product of a hatred* for the *other*. Not intended to be open to interpretation. The Other constitutes a love of sameness that has no recognition of itself as such and is raised to the dimension of a transcendent that ensures and guards the whole world entity. (ESD 112)

In such a strategy, "the one who offers or allows desire moves and envelopes, engulfing the other" (ESD 12). In Irigaray's own delineation of an appropriate response to this perversion of affairs, women have to refuse to be designated as love objects and as the focus of male projections and repressions. Women have to learn to live for themselves, to reclaim a female genealogy by which they affirm themselves in their own right (not simply designated by their relations to men) and also express their own desires. As such, they need to repudiate the otherness that has been foisted upon them in the guise of their own inadequacy, and their resultant dependency on the male of the species.

> Women can no longer love or desire the other man if they cannot love themselves. Women are no longer willing to be the guardians of love, especially when it is an improbable or even pathological love. Women want to find themselves, discover themselves and their own identity. (ESD 66)

But this program entails an obvious problem. Given, in Irigaray's description, the overwhelming and implacable nature of the system that is stacked against them, how are women to arrive at this state of self-sufficiency? How are they to attain this sense of self-worth that alone can guarantee the ethical exchange between men and women that Irigaray postulates as the solution to the present impasse in relations? Irigaray is lyrical and elliptical in her evocations of the connections that alone can foster this passionate communion that is generative at the same time as it assures the irreducibility of each participant. With reference to the female lover in such an enterprise, Irigaray's writing takes on the aspect of an extravagant incantation:

> Letting go and dwelling in the strength of becoming, letting the other go while staying contained and insistent, such is the wager that the female lover must make. Not holding back, but dwelling in that which wraps itself around a nonforgetfulness. That which is reborn, again and again, around a memory of flesh. Flourishing again around what, in herself, has opened up and dispersed itself in sowings. (ESD 215)

Where does this leave hermeneutics? For the erotic images and allusions tend to entice the reader into a poetic reverie rather than encourage concrete actions. And perhaps what Irigaray is encouraging is more a state of mind than a agenda of actual physical exercises. In this orientation, for Irigaray, the mind and body are inseparable, as are text and context. In order to depict this cohesion, Irigaray does not resort to the traditional format of philosophical explorations, even those of a hermeneutic variety. Throughout her work, Irigaray is nonetheless constantly conducting subversive conversations with the ideas of Western philosophers, interweaving delicate strands of observation and response that insistently introduce a woman's voice. Her poetic explorations both excavate and expand the received wisdom regarding the coincidence of singularity, rationality, and masculinity. Simultaneously, as a woman, she situates herself yet eludes capture by the forces of repetition and reduction. Conceptual and metaphorical at once, she is an animate exemplar of those postmodern interstices that can never be contained. Her writing serves to announce the presence of woman as infinite momentum, infinite transformation.

It is as if Irigaray defies any separating out of the two styles, of the rational and the figurative, as if to do so implies reinstatement of the old dichotomies of mind and body and the resultant exclusion of the female element. Irigaray positions herself both as interrogator of the established order of philosophical theory and practice at the same time that she beguiles her readers to remake the categories that have organized personal communication. There is a complex mix of critique, affirmation and utopian evocation. Margaret Whitford sensitively depicts this process:

> She [Irigaray] wants to *persuade* her readers, but she also wants to allow for the possibility of something new emerging from the dialogue between her and her readers. Within her texts, there is a tension between an invitation to create collectively an unknown future and a strong affirmative will, between openness to the other (woman) and the self-affirmation of her own vision.[17]

Whitford then concludes the first chapter of her own encounter with Irigaray:

> But ideally, the "male" and "female" readings should be linked ("both at once") in a kind of creative and fertile partnership, which would correspond to the amorous exchange that appears so often as an image in Irigaray's work. In the double gesture, neither would be elevated over the other, and interpretation would embody the symbolic possibilities of sexual difference. (PF 29)

Whitford's recommendations also bring to awareness several themes that are associated with hermeneutics but, as such, are not explicitly referred to by Irigaray. One is the inevitable linkage of rhetoric with hermeneutics, i.e., language in its persuasive mode. Another related idea is the place and role of metaphor (particularly in gendered applications) that do not have essentialist connotations. Finally, there is the inspiratory role of the imaginary/imagination—surely the stimulus that stirs those fortuitous rearrangements of words and ideas that, as Ricoeur would have it, sustain hermeneutic endeavors (RR 303–19).

It seems that excursions into these intimately interrelated topics are necessary, not only because they feature as unthematized components of Irigaray's explorations, but because they help to elucidate the nature of Irigaray's suggestions for the implementation of an ethics of sexual difference.

In "The Three Genders," Irigaray provides some guidelines as to how the new presence of woman is to be configured in a new relationship that is at once sexual and textual.

> But every text is esoteric, not because it hides a secret but because it constitutes the secret, that which has yet to be revealed is never exhaustively revealable. The only response one can make to the question of the meaning of the text is: read, perceive, experience. . . . *Who are you?*

is probably the most relevant question to ask of a text, as long as one isn't requesting a kind of identity card or an autobiographical anecdote. The answer would be: *how about you?* Can we find common ground? talk? love? create something together? What is there around us and between us that allows this?[18]

The answers to such questions are always multilayered and exuberant, resistant to conventional exposition or discussion. As such, Irigaray delights in a distinct contrapuntal style that keeps one off balance. Reception of her work oscillates between a visceral reaction that is captivated by the suggestive allure of the language, and also by an equally insistent need to ground the free-floating extrapolations so as to analyze the implications of their impression. There is also respect for her astuteness in dismantling the male dream of symmetry. Yet, how to express the resultant awareness? Irigaray is only too aware of her elusiveness, her duplicity, in her eliciting of this condition. This is illustrated by her reflections in an interview, which nonetheless indicate that she recognizes her involvement in a double movement of a hermeneutical nature:

> Thus, in my book *Ethics of Sexual Difference*, which relies on a larger number of earlier cultural analyses . . . there is no basic narrative, no possible commentaries by others, in the sense of an exhaustive decoding of the text. What is said in these books moves through a double style: a style of loving relationships, [and] a style of thought, of exegesis, of writing. The two are consciously or unconsciously linked, with a more corporeal and affective side in one case, a more socially developed style in the other. (SG 177)

It is the implementation of this "double style" which simultaneously incorporates but interrogates the accepted dialogical model of hermeneutics. Thus, Irigaray's textured and interwining motifs of difference[19]—applied to women and her sexual/textual articulations—disrupt old symmetries, yet allow a space at once imaginative and material for the expression of a new ethos of experience. At the same time, Irigaray insists on a radical mode of encounter that is never content with traditional formulas.

In this connection I would like to turn to a revised theory of metaphor, particularly as it occurs in the work of Paul Ricoeur. Such an appreciation of metaphor exploits the gaps between identity and difference, of the figurative and the literal. It is a similar form of metaphor that I believe sustains Irigaray's project. Such an approach, while originally influenced by a theory of metaphorical substitution (which is the mainstay of the Lacanian system, as well as by that of repetition and *usure* (which is a crucial element of Derrida's critique[20]), moves toward its own distinct alternative position.

The Imaginary and Intimations of Metaphor

In chapter two of *This Sex Which is Not One*, Irigaray refers to the absence of a female imaginary not just as the underside of the Freudian/Lacanian male-focused scenario, but of the entire Western mindset itself.

> The rejection, the exclusion of the female imaginary certainly puts woman in the position of experiencing herself only fragmentarily, in the little-structured margins of a dominant ideology, as waste, or excess, what is left of a mirror invested by the (masculine) "subject" to reflect himself, to copy himself. (TS 30)

This reference to the imaginary and the word "mirror" indicates the [change] influence of Lacan on Irigaray's work.[21]

But there is, however, a major problem for Irigaray with Lacan's construct. Lacan views the *imaginary* as the equivalent of the preoedipal phase from which the (paradigmatically male) child has to free himself from a symbiotic entanglement so as to consolidate an idealized sense of identity.[22] Irigaray wants to move beyond the seeming inevitability of Lacan's rigidity regarding social arrangements that result from a necessary rejection of the mother. Most especially, Irigaray wants to challenge the accompanying stereotypical roles of male and female. Her alternate construct of the *imaginary* would allow daughters to realize a productive bond with their mothers as women in their own right who are not confined to accessory roles in a male-ordered designer kit. This would enable female children in particular to constitute a milieu that is creative, fluid, prolific, versatile, capricious and subversive. The *imaginary* would thus not be a predetermined scene of rejection of the mother (and by association of women) but the basis of a positive appreciation.

I agree with Margaret Whitford when she remarks in her book *Luce Irigaray: Philosophy of the Feminine* that Irigaray does not restrict herself to Lacan's postulate of the *imaginary* (though she uses the same word), but construes the term according to her own purposes. Whitford detects elements of the thought of Sartre, Bachelard, and Castoriadis (among others) regarding the imagination in Irigaray's composite (though Irigaray often does not employ footnotes, so it is extremely difficult to document her sources with accuracy). Whitford then continues by remarking:

> Whenever we find the term "imaginary" in Irigaray's work, then, we have not only to look for the network of associations *within* her work that give the term its meaning, but also to bear in mind the network of associations circulating in the intellectual context within which she is writing and being read. (56)

It is precisely because of this specific intellectual context that I propose to focus in a critical way on the hermeneutic theory of Paul Ricoeur, in particular his theory of metaphor and imagination. While it is impossible to attribute any direct influence on Irigaray's work to his philosophy, I would like to explore the ideas of Ricoeur as being illuminative for certain aspects of Irigaray's *imaginary*. Ricoeur's work comes to mind principally because, in his own evolution regarding the imagination, he has been part of the same French intellectual milieu as Irigaray and has also engaged with the work of Sartre, Bachelard, and Castoriadis, in the process of refining his own phenomenologically based adaptations of the Aristotelian and Kantian accounts of imagination.[23] I am not alone in seeing the potential of the dynamic inherent in Ricoeur's definition of metaphor for Irigaray's work. Drucilla Cornell also remarks on it, especially in *Beyond Accommodation*, where she is also concerned with restoring a feminine imaginary, and realizes that a reformulation of the role of metaphor is vital.[24] Cornell appreciates the damage that has been done by Lacan's "rigid divide between the symbolic and the feminine imaginary" (p. 78) and is aware that Ricoeur's model of metaphor provides a possible creative alternative but she has not yet developed her own theory on this topic in detail (p. 168–78).

For Ricoeur, imagination is always linked with emergent meaning, beyond its former determinations as an intermediary between sensation and concept (as found in the Kantian model) in a purely reproductive version of mimesis, or as merely fantasy (*phantasia*, as in the work of Aristotle).

> Imaginative variations, play, metamorphosis—all these expressions point to a fundamental phenomenon, namely, that it is in *imagination* that this new being is first formed in me. . . . For the power of allowing oneself to be struck by new possibilities precedes the power of making up one's mind and choosing. (FTA 101)

But this imaginative enterprise is not simply confined by Ricoeur to mind-games, as it is for Sartre, where imagination as the domain of freedom and pure possibility remains simply a mental (and fictitious) formation. For Ricoeur, as for Castoriadis, these imaginative representations have practical implications, though they are initially entertained as potential modalities of existence.

> It is imagination that provides the milieu, the luminous clearing, in which we can compare and evaluate motives as diverse as desires and ethical obligations themselves as disparate as professional rules, social customs, or intensely personal values. (FTA 177)

It is this imaginative experimentation that then is the precursor of the application of the original insights that have been entertained and deemed appropriate, even requisite, measures for implementation.

> Without imagination, there is no action, we shall say. And this is so in several different ways: on the level of projects, on the level of motivations, and on the level of the very power to act. . . . And it is indeed through the anticipatory imagination of acting that I "try out" different possible courses of action and that I "play," in the precise sense of the word, with possible practices. (FTA 177)

Indeed, Ricoeur would even seem to suggest that it is imagination itself that injects the vital impetus that transforms fictive representations into actuality.

> I impute my own power to myself, as the agent of my own action, only by depicting it to myself in the form of imaginative variations on the theme of "I could." . . . What is essential from a phenomenological point of view is that I take possession of the immediate certainty of my power only through the imaginative variations that mediate this certainty. (FTA 178)

In all of Ricoeur's work, imagination becomes that aspect of ourselves by which we envisage and ultimately effect change—both in ourselves and in the world. It is fundamental to the process of understanding—in fact, it would appear that, in this context, imagination is virtually synonymous with understanding.

In his essay "The Philosophic Centrality of the Imagination," Gary B. Madison, with reference to Ricoeur, affirms this position accordingly:

> For us the imagination becomes, once we make the postmodern turn, the prime means for understanding reality, i.e., for forming interpretations of it, or, to be more precise still, for interpreting our lived experience in

such a way as to construct semantic objects to which the epithet "real" can conveniently be attached.[25]

Thus, these imaginative variations are not simply entertaining possibilities, they have the impact of an actual event. Ricoeur is quite precise on this issue. It is this sense of imagination that I believe sustains Irigaray's own imaginary diversifications. At the heart of her project is a desire to experience the world in a different way from accustomed impositions. There is a sense of play in her imaginative excursions, but her interventions are also serious play, with the purpose of introducing us to ways of seeing and living otherwise.

Irigaray's orientation of both critique and construction puts philosophic concepts under a microscope in such a manner that the masculinity of the logos is exposed. It also "reopens"

the figures of philosophical discourse—idea, substance, subject, transcendental subjectivity, absolute knowledge—in order to pry out of them what they have borrowed that is feminine, from the feminine, to make them "render up" and give back what they owe the feminine. (TS 79)

And it is this whole area of masculine/feminine qualities presented by Irigaray that has been the topic of heated discussion. There are those who decry her work as simply reiterating a simplistic essentialism, while others defend it as a nuanced stratagem of a deconstructive variety.[26] Yet what Irigaray would seem to be exploiting is the ambiguity of language that can have both literal and figurative applications. Her sexual/textual subversions are equivocal in the best sense of the word—shifting between the corporeal body and the body of the text in ways that expose multiple meanings that both disrupt accustomed patterns of thought and instigate original discoveries.

In this deliberate indulgence in the manifold transmutations of meaning, as well as in her "recovery" of a past that has been repressed in anticipation of a regenerated future, Irigaray would seem to be adopting the device of metaphor—at least as it is understood by Ricoeur:

The strategy of discourse implied in metaphorical language is neither to improve communication nor to insure univocity in argumentation, but to shatter and to increase our sense of reality by shattering and increasing our language. (RR 89)

For Ricoeur, it is metaphor that is at the core of hermeneutics; working in tandem with imagination as the agency by which change is facilitated. Ricoeur expands on this intrinsic interconnection between metaphor and imagination, as implicating memory and expectation in both theoretical and experiential ways: "In schematizing metaphorical attribution, imagination is diffused in all directions, reviving former experiences, awakening dormant memories, irrigating adjacent sensorial fields" (FTA 173).

But metaphor, at first glance, appears to be anathema to Irigaray, basically because she is undertaking a probing interrogation of its embeddedness in the lexicon of Western philosophy.

> What is called for instead is an examination of the *operation of the "grammar"* of each figure of discourse, its syntactic laws or requirements, its imaginary configurations, its metaphoric networks, and also, of course, what it does not articulate at the level of utterance: *its silences*. (TS 79)

It must be also admitted, however, that Irigaray is also engaged in an ambivalent reaction to Lacan's pronouncements regarding metaphor. As many commentators have remarked, Lacan's employment of the terms metaphor and metonymy is eccentric, even inconsistent. And it is the very intricacies of the metaphoric/metonymic interplay both in Lacan and in Irigaray's equivocal response that make it extremely difficult to pinpoint the nature of the problematic status of metaphor in Irigaray. A short survey of Lacan's views on metaphor provides a necessary background to Irigaray's own ambivalent attitude to this mode of language.

Metonymic Games

Lacan's extemporalizations relied heavily on both Saussure's system of linguistic differentials and Jacobson's characterizations of metonymy and metaphor. These finally coalesced into a system of signification that allied metaphor with condensation, and similarity and metonymy with displacement and contiguity. These two operations were then employed to account for the mechanism of the unconscious in the substitution of compensatory objects (or, more specifically their verbal signifiers) for repressed material. Yet, as David Macey observes, the usage of the two terms by Lacan is not particularly uniform:

> Although the metaphor-condensation and metonymy-displacement equations rapidly became an integral part of Lacanian linguistics or *linguisterie*, they rest upon highly unstable definitions. Lacan's own

classifications are uncertain: in "Fonction et champ" both metaphor and metonymy were "semantic condensations," but in the Seminar of 9 May 1956 condensation, displacement and representations are all said to belong to an order of metonymic articulation which allows metaphor to function. A week earlier, Lacan had been insisting that metonymy is the opposite of metaphor and established a polarity between the two.[27]

Perhaps Lacan's initial lack of precision is due to the ambiguity that is evident in Freud on this topic. Kaja Silverman, in her discussion of Freud's terms of description for unconscious mechanisms, remarks:

> Although it is most characteristic for condensation to proceed along lines of similarity, it is also possible for that operation to exploit relationships of contiguity. A parapraxis, for instance, often merges two words which the speaker intended to pronounce one after the other. Condensation is thus no more symmetrical with metaphor and paradigm than is displacement with metonymy and syntagm.[28]

Despite these seeming incompatibilities, Lacan's extrapolation of a chain of signifying verbal effects eventually solidified into an accepted dichotomous (though interactive) relation between metaphor and metonymy. Metaphor became associated with a process of substitution on a vertical axis of selection whereby there is a resolution involving fixation and repression. In contrast, metonymy, on a horizontal axis of combination, initiates a constant process of succession of one term by another.[29] This latter semiotic displacement demarcates theoretically for Lacan the interminable operation of a desire (for the repressed maternal) that can never be satisfied.

In all these mechanistic and austere calculations, with their certain sense of doomed inevitability, it is difficult to recognize the playful and seemingly unpredictable nature of metaphoric creativity. Or, as David Macey comments with reference to one of Lacan's cryptic pronouncements:

> Whether or not this is a true metaphor by any standard other than Lacan's own definition ("one word for another") must be open to doubt, particularly as the game in question relies upon a systematic and indeed stereotypical distortion which has little to do with the defiance of usage implicit in most effective metaphors. (p. 134)

Yet something rather dramatic has occurred as a result of Lacan's autocratic and inflexible posture—metaphor has become identified as a symptom of the Lacanian version of psychoanalysis's prohibition and denial of the feminine. In feminist theory, metaphor is tarnished as the epitome of patriarchal oppression—the implement of the phallus.[30]

There are those who would argue that in these operations the phallus with its symbolic sense remains distinct from the penis—i.e., that the psychic and the biological don't get confused. Yet, given Lacan's condescending slights regarding women, it is difficult to extricate the force of his symbolic pronouncements from a biologically grounded conviction of male superiority.[31] For all his posturings regarding metonymy and metaphor, Lacan appears simply to be manipulating language so as to serve his own metonymic purposes, which in actuality conform to his description of metaphor. He also continues the Freudian (dare I use the term) "phallusy" of confounding description with dogmatic prescription. David Macey describes this problematical situation.

> "One signifier (or word) for another" is Lacan's rather dubious definition of metaphor, and if that definition is taken at face value, "phallus" is little more than a metaphor or euphemism for "penis." Although the elaboration of the phallus concept is often said to represent a move away from psychoanalysis's residual biologism, it remains true to say that Lacan does not really depart from Freud's account of the castration complex and merely restates it in symbolic, metaphorical or structural terms. (p. 188)

This may well be a case of Lacan being hoisted on his own phallic petard of metaphor. And there is no doubt that Irigaray is suspicious of metaphor in this phallic mode. This wariness of Lacan's exclusive, if misguided, deployment of metaphor has led to it being dismissed by feminists simply as a tool of the fathers to keep them in their repressed and defective place. It remains questionable, however, whether Irigaray herself dispenses totally with metaphor, though initially she sees it as a masculine manoeuver. In her analysis of Freud, she states:

> Therefore the girl shuns or is cast out of a *primary metaphorization* of her desire as a woman, and she becomes inscribed into the phallic metaphors of the small male. And if she is no male, because she sees—he says, they say—that she doesn't have one, she will strive to become him, to mimic him, to seduce him in order to get one. (SW 84)

In response to the absence of the penis/phallus, in *This Sex Which is Not One* (1985), Irigaray introduced her notorious emblem of the two lips as her response to the monopoly of phallic symbolic to indicate the plurality and diffuseness that she believes is indicative of a female imaginary. This proposal has been labelled variously as "vaginal," "vulval," "labial," "hysteric," and inevitably, "essentialist." It is often regarded as merely the female counterpart of the phallus. But Irigaray is being far more ingenious than any such simplistic reversal. Whereas in Lacan's chain of metonymic signifiers, the phallic metaphor intervenes in such a way as to dominate and control proceedings, Irigaray wants to intimate that the process need not be so biased and determinate. For her, the free-play is open-ended in a spontaneous activity that does not promote closure and conformity.

There are those who say that Irigaray simply favors a labial/contiguous metonymic mode in place of the phallic metaphoric, but I believe Irigaray is more subtle than that, and continues to operate in a deconstructive mode of simultaneous critique and construct that itself redeploys metaphor. Diana Fuss gives one possible interpretation of Irigaray's usage:

> What is important about Irigaray's conception of this particular figure is that the "two lips" operate as a metaphor for metonymy; through this collapse of boundaries, Irigaray gestures toward the deconstruction of the classic metaphor/metonymy binaries. In fact, her work persistently attempts to effect a historical displacement of metaphor's dominance over metonymy.[32]

Such an alleged displacement of the binary works, however, only if one accepts Lacan's definition of metaphor as substitution.[33] There is no question that in both her early works, *Speculum* and *This Sex Which is Not One*, Irigaray favors metonymy and shares Derrida's distrust of the old metaphor/metaphysics affiliation,[34] but when she begins to investigate the question of difference and what that might imply for ethics, as she does in *An Ethic of Sexual Difference*, Irigaray's disposition changes. For though her earlier introduction of the feminine element has all the trappings of a Derridean exercise in *différance*, in *Ethics of Sexual Difference*, Irigaray becomes more insistent on the location of her feminine figure and its subjectivity within a social and cultural milieu. And it is in connection with this move (involving a reworking of the actual grounds of exchange between male and female) that a revised theory of metaphor, beyond the confines of a Lacanian substitution model, seems necessary. Far from being a compensatory measure, Irigaray's female-inspired mediation is a rebuttal of Lacan's system in a way that contests his metaphoric/metonymic division while exploring a more fluid and permeable syntax of expression. Her goal is one of metamorphosis. To do this, Irigaray exploits all possible gradations of meaning in her double style. Thus, for Irigaray, a woman's body is at once verbal, *imaginary*, carnal, social, and philosophical. It can have multiple pleasures as well as infinite ways of subverting established limits and thus realigning the terms of reference regarding sameness and otherness. These novel constellations are never absolute or final, yet their permutations have reverberations for both how women think and act—and how, in turn, males conceive of and relate to women.

Metaphoric Speculations

In this delicate exercise, perhaps a more nuanced reading of metaphor along and beyond the lines of Ricoeur would be of help, though this will involve a close scrutiny of Ricoeur's formula from a feminist perspective.[35] What seems to be needed is an appreciation of metaphor that does not regard it as simply a lexical substitution, but places it in a semantic and performative scheme, as in the work of Paul Ricoeur (pp. 110–33). Central to this mode of representation is an inherent paradox. This is because, according to Ricoeur's position, such a broadened and complex horizon of reference can produce a literal contradiction that is brought about by the clash of the accustomed and new meanings. Here, similarity is never identification—it is, in fact, an indulgence in a deliberate clash of literal and figurative meanings. For metaphoric meaning both "is" and "is not" (pp. 295–313). It is this element of metaphor, as developed by Ricoeur in *The Rule of Metaphor*, that is also invoked by Drucilla Cornell in her book *Transformations* in her discussion of a female imaginary, which draws on both Irigaray and Ricoeur:

> Metaphor as transformation and analogy always implies both the like and the not like. The definition of the feminine *is* only as metaphor. Metaphor, in turn, allows both for expansion of meaning and for reinterpretation . . . the realization of "feminine being" as metaphor is what allows us to reinterpret and, more important, to affirm the feminine as other, and *irreducibly other*, to any of the definitions imposed by patriarchy.[36]

Though Cornell uses the words "like" and "not like" rather than Ricoeur's "is" and "is not," she assumes that her position is analogous to Ricoeur's. However, it would seem that some clarifications of Cornell's view are in order. For, if taken in a simplistic way, as just the noncoincidence of literal and figurative references of two different frames of meaning, the resultant depiction of metaphor is somewhat problematic. Metaphor could simply be a logical or semantic inconsistency. Furthermore, if Cornell wants to identify the "feminine" with the "is not" as a figurative element that will contest the masculine "is" that has dominated the repertoire of Western lexicography, then the traditional binary structure remains unchallenged.

But if the feminine double style (as a hermeneutic strategy) is a metaphoric one (and I believe this is Cornell's point, though she does not stress this), then an innovative position emerges. This is because a metaphoric mode, from a feminine/feminist perspective, can juxtapose and revel in both figurative and literal elements in ways that subvert rigid formulations by which a male-identified system has designated feminine attributes and activities. Here Cornell concurs with Irigaray that women have been denied entrance to the mutually exclusive structures that have organized Western rational constructs. What Irigaray and Cornell then want to introduce is an alternate way of dealing with the world, but one that is not simply linguistically constrained by monological declarations. Hence the appeal to a double style which embraces the erotic, the carnal, the embodied nature of words. It is a duplicitous rather than a contradictory way of operating. It is also paradoxical, as it delights in invoking several registers at once.

Cornell also believes that a suspicious use of metaphor is in keeping with a feminine voice that can be articulated in a double style such as Irigaray's. The proviso is that any such utterance must never be given an ultimate or comprehensive status. As Cornell remarks in *Beyond Accommodation*:

> My contention then, is that the writing of the feminine, in spite of the "danger" of the reliance on metaphor, is perfectly consistent with the [doubled] "Derridean gesture" as long as the attempt to specify the feminine is understood as proceeding through a process of metaphorization that never fully captures Woman. There is always more to write.[37]

Such a polyvalent and tensional view of metaphor would permit Irigaray to utilize the full array of seemingly paradoxical ascriptions that her words may elicit, without their limitation to a single register. At the same time, the "as if" modality of metaphor reinforces the experimentation at the imaginative level (RM 212–15). Yet all of this improvisation is not simply whimsical—for the implication of the imaginative testing of boundaries, as in Ricoeur's version of hermeneutics, involves their eventual application. "There is a place in my book on metaphors when I say that when language is itself in the process of becoming once more

potential it is attuned to this dimension of reality which is itself unfinished
and in the making" (RR 462).

Irigaray is no less idealistic, no less utopian in her evocation of a
future that is to be realized by a process in which woman, as the excluded
other, transmutes her present ostracism by a strategy of metamorphosis:
"As an other that we have yet to make actual, as a region of life, strength,
imagination, creation, which exists for us both within and beyond, as our
possibility of a present and a future" (SG 72).

The morphological changes involved in such a transformation are
structural and practical as well as linguistic, somatic as well as intellectual. This marks a nexus of intersecting, multilayered currents which
characterize the space that women can explore and enact as uncharted
territory. Transformed and transformative dimensions arise—not just
as perceptions, but as realities to be implemented. As Drucilla Cornell
remarks in *Beyond Accommodation,* "Correctly understood, the feminine
also opens the space in which the performative powers of the metaphors
of the feminine can operate to enhance and expand our *reality*" (p. 83).

But Cornell's understanding of metaphor and imagination needs
to be grounded in a creative theory of metaphor such as Ricoeur's to
support the way that she claims metaphor can transform reality. Cornell
would appear to concur with the type of style and use of metaphor that
both Ricoeur and Irigaray employ, particularly the form of hermeneutical exchange where ethics is marked by an uncompromising stance of
deliberate refusal to contain and be contained.

It is this same strategy of metaphor that underlies Irigaray's most
recent work, particularly *I Love to You,* where Irigaray waxes lyrical about
the new form of exchange that is thus made possible. Here the newfound
terms of relation between man and woman is eulogized in a particularly
rhapsodic way. It is couched in terms that consummate Irigaray's own
odyssey in search of a fecund form of communication that rebukes not
just Hegel's dialectic, but Lacan's and Levinas's further expropriations
of the other:

> The man would cease to be the head of the woman's body-other—the
> Logos would cease to be the seed fertilizing mother nature. Man and
> woman breathe together, engender together, carnally and spiritually.
> Their alliance is flesh becoming word—the announcement, the question,
> the dialogue, the thanks, the poetry of the encounter, and word becoming
> flesh: love, child and so on, dialectically to infinity. (p. 124)

Irigaray extols another form of mediation where the negativity
implied by the other is surpassed in favor of a recognition that respects

and allows difference to flourish. And rather than remaining within a theoretical definition of hermeneutics, Irigaray personalizes her description of this process. As a woman she says:

> I am listening to you as another who transcends me, requires a transition to a new dimension. I am listening to you; I perceive what you are saying; I am attentive to it; I am attempting to understand and hear your intention. Which does not mean: I comprehend you, I know you, so I do not need to listen to you and I can even plan a future for you. No, I am listening to you as someone and something I do not know yet, on the basis of a freedom and an openness put aside for the moment. I am listening to you: I encourage something unexpected to emerge, some becoming, some growth, some new dawn, perhaps. I am listening to you prepares the way for the not yet coded, for silence, for a space for existence, initiative, free intentionality and support for your becoming. (ILY 116)

This recast relation is portrayed by Irigaray with an abundance of exuberant metaphors that illustrates the multivalent meeting of two separate, yet co-existent entities: male and female. Love, as the medium of exchange, no longer indicates possession. "I love to you means I maintain a relation of indirection to you. I do not subjugate you or consume you" (ILY 109). These very differences and their innovative exchange will foster new possibilities, not just of meaning, but of life itself.

And it is for this reason that Irigaray's eroticization of hermeneutics can never be reduced to a form of narcissistic indulgence or superficial sensual abandonment. For the deeply felt response that Irigaray wishes to elicit by her erotic encounters is that of wonder. Harking back to Descartes' primordial, even instinctive acknowledgement of that which eludes the sphere of comprehension, Irigaray envisions a world where:

> Wonder goes beyond that which is or is not suitable for us. The other never suits us simply. We would in some way have reduced the other to ourselves if he or she suited us completely. An *excess* resists: the other's existence and becoming as a place that permits union and/through resistance to assimilation or reduction to sameness. (ESD 74)

This aspect, both material and figurative, is a vital element in the delineation of Irigaray's ethics. This erotics of illumination, while it conjures up instances of poignant intimacy, also seeks to evade the stagnancy of mindless repetition—every encounter will be "as if" for the first time. Infinite possibility occurs at every moment.

In this context, it needs to be appreciated that with all her excesses, her extremes, her poetic extravagances, Irigaray is also bringing to our attention an indispensable and irrefutable fact. Most hermeneutics, from religious exegesis to radical interpretation, has never been sexually neutral. Even though it has conceded that each interpreter is influenced by his or her historical context, hermeneutics has been gender blind. Hermeneutics has, since its inception, been conducted in a masculine key. Otherness has always been incorporated or integrated to mesh with the dominant theory of interpretation. Thus, much of what has been regarded as reciprocity between male and female has been a controlled paternalistic protectiveness, romantic idealization, or defensive manipulation.

What Irigaray is attempting is to allow for the introduction of women's voices as well as of women's bodies, as the elements of differentiation, to be reclaimed and inserted into a dialogue of true equals. But this process is not a simplistic literal addition or a mere lexical substitution. Metaphor, as the agency of difference which can hold in tension seemingly paradoxical positions, puts into play unacknowledged dimensions in ways that promote innovative perspectives that, in turn, generate novel applications. Metamorphosis, both physical and conceptual, is the desired end. From this perspective, a hermeneutics of suspicion is but the first step in undermining entrenched ideologies. What needs to be added are utopian vistas, or *imaginary* invocations that provide the startling possibility that things could be otherwise. Irigaray, in depicting and insisting upon a consensual form of communion between male and female partners, promotes a paradigm that is not simply pleasurable, but engenders a world that revels in and honors difference. Such a disposition is both wondrous and disconcerting.

Thus, at one level, it could be said that Irigaray is striving to change the purely functional self-interest that has been advanced as normal, even egalitarian conduct between men and women. But her recognition of sexual specificity and its infinite variegations has subtler implications. And this is where, I believe, Irigaray exploits metaphor to its limit so as to introduce a new dispensation. This permits women to be an irreducible element in her otherness, and so interact spontaneously with another who cannot/will not ever again dictate the terms of reference. Women are no longer the irregular, the inferior of a divided species. Yet their integration will never be predictable, nor can the system itself ever be the same. This process is a never-ending, infinitely open one where discovery and creation go hand in hand.[38]

Irigaray intimates that a new ethical worldview can thus come into being. This worldview is both the promise and the result of the encounter of incarnate beings who exemplify a type of trust and vulnerability that moves beyond the clichés of reciprocity that reflect a romantic, exploitative system. Instead, a dormant creativity is awakened which generates possibilities of vibrant relationship by its sensitivity to the myriad forms of differentiation that can enliven all our intercourse, all our enlightenments, whether textual or bodily.

13

The Sense of Transcendence and the Question of Ethics

Charles E. Scott

I The Sense of Transcendence

Transcend implies space and place. It is opposed to words which denote placement within the limits of something or which denote present standing. In the context of this discussion, the word indicates a surpassing quality, a movement of crossing over, and continuation beyond 'here'. It has an inevitable suggestion of elevation and ascension on the one hand and excess on the other. Something that is said to transcend an individual, for example, is not only said to be present to the individual in some manner, but to escape the limits of the individual's presence and grasp and to be excessive in a way that is usually positive either in value or power. An individual may be said to transcend an intended object by virtue of the individual's structure or power of presentation—by virtue of an excess and difference that we might call apriori capacity for the appearing of things. This transcendence of the subject is often said to be grounds for truth and order. *Transcend* usually does not suggest badness, meanness, or lowliness.

This combination of meanings for *transcend* and positive value, for example, is particularly evident in our Platonic lineage. A crossing over is thought to take place in every occurrence. Timeless and deathless reality is present to the order and the determination of mortal things. In Aristotle's tradition we also expect to find indication of transcending unity in physical movement as well as in time. This sense of transcendence with determination is a part, I believe, of our historically developed ability to think in this sense: as we think or talk we are in lineages that give us to expect that in all specific events something that transcends the determinations is manifest in the determinations. We expect embodiments of something more than the passing occurrences in limited events. *In this way of thinking* we also often experience some kind of transcending unity as the necessary condition for finite orders and hence for finite values.

The connection between transcendence and unity in our lineage is also troubled. We are able to have a sense of unencompassable emptiness transcending us. We are able to think of being as pure transcendence without determinant unity, and we can think of indeterminate transcending possibility. But the issue of unity combined with transcendence is never far from western preoccupation.[1] Madness, whether in the form of insanity or nihilism, has often suggested in our history fragmentation instead of a grounding, unifying presence. Our sense of transcendence combined with unity is closely associated with 'healthy' spirituality, hope, and meaning. The possibility of transcending movement without definitive unity suggests fatal disruption of world order, loss of the possibility of truth, and life in a perverted ascendancy of death. The dominant sense of transcendence in our history tends toward feelings of meaninglessness and despair if it is disassociated from a recognition of unity in transcendence.

When our sense of transcendence is combined with a sense of unity and faces experiences of radical difference, we are thus predisposed to undergo a feeling of non-resolution, a threat of disorder in the space of transcendence. If that space is felt to be transvested by differences absent the unity that is 'required' to give them relation and order, we feel a perversion of order within order. It is the crazy-making sense that a unifying, determinate transcendence is disunified by limits internal to its occurrence, as though, for example, fragmentation transcended temporal unities, chaos yielded order, transcendence were nothing but another determination, or historical configurations of experience and practice provided the sense of transcendence. It is as though transcendence were transferred to non-transcendence in a process of discovering the meaning of our sense of transcendence.

When difference grows in value in our sense of transcendence, when, for example, empirical objects, nonorganic singularity of disciplined knowledge and truth, or human individuality without transcending human nature forcefully and oppositionally impact our sense of transcendence, our sense of unity is troubled. In such circumstances *transcend* and *transcendence* can be used to indicate the presence of difference which differentiates beyond experiential and reflective grasp and which gives no promise of continuing and transcending unity. *Troubled,*

I believe, is the right word. *Transcendence* is now appropriately associated with highly limited unities or with the loss of a sense of unity, with the crossings over among determinate unities in a departure from singular and transcendental unity. Differences seems to scan transcendence. This experience arises from a different sensibility when compared to that of both philosophers and theologians who discover a resurgence of unity in the transcendence that accompanies 'nature', 'mind', and 'value'. That resurgence may well be the self-articulation of one sense of transcendence in our lineage, its middle-voiced manifestation in some people's recognitions of limited orders. But however such resurgence of unity is found, the sense of unity in transcendence is troubled when transcendence is qualified in its own occurrence by differences-without-unifying-presence.

This qualification of transcendence by differences is probably as old as our traditional and dominant sense of transcendence. A recognition of absence, death, diversity, and time in the possibility of no pervasive unity seems to inhere in the dominant western experience of transcendence.[2] It is not a question of origins, of whether the sense of life without transcendence or a sense of mortal fragmentation gave rise to a sense of transcendence. My observation is rather that in the sense of transcendence a defining struggle takes place in which the possibility or threat of no defining transcendence is immediately palpable and imaginable. The possibility of no transcendent presence is palpable in the much discussed experiences in ontological anxiety, in mystical experiences of the soul's dark night, and in that doubt of which Descartes has become emblematic. There are many ways to experience and give image *within* the sense of transcendence to the possibility that the sense of transcendence is illusory, e.g., a deceiver God, our existence is only a dream, transcendence is an unconscious and fragmented projection. And there are many ways to counter such experiences and images. I believe that it is accurate to say that the large and diverse lineage that we call traditional metaphysics is defined in part by efforts to maintain, articulate, and upbuild the sense of transcendence before a contradictory sense that indwells the sense of transcendence. It is a troubled sense that struggles with its differences, re-visions itself endlessly, re-examines its evidence with calm obsession, and rethinks its own sensibility in logics and concepts that both reassure it and reenact the struggle in different patterns of differences that are ordered in a presence beyond difference.

Transcendence, however, is not limited in its meaning to traditional metaphysical thought. It functions in thought that is governed more by difference than by unity. The other 'transcends' me whether or not there is transcendental presence to define our difference. The other transcends me, for example, in such regional samenesses as species likeness, communal likeness, addresses to me, or likeness of occurrence. Language transcends the individual who speaks; the knowing, speaking individual transcends the known or addressed other; the other transcends the one who experiences it; lineages transcend their expressions and outcroppings; authorities transcend those within their rule; the ruled transcend by their obedience those who rule them: difference is transcendence, we might say. *Transcendence* need not suggest unity or even elevation and positive value. Any excess that differentiates itself in withdrawal from total inclusion in its specific determination might properly be called transcending.

Let us say, however, that our intention is to put thoroughly in question the sense of transcendence, to maximize the struggle that takes place within it, to interrupt the powerful suggestion of unity that the sense of transcendence often carries with it. If we intend to intensify the experience of fragmentation in the sense of transcendence and its languages and images, and if we agree with the descriptive claim that a certain obsession accompanies the sense of transcendence in its inclusion of its greatest opponent, a sense of fragmentation and mortality without transcendent presence or unity: if we intend to intensify fragmentation in the sense of transcendence we might well wish to set in motion a way of thinking that holds in question that sense and that turns the obsession with fragmentation and mortality against itself, a strategy already employed by Nietzsche in Book III of *The Genealogy of Morals* in his encounter with the ascetic ideal. We might well wish to turn toward a language that diminishes the meaning of transcendence on the assumption that that meaning will include, in spite of our intention, not only patterns of thought that inevitably tend toward the reinstatement of the sense of transcendence, but also include a quiet anxiety before mortal fragmentation. One of the most effective ways to continue our western obsession with death, absence, and emptiness would be to continue through languages of transcendence to reinstate the site of conflict between transcendental unity of whatever kind and difference without transcendental unity (or, difference with separate and mortal unities). To the extent that we use the language of transcendence, I suspect that the patterns that we wish to interrupt and break will reassert themselves in the breaking process. Hence the strategic advantage of interrupting the sense of transcendence and its many languages without an uninterrupted revision to the sense and the associated languages.

Levinas's thought in *Otherwise Than Being* is one of our most sustained attempts to interrupt both out traditional thought of transcendental immanence and the thought of transcendental immanence combined with the thought of unity. But he also retains the language of transcendence. In spite of the subtle turning that he effects in his thought as he thinks through and beyond the western traditions of transcendence, he nonetheless retains a sense of transcendence that one could hope that he would have put more radically in question. We shall turn to his thought after we consider an instance of thought that combines the sense of transcendence with the experience of withdrawal of transcendent presence, since the language and experience of such withdrawal are definitive of his effort as well as of the effort of this paper.

II Transcendence and Withdrawal of Transcendence

One experience of transcendence in our tradition gives priority to withdrawal of 'presence' over presence. I use the markers for *presence* to indicate, in the first instance, that in this experience transcendent presence is not experienced. We might use subjunctive and metaphorical constructions at first, even if we retract them later: it is as though there were presence that has disappeared and that leaves a strange space, like when you sense that someone might have left the room just before you entered it. Or, like when you sense that someone might be behind you, you turn around, and although you see no one it feels like someone had been there. Or—and here we draw closer to the language of Hölderlin and Heidegger (particularly Heidegger in *Die Beitraege*)—withdrawal of 'presence' is like when you are under some necessity in your language and tradition to speak of God and in the speaking you must also speak of a catastrophic loss of God. The withdrawal (or departure) signals nothing in particular, not even a determinate emptiness, as though God were *here* and God is not *here* any longer. It is like a trace of something lost when you have no clear idea that something was or could have been lost (and not like the trace of something that you are tracking and can reasonably expect to find). All you have are unconfirmable reports and, more importantly, a language that expects God, for example, to have been here at the same time that you are able to speak only in the loss of all grounds for continuing that expectation.

There are different opinions about how the 'presence' might have been, and different opinions about the withdrawal. For Heidegger, for example, the sense of withdrawal carries with it sadness as well as a hope for kindling a language that restores something of the life and vigor that has marked our lineage—and in his hope he also knows that this withdrawal 'means' the human destiny of open finitude and death cannot mean that a divine figure once literally filled a now empty space. The tragic loss and almost hopeless sensibility constitute an awareness of the appearing of things in a withdrawal of transcendence as continuing presence, of deathliness, of the immanent division of coming-to-life-with-dying. It also constitutes an awareness that the God's loss can be replaced by another kind of transcendental unity only at the cost of perpetuating 'what' is lost in its lostness. To avoid such substitute theology as might be found in any conception of transcendental unity, we need a language that arises from the withdrawal of transcendent presence and not from the 'unfilled space' of transcendence.

But that way of viewing the God's loss might also occasion relief and not much sadness if we were in a Nietzschean mood. It might be experienced as heralding an overcoming of a long nihilism of ascetic belief and hope, as giving rise to a cautious joy over the possibility of recuperation from both the sense of loss and the sense of a lost one, a release to new life. This difference between Heidegger and Nietzsche, which could be judged as expressing subtle, incommensurate sensitivities, at least has this agreement: we find the opening for whatever appears—its withdrawn 'foundation', if you will—not in any apriori structure or energy, not in any kind of reality, but in something like a space of withdrawn presence the occurrence of which is without reality and foundation.[3]

This linkage of 'transcendence' and withdrawal is lost if 'withdrawn presence' is given literal or symbolic meaning. Hölderlin's observation with regard to tragedy strikes me as accurate also in this context: in the experience of the God's withdrawal all signs regarding divine presence come to nothing. And Heidegger's observation also seems accurate: a different language from the language that has traditionally given appearance to things is emerging in the awkwardness and uncertainty of these words of withdrawal. For Heidegger this language began to emerge in poets', especially Hölderlin's, sense of mortal being, a sense which seems to arise from the language they are given to write and in which they find their possibility for writing. This sense brings us to our language's own event, its other beginning as it were, when compared to traditional meaning and thought, in a withdrawal of being that is immediate to the coming of being in the appearance of things. In this difficult language without common sense, language says or performs its own occurrence as Heidegger finds it, for example, in Hölderlin's poetry. Language appears in its withdrawal— *evaporation, dehiscence, dissipation,* and *caesura* come to mind in thinking of language's performance of its own origin and event. Language begins to give word and thought to its own strange event of coming to be/passing away as it lets its own withdrawal in the presence of things come to word. Such language comes to replace traditional concepts of transcendental subjectivity and of things' own transcendence of their experience and knowledge. A different problematic arises without the organizing power of the language and sense of transcendence.

In this language and its explorations the sense of transcendence is changing radically enough that *transcendence* becomes increasingly unfitting. I doubt that *transcendence* is fitting at all unless there is an operative sense of presence at least by virtue of a hypostatizing movement of belief, faith, or speculation, i.e., a movement of mind that requires a sense of presence, even if it is withdrawn presence, in connection to the space and transfer that is suggested by *transcendence*. Transcendent presence gives meaning and linkage for the loss that is incurred in the transferal as what is transcended undergoes a movement beyond itself. In Heidegger's language of withdrawal, on the other hand, nothing even possibly present gives meaning to the withdrawal of God or to being or time. No transcendental meaning happens 'there'. The nouns continually evaporate into dispersed aether until they return ontically and absurdly, always unsatisfactory, from their complete loss of reference and nomination.[4] *Withdrawal* in this context is not a word of 'continuation beyond here'. It is a word without suggested continuation, crossing over, ascension, or unity. In this sense I believe that Heidegger is accurate when he says in effect that the language of the withdrawal of the Gods gives a language of mortality that cannot determine its saying by any transcendental reference or movement of transcending.[5]

Of course, *transcendence* does not have to mean the transcendence of some transcendental thing. By accentuating the connotation of excess, we might say that *withdrawal from determination* means *transcendence* pure and simple. Whereas *transcendence* suggests at once determination and lack of determination, on Heidegger's account *withdrawal* does not suggest either determination or lack of determination in the traditional senses of these words, any more than it suggests atheism, agnosticism, or theism. Withdrawal is not *an* excess. It belongs to the occurrence of things' coming to pass, their appearing, their manifestness, in a simultaneous presencing and loss of presence. They happen as a foundationless loss of presence in presencing. That is not transcendence in a sense of crossing over. It is more like being crossed with no unity, no continuity, and no-where to go while one is also a singular and dynamic individual. Even the thought of a law of finitude became more and more doubtful for Heidegger as he thought in the caesura of the withdrawal of being.

Withdrawal marks a way of thinking that leaves the traditional experience of transcendence in the outer turning of the transcending orbit—in transcendence's own withdrawal as it moves, oscillating, from presence-to-consciousness through openings that it gives beyond presence: Heidegger's thought of withdrawal follows a movement of traditional experiences of transcendence, experiences of excess, in which withdrawal marks the movement of transcendent presence. In his thought transcendence seems to move through itself toward thinking that was lost when presence conjuncted with transcendence.

I wish only to indicate that transcendence and withdrawal of transcendence constitute an experience that Heidegger, often following his readings of Hölderlin, has brought to experimental language and thought. A more detailed study of this subject could show that Heidegger's way of thinking in the withdrawal of transcendence does not require the reinstatement of transcendence in spite of lapses in which he seems to falter before the horizon that begins to emerge in his own thought. In order to connect transcendence, withdrawal of transcendence, and the question of ethics, we leave aside such a study, however, and turn to aspects of Levinas's work in which an ethics accompanies a return of transcendence out of a withdrawal of transcendence.

III The Withdrawal and Return of Transcendence

I said at the beginning of this discussion that in our lineage we are determined by both a sense of transcendence and a sense of radical difference. The sense of radical difference both defines many experiences of transcendence and troubles the traditional linkage of transcendence and unity. In the preceding section we said that the withdrawal of God, Gods, or being can be thought—and is thought by Heidegger—in a movement of turning out of the sense of transcendence: while one can certainly find the language and images of transcendence in his thought, the language and images of withdrawal turn out of the language and imagery of transcendence toward 'an occurrence' that is not one of transcendence. At this point, that *turning* with its interruptive effect, rather than an 'occurrence' without transcendence, holds out attention.

I would like to consider the interruption of the sense of transcendence by considering aspects of Levinas's thought in which transcendence submits to its own withdrawal. We can see in his thought a clash between Hebraic and Greek emphases that is thoroughly a part of our lineage, and we can follow this clash in Levinas's way of thinking that both allows transcendence to withdraw and reinstates transcendence-in-withdrawal in a pre-philosophical experience of the other that is manifest in the Hebrew lineage and in departure from domination by the Greek lineage. In order fully to allow the question of ethics, we shall want a more intense interruption and release of transcendence than Levinas allows, but that question at least becomes apparent in Levinas's thought. We shall see that the question of ethics arises out of the withdrawal of transcendence in a sense of transcendent presence and that the positive value of the question of ethics bestows a positive value on that withdrawal.

Transcendent presence is almost eliminated in Levinas's thought.[6] And so is inference from experienced presence to a transcendent and necessary condition for that experience. I say 'almost' because one can speak of a radical transcendence that is known by trust, not because of transcending presence, but because of a religious and faithful Hebraic tradition. That means that in the context of Levinas's thought, we cannot *know* philosophically or reflectively any other individual in its transcending movement, i.e., in *its* 'presence'. Such 'knowledge', rather, comes from something prephilosophical—not from immediate experiences so much as from traditional Talmudic and Midrashic processes of commentary in their combination with faith.[7] These faithful processes give one to know of a transcendence that is beyond human comprehension and appropriation. Such transcendence is not found to happen originarily in thought, poetry, creativity, or worship. It happens for Levinas in God's lack of immanence in a context of a people's sense of being called by God. God is not present to traditional knowledge of him. One responds in a traditional faith that finds itself under sacred mandate without divine presence. Such a sense of transcendence pervades Levinas's thought; it is a sense that lacks an experience of immediate presence. I want to look more closely at the sense of difference, as distinct to the experience of immanent presence, that so heavily qualifies this sense of transcendence. Does this sense of difference provide a withdrawal of transcendence *in* the sense of transcendence?

When I said above that for Levinas the sense of transcendence happens originarily in a people's sense of being called by God and not in God's immediate presence to these people, I could also have said that the sense of transcendence happens for Levinas before the face of the other. The phrasing arises from my conviction that what Levinas addresses when he speaks of 'face-to-face' or of 'before the face of the other' is a thoroughly historical experience in the sense that the experience arises from a quite specific (and highly complex) lineage. Levinas's belief that what is ethically definitive of this tradition is universal in its truth also arises from a quite specific lineage. I do not, however, want to develop this observation. The genealogy of Levinas's belief is less important presently than the extreme emphasis on difference in his experience and interpretation of transcendence. But I want to note and later return to the possibility that 'the other' is constructed by a historically developed body of experiences and values that do not manifest anything outside of a lineage but rather show the core values and beliefs that constitute in part the perception of an ethos. That possibility does not deny the import of the other. It defines that import and interrupts the sense of transcendence more sharply than Levinas is prepared for—because he is still within the force and pattern of the sense of transcendence.[8]

The other, as Levinas writes of the other, takes place pre-philosophically 'beyond essence' in the sense that the other is not constituted by 'being' or consciousness or experience. The other is not an event of consciousness, not subject to any ideality, never an aesthetic occurrence, not a projection, not a perceived immanence, and thus is not a presence-to-consciousness. The other makes requirements of consciousness before consciousness is.[9] Transcendence, if we are to use this word—and its use is still in question—takes place in this 'before', and this 'before' is proximity prior to any signification, appropriation, or assignation. Proximity is incommensurable with consciousness; it would not become conscious. Proximity is before appearance. It is contact without visibility, without appropriation in a system of signs and symbols. This proximity is "absolute exteriority. . . . It is the very transcending characteristic of this beyond that is signification" (OTB 100). Or, to use a type of phrasing characteristic of Levinas's writing, this proximity, this 'transcending', is different before there is difference, so different that 'other' must require its signification to pass away into the non-categorical and pre-signified concrete responsibility of the 'I' for the neighbor before 'other' can, as it were, be 'understood'. The other is 'understood' pre-reflectively in the 'one-for-the-other', in the self's responsibility for the other that comes totally without benefit of the self's initiation or apriori structure.

In the one-for-the-other the self is given to be responsible for the other by the other's assigning the self, making the self to be already responsible before the self can enact itself or 'be' itself. The self is already responsible for the other when the self acts spontaneously because the other is always already in calling proximity as other to the self, as unbound and undefined by the self. The self is always in the accusative before the other. In our context, this means that the other's 'transcendence' does not belong to consciousness, selfhood, or any apriori structure of truth or condition for possible existence. This is what I have in mind by 'extreme difference': difference that as difference is totally ungraspable by a knowing identity. And this difference, in Levinas's thought, may be taken as transcendence, not the transcendence of something immanent to the consciousness but of something that withdraws its immanence in its accusative relation with the self. Levinas's term 'proximity' does not mean presence to consciousness. 'Proximity' means, rather, not present to consciousness. The other's proximity surpasses presence in its difference before the self. The self, Levinas says, is for-the-other before it can enact itself.

The self on Levinas's accounting of it thus finds itself already responsible for the other, already "substituted" for the other, already one-for-the-other. The self's (or consciousness') presence to itself is interrupted in its immediacy *in* the other's proximity. The missing other is missed (is traced) in the self's most intimate event of self-presence, and that missing is testimony to the other's utterly different life outside of the self *and* testimony to the call of that life in the self's own event: not testimony in presence but in its life before presence could occur, in its call that defines the self's own life and in its interruption of the self's ownness and self-presence. Levinas's sense of transcendence is defined by a withdrawal of presence and something like a remainder of missing and call, by traces of difference without presence. In this context we can say that Levinas's sense of transcendence is one in which transcendence is lost in transcending, that transcendence submits to its own withdrawal in a loss of presence and in extremity of difference.

How are we to describe Levinas's perceptions and descriptions? On the one hand he clearly intends them to be accurate about human life. He intends to counter what he perceives to be a domination in western culture on the part of Greek logos of a body of experiences in the Hebraic tradition. He thinks that these experiences show 'truths'—not Greek truths but non-Greek ones that are not subject to 'normal' laws of thought and communication.[10] These different rightnesses are right about us in our lives, and if they are learned and lived we would not have such an aestheticized culture that gives rise to and tolerates multiple kinds of murder and human destruction. In his intention to communicate his 'knowledge' to western thought and to occasion its overturning, Levinas intends for his perceptions and descriptions to submit to the processes that establish their universal validity, although the criteria for universal validity might well change in the process. He does not see himself to be giving a Hebraic homily that is intended only for a believing, Jewish audience, or a poetic articulation of a local piety.

On the other hand, Levinas thinks that his thought arises from something more originary than either thought or consciousness. It arises, as we have seen, from the 'facts' of responsibility, the face-to-face, the one-for-the-other. That is, they arise from something prior even to phenomena, from the already given testimony to the extreme difference of the other and to the self's indebtedness to the other. Levinas's thought arises, I have said, from a withdrawal of transcendence that occurs in his sense of transcendence, a withdrawal richly prefigured in the Hebraic experience of the simultaneity of being a chosen people and of lacking immediate divine presence. As being chosen is a non-voluntary and definitive aspect of a Jew's life, so is responsibility for the other in the other's call a nonvoluntary and definitive aspect of the self's life. As God is not present in His continuing covenant with the people of Israel, so the other is not present in the other's call before the self.[11] Traced as missing, we said following Levinas, but not present-to-consciousness. There is no reason to doubt that Levinas's philosophical thought is prefigured in Hebraic experience (or to doubt that Hebraic experience undergoes a considerable change of expression and appearance in his thought). Yet, his claim that the prephilosophical origins of his thought are not only articulations of a lineage, but that they are also origins for all of us, means that on its own terms Levinas's thought is trying to persuade us in the very court of western thought that he is in the process of overturning. On his terms, the goal is to persuade, not to proselytize. That is part of the meaning of God's call—to bring all people to God's truth. In this bringing people to God's truth, not by physical conquest or force but by descriptive accounts of human life in contesting conversations and argument with contrary accounts and by the cultivation of a different (not yet dominant) ethic of responsibility for western culture. War by other means?

The relation of universality and locality is a hard one to bring about in the context of Levinas's work. I want to raise the problem of this relation only this far: the play of originary and prephilosophical grounds for thought in which transcendence submits to its own withdrawal has the effect of returning us again and again—some of Levinas's most fetching prose has to do with obsession[12]—to the originary, withdrawn transcendence of the other *as though* the other were continuously present to the self. That is like the movement and obsession of a faith that finds its trust as it returns again and again to its originary experience and claims, no matter how severe the doubt and opposition concerning them.[13] The returning movement manifests a troubled identity-in-faith, one based on trust of something that is not subject to confirmation except in the language and experience of faith. But in Levinas's thought this locality of faith is attached to a claim for universality. One-for-the-other is not a situation for a few selves or only of Jewish selves. *All* human beings suffer the passivity of given responsibility. *Responsibility* implicates all of us. This language of universality suggests a strange continuing presence of transcendence-in-withdrawal as traced in the interrupted self. And it *requires* in Levinas's account an ethics of responsibility as though such an ethics were commanded. It is not necessarily an authoritarian ethics that is to be enforced by an external authority (although Levinas often seems to me to be inclined toward an authoritarian ethics). Levinas's is an ethics that requires each individual to suffer its own responsibility, its own unovercomeable indebtedness to the other. But each of us is under that requirement. The requirement is universal because we are all in a situation of life that is known within the Hebraic tradition. Levinas's is an original version of an ethics that universalizes moral aspects of his own lineage.

The movement of faithful if obsessive return to originary, local experiences defines the *almost*, when I said above that Levinas almost eliminates transcendence. I had in mind this movement of return that has the effect of organizing his discourse as though the other were present in a transcendent sense, as though the other were present to the self all of the time by means of its trace in spite of the loss of the other's immediacy in our experience of the other. The loss of presence in Levinas's thought, we have seen, gives transcendence to submit to its own withdrawal and suggests an overturning of *transcendence* in its power to organize our thought and practice. The returning movement of what we can call quasi faith in his philosophical thought, however, holds the other in place. Not letting the other go—that obsession—grants a sense of transcendence when otherwise the submission to withdrawal might continue its work toward thought and practice without a sense of transcendence. I believe that this loss of the submission of transcendence to its own withdrawal is due in part to Levinas's commitment to the universal 'truth' of a Hebraic sense of call and responsibility.

IV The *Question* of Ethics

It is often counterintuitive to think that our commitment, our trusting and faithful, if often critical obedience to a body of values may be generative of some of our most unfortunate suffering. Such a thought means that the manner in which we hold values might be as significant as the content of the values in giving rise to what we experience as worthwhile or as pain and sorrow. The thought becomes less counterintuitive if I hold in mind that what is experienced as worthwhile and as pain and sorrow also shifts, that what can devastate one person can elevate or not affect another. And the thought becomes almost obvious if I also hold in mind that many systems of valuation manifest the tribal characteristic of wanting dominance over other, different systems and of believing that 'this' core group of values will give better times if people will only turn to it and follow it. Usually there is a transcendental presence to the values that guarantees their importance. When strong commitment to a system of valuation combines with a universal intent we have a movement that makes difficult, if not impossible, what I would call the question of ethics. This difficulty is often dependent on a sense of transcendence. I would like to close with a few observations about the collusion of the questions of ethics and the withdrawal of transcendence.

If Levinas had thoroughly interrupted the obsessive force of the other in his discourse, I believe that he could have allowed a fading of the tendency to universalize that is at the core of his own ethos, i.e., he could have allowed ethics as he understands it to fall into question and he could have allowed a movement in his own thought toward values that arise from the withdrawal and loss of transcendence.[14] In his discourse, however, and in spite of the non-foundationalist direction of his thought, the movement of transcendence-in-withdrawal toward a return of the sense of transcendence provides an imperative to ethics as though it were a command from God. Not literally law, but like law in the sense that one finds him- or herself unavoidably under the requirement for responsibility to the other and under the necessity of suffering the passivity of the self as it is occasioned by the other's proximity.

Levinas is speaking of an ethics that at its core opposes murder and other destruction of human life. He says that we are never free of our responsibility for the other's life, that we are under a mandate to respond to the other's need even when the other-in-need strikes out against us. He says that we are living in lineages that lead us away from the other's life, lineages that forget the primal value of human life, forget life sometimes even in the name of God, lineages in which language itself functions in a silently murderous way. Why would a westerner want to oppose Levinas's values when they arise from the Hebraic heart in the body of our ethos?

The *question* of ethics arises not out of questionable values but out of ethics as such, regardless of the values that compose it. The phrase question of ethics does not refer primarily to questions about values but to conflicts and oppositions within the systems of values by which an ethos establishes a hierarchy of goods and bads. Our emphasis now is on the relation of such a hierarchy to universalization. *Ethics* names a way of valuing in which the definitive forces (definitive valences or values) of a tradition—of an ethos—come to expression in more or less normative ways. On the one hand, such normativity appears to be necessary for the practice of the ethos. On the other, the movement of normativity, as it normalizes differences and establishes identity within its domain, appears to spill over to application to different ethea: it seems to tend toward universalization in its sense of right and in the experiences of familiarity and well being that it provides. The frequent and recent criticisms of universalization are right in their claims that this movement itself, regardless of the specific values, incites something like tribal wars, now conducted as struggles for cultural domination and refusal of amalgamation (i.e., of transformation of identity), and that this movement encourages a sense of universal authority for the ethnic, transcendental beings which ground and justify a people's experience of the rights and wrongs—whether such beings are Gods or transcendental subjectivity or human nature. The *question* of ethics arises from such movements. The question arises from a limited ethos combined with its universalization, which transgresses its own limits, and its claim to authority over other ethea. Out of this question we may reserve these universalizing, normalizing movements for critical attention. I do not know if an ethics without universalization is possible, but I assume that in our western lineage universalization is inevitable if our values are founded on universal movements or entities that are taken to be universal. Hence, the importance in the context of the question of ethics that I am placing on interruptation of the sense of transcendence. Such interruptions are ways whereby we can respond appropriately to the incommensurability of ethnic limits and universalizing.

I do not have an alternative to ethics to suggest. I am convinced that presenting a reconstruction of ethics would be premature until we learn how to think *in* the question. A strategy of interrupting the sense of transcendence and our axiomatic sense of fundamental values appears to be more appropriate. The question of ethics might be maintained not only by giving focus to the dangers of ethics, such as that of universalizing, but also by intensifying the conflicts that disturb the sense of transcendence and by cultivating language and thought that direct themselves away from that sense.

We have considered thought in which the withdrawal of the language of transcendence appears to be required by virtue of the withdrawal of the Gods or the loss of vitality in traditional thought. We have noted the submission of transcendence to its own withdrawal in the thought of Levinas. And we are aware that all of these accounts retain the sense of transcendence in their ways of putting that sense in question. To the extent that the sense of transcendence is in question, the grounding for our universalizing thought appears to be in question. I have said that to the extent that the sense of transcendence falls in questions, our seemingly inevitable inclination to universalize our values also falls in question. I suspect that the present, renewed interest in transcendence among some philosophers arises out of the feeling that our axiomatic and universalized values are threatened by a growing threat to transcendental grounding. The sense of transcendence weakens the question of ethics to the extent that the sense of transcendence posits a movement that surpasses the locale and gives expanded, transcending voice to the local constructions of right, true, and good. That is why the question of ethics in Levinas's thought reverts to an ethics with universal import even when the question is strongest: the question of ethics in his thought maintains a (faithful) sense of transcendence while it radically questions the traditional western experiences of immanent transcendence.

I close this discussion with a difficulty that it raises for itself. On the one hand, we find in a universalized locale a perhaps optional source of destructive conflict that is spawned by an ethical sense that some differences in other locales must be changed under the guidance of the universalized ethos. We have said that the sense of transcendence enhances this movement of universalization. On the other hand, we have suggested that intensifying the fragmentation that can be found within the sense of transcendence is worthwhile in order to allow for a more open, less anxious, less protective sense of difference, mortality, and ungroundedness. Such allowance may lead us away from the disasters associated with the traditional ways in which we attempt to avoid experiences of fragmentation, mortality, and difference in the absence of transcendental 'reality'. But the weakening of the sense of transcendence does indeed occasion a weakened sense of unity and commonality. Perhaps it would occasion a weakened sense of human responsibility and human community—a weakened sense of universal humanity. Would that not allow for acts of violence that are free of any ethical sense regarding those 'others' whom we oppose? Would a heightened sense of difference generate values that respect differences? Does not such respect assume a certain transcending and universal human reality? In a word, does not this suspicion of universalized locales with their transcendental grounding lead to a fragmentation of locales with no sense of respect and responsibility for the others, a situation that places no blockage to all out war for conquest and control?

These questions certainly articulate a well founded fear in our tradition. Universal values and transcendent 'natures', with the consequences of western humanism and/or an obligation to a caring, universal God, have given us hope and hedge against unending wars of conquest. But the patterns of these wars of conquest appear to have persisted at the level of universalization and normalization. Can the persisting patterns that require such conflict be changed? Can the sites of those patterns— such sites as ethics and the sense of transcendence—be changed? Those are questions that motivate our attention to the question of ethics and restrain us in our ethical responses to the question. Hearing the question, changing our languages of evaluation and recognition, changing the patterns of thinking, submitting and resubmitting our ways of judging and perceiving to questions: turning our obsessions on themselves. Not waiting for the Light, but encouraging more transformation without transcendence. Participating in the transformation of the sense of transcendence and the question of ethics without expecting or desiring a new transcendence or a new ethics. Being ethical in the process: such activity is part of thought that is moved by the fragmentation and mortality in our traditional experiences of transcendence and value.

Notes

Gary B. Madison and Marty Fairbairn, Introduction

1. Paul Ricoeur, *Lectures 1: Autour du politique* (Paris: Editions du Seuil, 1991), p. 278.

2. The remark is that of Barry Allen as appropriated by Gary Madison in his introduction to *Working Through Derrida* (Evanston, Ill.: Northwestern University Press, 1993), p. 4.

3. Donald M. McCloskey, *Knowledge and Persuasion in Economics* (Cambridge: Cambridge University Press, 1994), p. xv. To McCloskey's list of "English-writing philosophers" should be added Joseph Margolis, one of the contributors to this volume.

4. As is evidenced in the essays and discussions gathered together by Evan Simpson in his edited volume, *Anti-Foundationalism and Practical Reasoning: Conversations between Hermeneutics and Analysis* (Edmonton, Alberta: Academic Printing and Publishing, 1987).

5. It should be clear to the reader that we are using the term "postmodern" in a rather wide sense. The term is often used to refer only to various forms of poststructuralist thought (e.g., deconstruction), with their characteristically relativistic (if not nihilistic) tendencies. We view this as an unduly restrictive usage of the term. As we see the matter, phenomenological hermeneutics is as "postmodern" as is deconstruction. The trait which chiefly serves to mark a form of thought as postmodern, in our view, is the degree to which it is *anti-* or *postfoundational* (in regard to antifoundationalism see the remarks of Evan Simpson quoted in note 8 below), i.e., the degree to which it rejects the modernist search for Cartesian certainty and ultimate foundations. There are, to be sure, different ways in which this can be attempted, and it is precisely these differences which serve to delineate various forms of postmodernism. For further observations on this matter, see Madison, "Coping with Nietzsche's Legacy: Rorty, Derrida, Gadamer," *Philosophy Today* (Winter 1991) and "Philosophy Without Foundations," *Reason Papers* 16 (Fall 1991).

6. "Applied ethics" (biomedical ethics, business ethics, engineering ethics, etc.) is, to be sure, big business now for philosophy departments (which have moved into this field in a massive way, due mainly to pressures emanating from governments to make themselves "relevant" to the modern, work-a-day world). This is no way undermines our claim that "ethics" is now dead; it simply means

that applied ethics is the habitat of the living dead (postmodern thought has managed to make exceedingly few inroads in this domain). Postmodernism signals the death of metaphysics, but the death of metaphysics does not mean its *end* (zombies, as Nietzsche might say, can go on "living" for quite a long time). In any event, postmodernity is not a historical epoch coming after, and displacing, modernity; it denotes, rather, a critical stance toward modernity (see in this regard Gary Madison's "Visages de la postmodernité," *Etudes littéraires* 27, no. 1 [été 1994]).

7. As Zygmunt Bauman points out in his *Postmodern Ethics* (Oxford: Blackwell, 1993).

8. Evan Simpson describes what is at issue in the antifoundationalist debate in the following manner:

> Foundationalism and anti-foundationalism remain positions best understood by their relation to epistemology. The one seeks, and the other dismisses the notion of, criteria defining conditions in which some beliefs are finally justified. Few deny that beliefs need foundations, that is, the more or less secure grounds which make the conclusions of argument as solid as they can be. Any pure foundationalism, however, supposes that genuine grounds for judgment are not merely confident assumptions but absolutely secure bases which are not subject to amendment, or are amendable only in the direction of greater accuracy. Only in this way could they serve as arbiters of rational judgment. This is the notion of a single, over-arching ahistorical standard against which any claim can be tested, so that it is possible in principle to decide between rival points of view. (*Anti-Foundationalism and Practical Reasoning*, pp. 2–3)

9. Charles Scott, *The Question of Ethics: Nietzsche, Foucault, Heidegger* (Bloomington: Indiana University Press, 1990), p. 7.

10. Bauman, *Postmodern Ethics*, p. 245.

11. See Ricoeur, *Soi-même comme un autre* (Paris: Editions du Seuil, 1990): "*Soi-même comme un autre* suggère d'entrée de jeu que l'ipséité du soi-même implique l'altérité à un degré si intime que l'une ne se laisse pas penser sans l'autre, que l'une passe plutôt dans l'autre, comme on dirait en langage hégélien" (p. 14).

12. See Ricoeur, *Lectures 1: Autour du politique*, p. 257.

13. This is a point that Anna Yeatman convincingly argues in her *Postmodern Revisionings of the Political* (New York: Routledge, 1994).

14. Ibid., p. 78.

Richard Kearney, The Crisis of the Image: Levinas's Ethical Response

1. See my *The Wake of Imagination* (London: Hutchinson, 1987; Minneapolis: University of Minnesota Press, 1988) and *Poetics of Imagining* (London: Routledge, 1991).

2. Levinas, "Ideologie et Idéalisme," in *De Dieu qui vient à l'idée* (Paris: Vrin, 1982), p. 31. Hereafter II. Trans. in *The Levinas Reader*, ed. S. Hand (Oxford: Basil Blackwell, 1989). Hereafter LR.

3. Levinas, "La Réalite et son Ombre," in *Les Temps Modernes*, no. 38 (1948). Hereafter RO. Trans. in LR. *Sur Maurice Blanchot* (Paris: Fata Morgana, 1975). "La Transcendence des Mots" (on the writing of Michel Leiris) in *Les Temps Modernes*, no. 44 (1949). "Agnon/Poésie et Resurrection," "Paul Celan/De L'Etré à L'autre," and "L'autre dans Proust" in *Noms Propres* (Paris: Fata Morgana, 1986). Hereafter NP.

4. See M. P. Hederman's critique of Levinas's position on art and poetry, "De l'interdiction à l'écoute," in *Heidegger et la Question de Dieu*, ed. R. Kearney and J. O'Leary (Paris: Grasset, 1981), pp. 285–96.

5. Levinas, *Totalité et infini* (The Hague: Nijhoff, 1961). Hereafter TI.

6. Jean Baudrillard, "Simulations," in *Semiotext(e)* (1983). Hereafter S.

7. Jean-François Lyotard, *Heidegger et le 'Juifs'* (Paris: Galilée, 1988), p. 51.

8. "Un Dieu Homme?" in Levinas, *Exercises de la Patience* (Paris: Obsidiane, 1980), p. 74.

9. Levinas, "Sur la Mort de Ernst Bloch," in *De Dieu qui vient à l'idée*, p. 65n.

10. For a contrary reading of Proust on this issue, see Martha Nussbaum, *Love's Knowledge* (Oxford: Oxford University Press, 1990), pp. 261–85.

11. "The Transcendence of Words," in LR, pp. 144–49. Hereafter TW.

12. See in particular Herbert Marcuse, *The Aesthetic Dimension* (Boston: Beacon, 1988); George Steiner, *Real Presences* (London: Faber and Faber, 1989); Michel Henri, *La Barbarie* (Paris: Grasset, 1987).

13. Contribution to Cerisy Colloque on Levinas, August 1987.

14. Levinas, "L'idée de la Culture," in *Entre Nous* (Paris: Grasset, 1991), pp. 207–8.

15. Paul Ricoeur, *Time and Narrative* (Chicago: University of Chicago Press, 1988).

16. Jean-Paul Sartre, *Existentialism and Literature* (New York: Citadel, 1972).

Robert Bernasconi, The Truth that Accuses: Conscience, Shame, and Guilt in Levinas and Augustine

1. E. Levinas, *Ethique et Infini* (Paris: Fayard, 1982), p. 950; *Ethics and Infinity*, trans. R. Cohen (Pittsburgh: Duquesne University Press, 1985), p. 90.

2. E. Levinas, *Autrement qu'être ou au-delà de l'essence* (The Hague: Martinus Nijhoff, 1974), p. 166; *Otherwise than Being or Beyond Essence*, trans. A. Lingis, (The Hague, Martinus Nijhoff, 1981), p. 129. Henceforth AE and OB.

3. R. Kearney, *Dialogues with Contemporary Continental Thinkers* (Manchester: Manchester University Press, 1984), p. 61. I am reading "within" in place of "without" in the question. The status accorded the instances cited by Levinas can be clarified by comparing this list with a parallel list that includes the names of Plato, Aristotle, Descartes, Kant, Hegel, Bergson and Heidegger, and which arises in answer to the task of finding transcendence named "non-ontologically"

in philosophies that nevertheless immediately revert to Being. *De Dieu qui vient à l'idée* (Paris: Vrin, 1986), pp. 184–85. Henceforth DVI.

4. E. Levinas, *De l'existence à l'existant* (Paris: Vrin, 1947), p. 11; *Existence and Existents*, trans. A. Lingis (The Hague: Martinus Nijhoff, 1978), p. 15.

5. E. Levinas, "La philosophie et l'idée de l'Infini," *En découvrant l'existence avec Husserl et Heidegger* (Paris: Vrin, 1974), pp. 171–72; "Philosophy and the Idea of Infinity," *Collected Philosophical Papers*, trans. A. Lingis (Dordrecht: Martinus Nijhoff, 1987), pp. 53–54. Henceforth EHH and CP.

6. E. Levinas, "De la signifiance du sens," in *Heidegger et la question de Dieu*, eds. Richard Kearney and Joseph Stephen O'Leary (Paris: Bernard Grasset, 1980), pp. 238–47. The introduction and first part of the essay was subsequently republished under the same title in *Hors sujet* (Montpelier: Fata Morgana, 1987), pp. 137–42; *Outside the Subject*, trans. Michael B. Smith (Stanford: Stanford University Press, 1993), pp. 90–95. Henceforth HS and OS. The second part of the 1980 text was republished as "Façon de parler" in DVI 266–70.

7. Stanislaus Breton in his contribution to the volume also recalls this discussion. "La querelle des dénominations," *Heidegger et la question de Dieu*, p. 256. Although we as yet do not know what Heidegger's reading of this distinction would be, we do know that Heidegger addressed this sentence in his course "Augustinus und der Neoplatonismus" (1921), to be published as volume 59/60 of the Gesamtausgabe. See T. Kisiel, *The Genesis of Heidegger's Being and Time* (Berkeley: University of California Press, 1993), p. 200.

8. For example, in his classic study, Snell argues that in Greece the religious gave way to the ethical. Bruno Snell, *Die Entdeckung des Geistes* (Göttingen: Vandenhoeck and Ruprecht, 1980), p. 162; *The Discovery of the Mind*, trans. T. G. Rosenmeyer (New York: Harper and Row, 1960), pp. 167–68.

9. E. Levinas, *Difficile Liberté* (Paris: Albin, 1976), p. 33; *Difficult Freedom*, trans. S. Hand (Baltimore: Johns Hopkins University Press, 1990), p. 17. Henceforth DL and DF.

10. E. Levinas, "Notes sur le sens," *Le nouveau commerce* 49 (1981): 97–127 and DVI 231–57.

11. R. Kearney, *Dialogues*, p. 61.

12. E. Levinas, "Vérité du dévoilement et vérité du témoignage," *La testimonianza*, ed. Enrico Castelli (Padua: Cedam, 1972), pp. 101–10.

13. E. Levinas, *Totalité et Infini* (The Hague: Martinus Nijhoff, 1961), p. 62; *Totality and Infinity*, trans. A. Lingis (Pittsburgh: Duquesne University Press, 1969), p. 90. Henceforth TeI and TI.

14. Hermann Fränkel, *Early Greek Poetry and Philosophy*, trans. Moses Hadas and James Willis (Oxford: Blackwell, 1975), p. 221.

15. *The English Works of Thomas Hobbes. Vol. III. Leviathan*, ed. William Molesworth (Darmstadt: Scientia Verlag Aalen, 1966), p. 53.

16. Ludwig Feuerbach, *Das Wesen des Christentums*, Theorie Werkausgabe 5 (Frankfurt: Suhrkamp, 1976), p. 188; *The Essence of Christianity*, trans. George Eliot (New York: Harper & Row, 1957), p. 158.

17. E. Levinas, *Humanisme de l'autre homme* (Montpelier: Fata Morgana, 1972), p. 49; *Collected Philosophical Papers*, p. 97.

18. I have borrowed the distinction between executive and legislative conscience from Eric D'Arcy, *Conscience and its Right to Freedom* (London: Sheed and Ward, 1961).

19. For an introduction to the distinction between *synderesis* and *conscientia* see T. C. Potts, *Conscience in Medieval Philosophy* (Cambridge: Cambridge University Press, 1980). See also Jacques de Blic, "Synderese ou conscience?" *Revue d'ascétique et de mystique* 15 (1949): 146–57.

20. Augustine, *Les Confessions*, Oeuvres de Saint Augustin, vol. 14 (Paris: Desclée de Brouwer, 1962), X.16.25. I have used the translation by John K. Ryan except where otherwise stated: *The Confessions of Augustine* (New York: Doubleday, 1960).

21. From the extensive secondary literature see especially Winfried Weier, "Die introspektive Bewusstseinswahrnehmung beim hl. Augustinus und bei Descartes," *Franziskanische Studien* 50 (1968): 239–50.

22. See R. Bernasconi, "The Silent Anarchic World of the Evil Genius," *The Collection Phaenomenologicum. The First Ten Years* (Dordrecht: Kluwer, 1988), pp. 257–72.

23. There is a hint in the Preface to *Totality and Infinity* that Levinas remains sufficiently close to the phenomenological method for the notion of destruction to be not altogether alien to him: "What counts is the idea of the overflowing of objectifying thought by a forgotten experience from which it lives" (TeI xvi; TI 28). Transferred to the historical realm this is Heidegger's *Destruktion*.

24. Terence, *Andria* line 68, trans. John Sargeaunt, Loeb ed., vol. I (London: Heinemann, 1920), p. 11.

25. I have quoted here the translation by Vernon J. Bourke as it more closely follows the original. *Augustine's Love of Wisdom* (West Lafayette: Purdue University Press, 1992), p. 101.

26. H. Arendt, *The Human Condition* (Chicago: University of Chicago Press, 1958), p. 10n.

27. On the importance generally of the *coram Deo* for Augustine's conception of conscience, see Johannes Stelzenberger, *Conscientia bei Augustinus* (Paderborn: Ferdinard Schöningh, 1959), pp. 35–40.

28. Philo, "On the Special Laws" I. 235, trans. F. H. Colson, Loeb ed. (London: Heinemann, vol. VII, 1937), pp. 236–37. For a discussion of this passage in the light of its Jewish sources, see Jacob Milgrom's response to R. T. Wallis, *The Idea of Conscience in Philo of Alexandria* (Berkeley: The Center for Hermeneutical Studies, 1975), pp. 16–18.

29. F. Nietzsche, *Zür Genealogie der Moral*, Kritische Studienausgabe 5 (Berlin: De Gruyter, 1980), I, 8, pp. 305–6; *On the Genealogy of Morals*, trans. W. Kaufmann and R. J. Hollingdale (New York: Random House, 1989), p. 70.

30. See also E. Levinas, "Transcendance et Hauteur," *Bulletin de la Société Française de Philosophie* 14 (1962): 100. Henceforth TH.

31. E. Levinas, "Ethique comme philosophie première," *Justifications de l'éthique*, ed. G. Hottois (Brussels: Editions de l'Universite-de Bruxelles, 1982), p. 49; *The Levinas Reader*, trans. Sean Hand and Michael Temple, ed. Sean Hand (Oxford: Basil Blackwell, 1989), pp. 83–84.

32. E. Levinas, "De l'évasion," *Recherches Philosophiques*, 5, 1935–36, p. 385.

33. M. Heidegger, *Sein und Zeit* (Tübingen: Max Niemeyer, 1967), p. 291; *Being and Time*, trans. J. Macquarrie and E. Robinson (Oxford: Basil Blackwell, 1967), p. 337.

34. An important statement of the thesis about the first stages of the internalizing of conscience is found in Friedrich Zucker, *Syneidesis-Conscientia*, Jenaer Akademischer Reden 6 (Jena: Gustav Fischer, 1928). It subsequently was taken up by E. R. Dodds to form the basis for an account of Greece as making the passage from a shame-culture to a guilt-culture. *The Greeks and the Irrational* (Berkeley: University of California Press, 1963).

35. The distinction between shame and guilt has given rise to a widespread characterization of a difference between shame-cultures and guilt cultures. In an important new study, Douglas Caims has put the usefulness of this distinction in doubt and throws a great deal of light on the issues discussed here. *Aidos. The Psychology and Ethics of Honour and Shame in Ancient Greek Literature* (Oxford: Oxford University Press, 1993). However, Caims does not allow for the radical rethinking of conscience that takes place in Levinas. Indeed, he insists on thinking of conscience as inward.

36. Levinas is not altogether consistent on this point. There is a definite tendency counter to the one I have chosen to emphasize, as for example, when he writes: "To know God is to know what must be done" (DL 34; DF 17). As this quotation suggests, a reflection on these two tendencies belongs in the space opened up by the relation of Levinas's philosophical writings to his confessional writings.

37. E. Levinas, *Du sacré au saint* (Paris: Minuit, 1977), p. 38; *Nine Talmudic Writings*, trans. A. Aronowicz (Bloomington: Indiana University Press, 1990), p. 109. Henceforth SS and NTR.

38. See R. Bernasconi, "The Ethics of Suspicion," *Research in Phenomenology*, 20 (1990): 3–18.

Joseph Margolis, Moral Optimism

1. See Bernard Williams, *Shame and Necessity* (Berkeley: University of California Press, 1993); "Moral Standards and the Distinguishing Mark of Man," *Morality: An Introduction to Ethics* (New York: Harper and Row, 1972); *Ethics and the Limits of Philosophy* (Cambridge, Mass.: Harvard University Press, 1985), ch. 4.

2. See Karl-Otto Apel, "The Transformation of Transcendental Philosophy," *Understanding and Explanation*; *A Transcendental-Pragmatic Perspective*, trans. Georgia Warnke (Cambridge, Mass.: MIT Press, 1984); and "Is the Ethics of the Ideal Communication Community a Utopia? On the Relationship between Ethics, Utopia, and the Critique of Utopia," in *The Communicative Ethics Controversy*, ed. Seyla Benhabib and Fred Dallmayr (Cambridge, Mass.: MIT Press, 1990).

3. See Thomas S. Kuhn, *The Structure of Scientific Revolutions*, 2nd ed. enlarged (Chicago: University of Chicago Press, 1970); Imre Lakatos, "Falsification

and the Methodology of Scientific Research Programs," *Philosophical Papers*, Vol. 1, eds. John Worrell and Gregory Currie (Cambridge: Cambridge University Press, 1978); and Arthur Fine, *The Shaky Game: Einstein, Realism, and the Quantum Theory* (Chicago: University of Chicago Press, 1986).

4. See Donald Davidson, "Mental Events," *Essays on Actions and Events* (Oxford: Clarendon, 1950); also Alvin I. Goldman, *Liaisons: Philosophy Meets the Cognitive and Social Sciences* (Cambridge, Mass.: MIT Press, 1992).

5. I have explored the difference between progressivism and traditionalism in *The Flux of History and the Flux of Science* (Berkeley: University of California Press, 1993). See also my *Pragmatism without Foundations: Reconciling Realism and Relativism* (Oxford: Basil Blackwell, 1986), ch. 2.

6. Hilary Putnam, *The Many Faces of Realism* (La Salle: Open Court, 1987), Lecture III, pp. 53–54. Hereafter MFR.

7. See Immanuel Kant, *Grounding for the Metaphysics of Morals*, trans. James W. Ellington, in *Immanuel Kant. Ethical Philosophy* (Indianapolis: Hackett Publishing Co., 1983), Third Section; and Immanuel Kant, *Lectures on Ethics*, trans. Louis Infeld (Indianapolis: Hackett Publishing Co., 1963), "The Supreme Principle of Morality."

8. Hilary Putnam, *Reason, Truth and History* (Cambridge: Cambridge University Press, 1981), p. 124. Hereafter RTH.

9. See Hilary Putnam, *Realism with a Human Face*, ed. James Conant (Cambridge, Mass.: Harvard University Press, 1990).

10. See, for instance, MFR 17. See also W.V. Quine, *Pursuit of Truth*, rev. (Cambridge, Mass.: Harvard University Press, 1972), pp. 32–33; and *Word and Object* (Cambridge, Mass.: MIT Press, 1960), §§15–16.

11. Hilary Putnam, *Philosophical Papers*, vol. 3 (Cambridge: Cambridge University Press, 1983): Introduction, pp. xvi—xvii. See also, in the same volume, "Models and Reality" and "Reference and Truth."

12. Putnam, "Reference and Truth," p. 85.

13. For a sense of Putnam's former confidence, when he shared certain views of science with Richard Boyd regarding reference and explanation, see Hilary Putnam, *Meaning and the Moral Sciences* (London: Routledge and Kegan Paul, 1978), Lecture II of the 1976 John Locke Lectures, where he explains what he means by "convergence," particularly at pp. 21–25. He has given up this view; accordingly, he is entitled to adjust his view of "convergence"; but he has not satisfactorily recovered any viable such sense, and it now looks impossible to do.

14. MFR 44–45. Compare here Richard Rorty, "Science as Solidarity," *Philosophical Papers*, vol. 1 (Cambridge: Cambridge University Press, 1991); and "Habermas and Lyotard on Postmodernity," *Philosophical Papers*, vol. 2 (Cambridge: Cambridge University Press, 1991).

15. Karl-Otto Apel, "The *a priori* of the Communication Community and the Foundations of Ethics: The Problem of a Rational Foundation of Ethics in a Scientific Age," in *Towards a Transformation of Philosophy*, trans. Glyn Adey and David Frisby (London: Routledge and Kegan Paul, 1980), pp. 266, 268.

16. On this matter, see Michel Foucault's notion of the "historical a priori," in *The Order of Things; An Archaeology of the Human Sciences* (New York: Vintage, 1970), ch. 10.

17. Hans Albert, *Treatise on Critical Reason*, trans. Mary Varney Rorty (Princeton: Princeton University Press, 1985), pp. xvi, 13. Hereafter TCR.

18. Jürgen Habermas, "Discourse Ethics: Notes on a Program of Philosophical Justification," *Moral Consciousness and Communicative Action*, trans. Christian Lenhardt and Shierry Weber Nicholsen (Cambridge, Mass.: MIT Press, 1990), pp. 78–79. Hereafter DE.

19. As a matter of fact, Habermas himself admits the point, in defending his own procedure, which requires a "maieutic" strategy in moving from "knowing how" to "knowing that" (that is, legitimatively). I shall come to the passage in a moment. See DE 97.

20. See A.J. Watt, "Transcendental Arguments and Moral Principles," *Philosophical Quarterly*, XXV (1975); and R.S. Peters, *Ethics and Education* (London: Allen and Unwin, 1974). Both are favorably cited by Habermas.

21. Watt, "Transcendental Arguments and Moral Principles," p. 40.

22. John Rawls, *Political Liberalism* (New York: Columbia University Press, 1993), p. 61n16. Hereafter PL.

23. On "reflective equilibrium," see John Rawls, *A Theory of Justice* (Cambridge, Mass.: Harvard University Press, 1971), pp. 20f., 48–51, 120f. See also Thomas McCarthy's introduction to *Moral Consciousness and Communicative Action*, particularly pp. viii–ix.

24. Isaiah Berlin, *The Crooked Timber of Humanity* (New York: Knopf, 1991), p. 13; cited in PL 197n.32; see also p. 57.

25. I pursue Rawls's account in greater depth in "Rawls on Justice—Once Again," forthcoming.

26. See Joseph Margolis, "The Locus of Coherence," *Linguistics and Philosophy* VII (1984).

27. DE 88. See also Jürgen Habermas, *The Theory of Communicative Actions*, trans. Thomas McCarthy (Boston: Beacon, 1984), vol. 1, pp. 22–42.

28. See Paul K. Feyerabend, *Against Method; Outline of an Anarchistic Theory of Knowledge* (London: Verso, 1975).

29. See Karl-Otto Apel, "The Problem of Philosophical Foundations in Light of a Transcendental Pragmatics of Language," modified, translation (by Karl Richard Pavlovic) also modified, in *After Philosophy*, eds. Kenneth Baynes, James Bohman, and Thomas McCarthy (Cambridge, Mass.: MIT Press, 1987), particularly pp. 280–81.

30. See Robert Alexy, "A Theory of Practical Discourse," trans., in *The Communicative Ethics Controversy.*

31. See further Joseph Margolis, "The Passing of Peirce's Realism," *Transactions of the Charles S. Peirce Society* XXIX (1993).

32. Alexy, "A Theory of Practical Discourse," pp. 174–75. (I have abbreviated 5.2.1 and 5.2.2).

33. W. V. Quine, "Epistemology Naturalized," *Ontological Relativity and Other Essays* (New York: Columbia University Press, 1969).

Tom Rockmore, More Hegelian Doubts about Discourse Ethics

1. See "Morality and Ethical Life: Does Hegel's Critique of Kant Apply to Discourse Ethics," in Jürgen Habermas, *Moral Consciousness and Communicative Action*, trans. Christian Lenhardt and Shierry Weber Nicholson (Cambridge, Mass.: MIT Press, 1990, 1993), p. 201. Hereafter MCCA. For discussion, see *Moralität und Sittlichkeit, Das Problem Hegels und die Diskursethik*, ed. Wolfgang Kühlmann (Frankfurt: Suhrkamp, 1986).

2. See Tom Rockmore, "Philosophy, Literature, and Intellectual Responsibility," *American Philosophical Quarterly* 30, no. 2 (April 1993): 109–22.

3. See Tom Rockmore, *On Heidegger's Nazism and Philosophy* (Berkeley: University of California Press, 1992).

4. See "Traditional and Critical Theory," in Max Horkheimer, *Critical Theory*, trans. Matthew J. O'Connell and others (New York: Herder and Herder, 1968), pp. 188–243.

5. For a recent discussion of Habermas's theory as a response to Rawls, see Kenneth Baynes, *The Normative Grounds of Social Criticism: Kant, Rawls, and Habermas* (Albany: SUNY Press, 1992).

6. For discussion of Habermas's view of discourse ethics, see William Rehg, *Insight and Solidarity: A Study in the Discourse Ethics of Jürgen Habermas* (Berkeley: University of California Press, 1993).

7. See John Rawls, "The Idea of an Overlapping Consensus," *Oxford Journal of Legal Studies* 7, no. 1 (Spring 1987).

8. See Maurice Merleau-Ponty, *Humanism and Terror*, trans. John O'Neill (Boston: Beacon, 1969).

9. See Maurice Merleau-Ponty, *Les Aventures de la dialectique* (Paris: Gallimard, 1955).

10. See Tom Rockmore, *Habermas on Historical Materialism* (Bloomington, In.: Indiana University Press, 1989).

11. See Jürgen Habermas, *Zur Rekonstruktion des historischen Materialismus* (Frankfurt: Suhrkamp, 1976).

12. See Tom Rockmore, *Irrationalism: Lukács and the Marxist View of Reason* (Philadelphia: Temple University Press, 1992).

13. See "Labor and Interaction: Remarks on Hegel's Jena *Philosophy of Mind*," in Jürgen Habermas, *Theory and Practice*, trans. John Viertel (Boston: Beacon, 1974), pp. 142–69.

14. See Habermas, *Justification and Application: Remarks on Discourse Ethics* (Cambridge, Mass.: MIT Press, 1993), pp. 20–111. Hereafter JA.

15. See Alasdair MacIntyre, *After Virtue: A Study in Moral Theory* (Notre Dame: University of Notre Dame Press, 1981, 1984).

16. See Alasdair MacIntyre, *Three Rival Versions of Moral Enquiry: Encyclopedia, Genealogy and Tradition* (Notre Dame: University of Notre Dame Press, 1990).

17. See "Die Moderne-ein unvollendetes Projekt," in Jürgen Habermas, *Kleine politische Schriften (I–IV)* (Frankfurt: Suhrkamp, 1981), pp. 444–64.

18. See Kant, *Critique of Pure Reason*, trans. N. K. Smith (London/New York: Macmillan/St. Martin's, 1962), B 508, p. 433. Hereafter CPR.

19. According to Habermas, the idea of mutual understanding rooted in language provides for the consensus about democratic will formation and law that undergird the modern state. See Jürgen Habermas, *Theory of Communicative Action* (Boston: Beacon, 1984), 2 vols, II, p. 96. See also Jürgen Habermas, *Philosophical Discourse of Modernity: Twelve Lectures* (Cambridge, Mass.: MIT Press, 1987), pp. 344–45.

20. See "Morality and Ethical Life: Hegel's Controversy with Kantian Ethics," in Joachim Ritter, *Hegel and the French Revolution*, trans. Richard Dien Winfield (Cambridge, Mass.: MIT Press, 1982), pp. 151–83.

21. See G. W. F. Hegel, *Hegel's Philosophy of Right*, trans. T. M. Knox (London: Oxford University Press, 1952, 1967), § 4, p. 20.

22. See Immanuel Kant, *Fundamental Principles of the Metaphysics of Morals*, trans. Thomas K. Abbott (New York: LLA, 1949), p. 3.

23. See Hegel, *Phenomenology of Spirit*, trans. A. V. Miller (New York: Oxford University Press, 1977), p. 259.

24. See Nicholas Rescher, *Pluralism: Against the Demand for Consensus* (Oxford: Oxford University Press, 1993), pp. 195–99.

25. See Thomas Kuhn, *The Structure of Scientific Revolution* (Chicago: University of Chicago Press, 1962, 1970).

26. See Ludwik Fleck, *Genesis and Development of a Scientific Fact*, trans. Fred Bradley and Thaddeus J. Trenn (Chicago: University of Chicago Press, 1979).

27. See Thomas McCarthy, "Introduction" to Habermas, *Moral Consciousness and Communicative Action*, p. vii.

28. See Edmund Husserl, *Logische Untersuchungen* (Tübingen: Max Niemeyer, 1900, 1968), I: *Prolegomena zur reinen Logik*, pp. 110–53.

29. See Werner Jaeger, *Aristotle: Fundamentals of His Development*, trans. Richard Robinson (London: Oxford University Press, 1934, 1962).

30. See Joseph Margolis, *The Flux of History and the Flux of Science* (Berkeley: University of California Press, 1993).

Caroline Bayard, Lyotard's Ethical Challenges: Meditations for the End of a Century

1. Two special issues on Lyotard critically cover the vast spectrum of his works. See *L'Esprit créateur* 31, no. 1 (Spring 1991), and *Philosophy Today* 36, no. 4 (Winter 1992). An earlier issue of *Diacritics* specifically examines *Le Différend* and the discourse of the "other" in Lyotard's writings.

2. Essays by Lyotard in *Socialisme ou Barbarie* range from 1956 to 1963, although, as Cornelius Castoriadis points out, this journal should not be narrowly circumscribed around Lyotard's participation in it, however important the latter may have been. Castoriadis, introduction to *Political and Social Writings*, ed. David Ames Curtis (Minneapolis: University of Minnesota Press, 1988).

3. The accusation Habermas leveled against the author of *La condition postmoderne*—his irresponsibility, his jeopardizing the heritage of modernity—first appeared in English in "Modernity versus Postmodernity," *New German Critique* 22

(Winter 1981): 3–14. A broader context for Habermas's frustration can also be found in his "Neoconservative Culture Criticism in the United States and West Germany: An Intellectual Movement in Two Political Cultures," trans. Russell A. Berman, *Telos* 56 (1983): 75–87. Lyotard's chartering of modernity, of the demise of its various concepts of progress, in 1979 with *La condition postmoderne* has since been acknowledged and substantiated by various philosophers and social scientists, including Agnes Heller, Alain Touraine, Zygmunt Bauman, and Leslek Kolakowski.

4. For a translation in English of this particular essay, see "The Wall, the Gulf, the Sun: A Fable," written in English with the help of Thomas Cochran, in *Politics, Theory and Contemporary Culture*, ed. Mark Poster (New York: Columbia University Press, 1993), pp. 261–76.

5. On liberalism, on European nations making their peace with liberal theory and practice, after rejecting them for the benefit of Marxism (Lyotard, Derrida, Foucault), or of a Third Way which embraced a radical, utopian Enlightenment (Habermas), see Mark Lilla, "The Other Velvet Revolution: Continental Liberalism and its Discontents," *Daedalus* 123, no. 2 (Spring 1994): 129–58. See also Pierre Manent, *An Intellectual History of Liberalism*, trans. Rebecca Balinski (Princeton: Princeton University Press, 1994). Two special issues on liberalism— *Social Research* 61, no. 3 (Fall 1994), and *East European Cultures and Politics* 5, no. 1 (Winter 1991), "Rediscovery of Liberalism in Eastern Europe"—would also be relevant.

6. See *Le postmoderne expliqué aux enfants* (Paris: Galilée, 1987), pp. 41– 59, but specifically p. 59. See also Caroline Bayard, "The Intellectual in the Postmodern Age," *Philosophy Today* (Winter 1990): 291–302.

7. For an overview of the journal *Socialisme ou Barbarie*, see Castoriadis, introduction to *Political and Social Writings*. Lyotard, "The Situation in North Africa" and "Algerians' Contradictions Exposed," in *Jean-François Lyotard: Political Writings*, trans. Bill Readings and Kevin Paul Geiman (Minneapolis: University of Minnesota Press, 1993), pp. 171–78, 187–96. Note also what Lyotard said in 1991 to Gilbert Larochelle: "I began my philosophical career fifteen years late, years that were dedicated to being an activist in the group *Socialisme ou Barbarie* where I wrote only *that which was asked of me and nothing else*" (emphasis mine), in "That Which Resists After All," *Philosophy Today* 36 (4): 402.

8. For an assessment of the political and social situation in Algeria in the mid nineties, see Ignacio Ramonet, "Algérie panique," *Le Monde Diplomatique* 486 (September 1994): 1. See also the special issue of *Manière de voir* 24 (January 1995) dedicated to fundamentalist and populist conflicts.

9. "Proud struggles for independence end in young, reactionary States." *Le Differend* (Paris: Minuit, 1983), p. 181.

10. "Algeria Seven Years Later" and "Algeria Evacuated," in *Jean-François Lyotard: Political Writings*, pp. 286–92, 296–326.

11. Jean-François Lyotard, "The Name of Algeria," in *Jean-François Lyotard: Political Writings*, pp. 165–170, esp. p. 168.

12. Jean-François Lyotard, *La condition postmoderne* (Paris: Minuit, 1979),

p. 7. Lyotard identifies the term postmodernity as one in usage on the North American continent, although mostly among sociologists and critics.

13. On Lyotard's brief meditation on "1968," as seen from 1993, one could consult "A l'insu," in *Moralités postmodernes*, pp. 161–70, in particular his thoughts on the meaning of this particular event: "The event called 1968, or "the events" as they were called later, drained anxieties. Childhood is not happiness, but a condition of dependence. May 68 expressed a disconsolate grief: that of being born unfree. As in a tragic chorus, the adults commiserated with the grief of children-heroes" (p. 169; translation mine). On different perspectives about the various philosophical decoys of 1968, see Luc Ferry and Alain Renaut, *La pensée 68: essai sur l'anti-humanisme contemporain* (Paris: Gallimard, 1988), pp. 60–77, which is a strong critique of Lyotard's positions. On Lyotard's response to Ferry's attack, see Jean-François Lyotard and Jacob Rogozinski, "La police de la pensée," *L'Autre journal* December 1985: 27–34. In a possibly less partial vein, see also Hervé Hamon and Patrick Rotman, *Génération: les années de rêve* (Paris: Seuil, 1987).

14. This book was published in French as *Heidegger et les juifs* (Paris: Galilée, 1988), then subsequently translated as *Heidegger and the Jews* by Andreas Michel and Mark S. Roberts (Minneapolis: University of Minnesota Press, 1990). It aroused considerable interest among French readers, although it also caused sizable discomfort, since Lyotard defines the "Jews" as "that which cannot be either integrated within the economy of the Occident, nor converted to it. Nor can they be expelled from the West even by extermination" (*Heidegger and the Jews*, p. 22–23). Such statements, while they are intent on challenging Heideggerian thought, curiously duplicate some of its most disturbing moments. If they never fall into Lacoue-Labarthe's scholarly decoy, which consists in providing substantial support to the Heideggerian argument while seemingly deconstructing it, they nevertheless raise more questions than they are able to answer. The unease aroused by Philippe Lacoue-Labarthe and Jean-Luc Nancy in *Rejouer le politique* (Paris: Galilée, 1982)—"L'extermination n'est à l'égard de l'occident que la terrible révélation de son essence" (p. 61)—is only one moment of such a process. On the discomfort provoked by *Heidegger and the Jews*, see Robert Bernasconi's review in *L'Esprit créateur* 31, no. 1 (Spring 1991): 162–63.

15. "Thanks to the precept of love, all of the events already told in the narratives of infidels and unbelievers can be retold as so may signs portentous of the new commandments. . . . Christian narration not only tells what happened, thereby fixing a tradition, but it also prescribes the *caritas* for what may happen, whatever it might be." *Le Différend*, p. 168. On Marxism as critical passion in *Socialisme ou Barbarie*, see "The Name of Algeria" and "Algerians' Contradictions Exposed," pp. 169, 197–99.

16. *Le Différend*, pp. 112–17.

17. On the exploration of an epilogue for modernity following Kant's lead, see *Le postmoderne expliqué aux enfants:* "Kant himself indicates which direction to take when he names shapelessness, the absence of form as: that which cannot be presented [*l'imprésentable*]" (p.26). For the English translation of the same, *The Postmodern Explained to Children*, ed. Julian Pefanis, trans. Don Barry (Minneapolis:

University of Minnesota Press, 1992). See also "Kant/Ethical Time" in *Le Différend*, pp. 126–27. On an honorable postmodernity and Wittgenstein, see "Genre, Norm" in *Le Différend*, pp. 128, 136.

18. "It puts off the idea of a cosmopolitical history." *Le Différend*, p. 181.

19. Ibid., p. 178.

20. Ibid., p. 179.

21. "Intime est la terreur," in *Moralités postmodernes*, p. 171–72.

22. "The Wall, the Gulf, the Sun: A Fable," pp. 264–65. See also, on the efficiency of an open system: "The Fall of the Wall, on the one hand, provides evidence that the more open the system, the more efficient it is: while on the other it shows that closed and isolated systems are doomed to disappear, either by competition or merely by entropy (Brezhnev should have studied thermodynamics a bit)." Ibid., p. 269.

23. "Note sur les sens du post-," in *Le Postmoderne expliqué aux enfants*, p. 116.

24. "The Wall, the Gulf, the Sun," pp. 265, 268–69.

25. *Le Différend*, p. 181.

26. "The Name of Algeria," pp. 168–69. It is interesting to read in 1995 a analogous analysis from Ignacio Ramonet: "The modern dogmatism, articulated by the International Monetary Fund, the Banque de France, financial and industrial groups which incant ten new commandments ad nauseam in a new, sticky dogma, surreptitiously engulfing any contrary way of thought by inhabiting it and squeezing it shut." "La Pensée unique," in *Le Monde Diplomatique* 490 (January 1995): 1.

27. *Le Différend*, p. 169.

28. "It is inaccurate and intellectually dishonest to impose the hope, or to pretend that as Marxists we should invest in the revolutionary activity of the proletariat, upon the freely spontaneous activity of young people, immigrants, women, homosexuals, prisoners, or the people of the Third World." "In the Name of Algeria," p. 169.

29. *Le tombeau de l'intellectuel et autres papiers* (Paris: Galilée, 1954). For an excerpt of this important text, see "Tomb of the Intellectual," in *Political Writings*, pp. 3–7.

30. See Caroline Bayard, "The Intellectual in the Postmodern Age: East/West Contrasts," *Philosophy Today* 3, no. 3 (Winter 1990): 291–302.

31. See "Lettre à David Rogocinski June 21st Prague," in "Glose sur la résistance" in *Le postmoderne expliqué aux enfants*, pp. 131–43, esp. 141–42.

32. On the strength of open systems versus closed/totalitarian ones and the hiatus present in the very definition of democracies, see *Moralités postmodernes*, p. 76. On the opposition his stance on the Gulf War encountered, see Etienne Balibar, Ben Jalloun, and Pierre Bourdieu, "Contre la guerre," *Libération*, 21 February 1991, p. 13. On his stance, along with Alain Finkielkraut, Elisabeth de Fontenay, Jacob Rogocinski, Pierre André-Taguieff, and Alain Touraine, see "Une Guerre requise," *Libération*, 21 February 1991, p. 12.

33. See "The Wall, the Gulf, the Sun" and the appeal "Une Guerre requise": "Against the combined temptations presented by moral angelism and cynical realism, it is essential to preserve the exacting demands an ethical politics confers

upon us all [*la voie difficile d'une politique morale doit être préservée*]. It is our duty to ensure that victory against Iraq promote democracy, justice as much as peace opportunities" (p. 12). One should also mention in this context the interventions published by Michel Serres, who explicitly addressed such ethical responsibilities in his *Eclaircissements* (Paris: François Bourin, 1992), particularly when he focuses on the "blind spot of philosophy, when everything starts again" [*le point aveugle de la philosophie, tout recommence*; translation mine] (pp. 235–40).

34. See his stance on the issue of the intractable [*l'intraitable*] when he insists upon his respect of the very notion of gap, hiatus, pause, not just in a text, or within his philosophical ear, but also within political and cultural systems, in *Le Différend*. See his definition of postmodernity as the end of the "peuple-roi des histoires," hence the end of any possibility of emancipation, revelation or wisdom, in *Le postmoderne expliqué aux enfants*, p. 39. On indeterminacy within democracy, the hiatus within it, see "The Wall, the Gulf, the System," p. 270. On the irremediable opacity of language itself, see "A Svelte Appendix to the Postmodern," in *Political Writings*, p. 27.

35. "Adresse au sujet du cours philosophique," *Le postmoderne expliqué au enfants*, p. 157; see also "Zone," in *Moralités postmodernes*, p. 36.

36. Seyla Benhabib, "Epistemologies of Postmodernism: A Rejoinder to Jean-François Lyotard," *New German Critique* 33 (1984): 103–26.

37. Larochelle, "That Which Resists, After All," pp. 402–18.

38. See *Women, Culture and Society*, ed. Michelle Zimbalist Rosaldo (Stanford: Stanford University Press, 1974). Linda J. Nicholson and Nancy Fraser suggest that such an approach allowed for diversity and ubiquity in its study of the manifestation of sexism, thus alternatively separating and correlating domestic and public spheres. "Social Criticism without Philosophy: An Encounter between Feminism and Postmodernism," in *Feminism/Postmodernism*, ed. Linda J. Nicholson (London: Routledge, 1990), p. 28.

39. "La mainmise," in "The Grip," in *Political Writings*, p. 148–58.

40. "Un partenaire bizarre," in *Moralités postmodernes*, pp. 119–30, explores Donald Davidson's and Richard Rorty's different interpretations of dialogue and consensus when faced with contemporary conflicts. While Lyotard focuses upon a number of Franco-American misunderstandings in this essay (explicit since the special issue of *Critique* 456 (May 1985), subtitled "La traversée de l'Atlantique"), he also rejects the reduction both Rorty and Davidson enact upon the purpose and function of language. See esp. pp. 119–20.

41. "Ligne générale," in *Moralités postmodernes*, pp. 105–10. In the original text: "L'invite répétée à exercer les droits et à en surveiller l'observance peut-être pressante jusqu'à l'oppression.[. . .]. Que l'exercice des droits et la vigilance quant à leur respect soient requis comme des devoirs, il y a là une sorte d'évidence, aussi infaillible qu'une disposition totalitaire peut l'être" (p. 108; translation mine).

42. *Moralités postmodernes*, p. 121.

43. Jean-François Lyotard, "La terre n'a pas de chemins par elle-même," in *Moralités postmodernes*, pp. 95–102.

44. See "The Rise and Fall of Yugoslavia: Stations of a European Tragedy," a special issue of *Praxis International* 13, no. 4 (January 1994).

Barry Allen, Disabling Knowledge

1. Bruno Latour, *We Have Never Been Modern*, trans. Catherine Porter (Cambridge, Mass.: Harvard University Press, 1993), p. 132.

2. Ivan Illich, *Toward a History of Needs* (Berkeley: Heyday, 1978), p. 39; and *Limits to Medicine: Medical Nemesis — The Expropriation of Health* (London: Marion Boyars, 1976; Harmondsworth: Penguin, 1990), pp. 35, 44.

3. Illich, *History of Needs*, pp. 37–38.

4. Michel Foucault, *Power/Knowledge: Selected Interviews and Other Writings 1972–1977*, ed. C. Gorden (New York: Pantheon, 1980), pp. 51–52. Paolo Rossi observes that Bacon's identification of knowledge and power "is never presented as a simple confirmation of fact, but assumes the characteristic and solemn tone of a manifesto addressed to mankind so that it may choose between two different paths and between two different concepts of 'truth.' In Bacon's view what was at stake was the closure of an epoch of civilization." "Truth and Utility in the Science of Francis Bacon," *Philosophy, Technology, and the Arts in the Early Modern Era*, trans. S. Attanasio (New York: Harper & Row, 1970), p. 171.

5. On "discipline," see Foucault, *Discipline and Punish*, trans. Alan Sheridan (New York: Vintage, 1979). See also my "Government in Foucault," *Canadian Journal of Philosophy* 21 (1991): 421–40. For a historical example of the reciprocity of power and knowledge worked out in some detail, see my "Demonology, Styles of Reasoning, and Truth," *International Journal of Moral and Social Studies* 8 (1993): 95–122. For discussion of the relationship among knowledge, truth, and politics, see my *Truth in Philosophy* (Cambridge, Mass.: Harvard University Press, 1993), chap. 8. I discuss Foucault's place in the tradition of modern political philosophy in "Foucault and Modern Political Philosophy," *The Later Foucault*, ed. Jeremy Moss (Sage, forthcoming).

6. Writing of the deaf and the "audist" professionals who claim to care for their supposed special needs, Harlan Lane says, "audist professionals have no difficulty in overruling the parents' wishes with respect to the Individualized Education Plan [mandated by US law] for their child. The parents can appeal, and if the appeal fails they can go to court, but at both levels of review there is a presumption that the experts have made the right decision." *The Mask of Benevolence: Disabling the Deaf Community* (New York: Knopf, 1992), p. 236. Hereafter MB.

7. Michael Ignatieff takes from *King Lear* the lesson that "what a man needs is his due, and what is his due, he needs," but also that Lear, like anyone else, "needs not only raiment, bed, and food, but such raiment, bed, and food as is due his rank, his virtue, his history." Hence the paradox "that to treat men equally—only as men—is to deny them the respect due to their humanity. . . . To treat each person as a human being is to give to each according to their merit, rank, quality, and deserving—that is, unequally." *The Needs of Strangers*

(London: Chatto & Windus, 1984), pp. 35–36. See also William Leiss, *The Limits to Satisfaction* (Toronto: University of Toronto Press, 1976); and Ivan Illich, "Needs," *The Development Dictionary: A Guide to Knowledge as Power*, ed. W. Sachs (London: Zed Books, 1992).

8. The theory of mimetic needs was originally developed for a theory of the novel; see René Girard, *Deceit, Desire, and the Novel: Self and Other in Literary Structure*, trans. Y. Freccero (Baltimore: Johns Hopkins University Press, 1965). The extension to communications and advertising is suggested; see pp. 222–24.

9. Peter Brown, *Power and Persuasion in Late Antiquity* (Madison: University of Wisconsin Press, 1992), pp. 77, 152, 153.

10. St. Gregory the Great, *Pastoral Care*, trans. H. Davis (New York: Neuman Press, 1950) I.1, I.9, III. Prologue (pp. 21, 38, 89). On "pastoral power," see Foucault, "The Subject and Power," in H. Dreyfus and P. Rabinow, *Michel Foucault: Beyond Structuralism and Hermeneutics*, 2d ed. (Chicago: University of Chicago Press, 1983), pp. 213–15. The penitential handbooks constantly reiterate the comparison of the pastor to a physician; see J. T. McNeill and H. M. Gamer, ed., *Medieval Handbooks of Penance* (New York: Columbia University Press, 1938, 1990), pp. 148–49, 221–23, 323, 347–48, 413–14. See also R. I. Moore, "Heresy as Disease," *The Concept of Heresy in the Middle Ages*, ed. W. Lourdaux and D. Verhelst (Louvain: Louvain University Press, 1976), and *The Formation of a Persecuting Society: Power and Deviance in Western Europe, 950–1250* (Oxford: Blackwell, 1987).

11. "*Need* expresses how this system [Freud's system ø], which is a special system within the organism, connects up with the general homeostasis of the organism." *The Seminar of Jacques Lacan*, Book II: *The Ego in Freud's Theory and in the Technique of Psychoanalysis 1954–1955*, ed. Jacques-Alain Miller, trans. Sylvana Tomaselli (New York: Norton, 1988), p. 106. Perhaps the most illuminating development of Lacan's argument for the difference between need and desire is in Laplanche, *Life and Death in Psychoanalysis*, trans. J. Mehlman (Baltimore: Johns Hopkins University Press, 1976), chaps. 1–2.

12. Lacan, *Écrits: A Selection*, trans. Alan Sheridan (New York: Norton, 1977), p. 287; and *The Seminar of Jacques Lacan*, Book I: *Freud's Papers on Technique 1953–1954*, ed. Jacques-Alain Miller, trans. John Forrester (New York: Norton, 1988), p. 214. Italicized words are Lacan's English.

13. Malcolm Bowie, *Lacan* (London: Fontana, 1991), pp. 135–36.

14. See Barbara Duden, *The Woman Beneath the Skin*, trans. Thomas Dunlap (Cambridge, Mass.: Harvard University Press, 1991), pp. 94–95, 156.

15. Ivan Illich, "Disabling Professions," in Illich et al., *Disabling Professions* (London: Marion Boyars, 1977), pp. 15–16, 23, 17–18; and *History of Needs*, p. 24. A self-certifying quality is common among established sciences; see Ian Hacking, "'Style' for Historians and Philosophers," *Studies in the History and Philosophy of Science* 23 (1992), esp. pp. 13–16.

16. John Dewey, *Political Writings*, ed. D. Morris and I. Shapiro (Indianapolis: Hackett, 1993), p. 1.

17. On the far-ranging implications of the shift from craft to industrial forms of organization in science, see Jerome R. Ravetz, *Scientific Knowledge and its Social Problems* (Oxford: Oxford University Press, 1971).

18. John McKnight, "Professionalized Service and Disabling Help," in Illich et al., *Disabling Professions*, p. 83.

19. Gary L. Albrecht, *The Disability Business: Rehabilitation in America* (Newbury Park, Calif.: Sage, 1992), pp. 19–20, 22, 120, 122. I am grateful to Shelley Tremain both for the reference to this book and for our discussion of disability and rehabilitation.

20. McKnight, "Professionalized Service," p. 89. I do not mean that clients are not expected to internalize some of the vocabulary of the service professional's discipline, which demand is, on the contrary, a common strategy of "rehabilitation."

21. Contrary to a widespread assumption, there is no connection between being healthier and having greater access to professional health care. Most modern health techniques (for instance contraception, smallpox vaccination, and treatment of water and sewage) were developed only in part by physicians and are most effective without professional delivery. Rather than having made some heroic contribution to human well-being, modern medicine, especially when operating as a branch of the welfare state, "has immeasurably increased the number of the needy." Illich, *History of Needs*, p. 33. See also *Limits to Medicine*, p. 23; I. K. Zola, "Healthism and Disabling Medicalization" in Illich et al., *Disabling Professions*; and Michael Mulkay, "Knowledge and Utility," *Sociology of Science* (Bloomington: Indiana University Press, 1991), pp. 100–101.

22. Georges Canguilhem, *The Normal and the Pathological*, trans. C. R. Fawcett (Cambridge, Mass.: MIT Press, 1989), p. 93.

23. Barbara Duden, "History Beneath the Skin," Interview with David Cayley, *Ideas* Transcripts ID9151 (Toronto: Canadian Broadcasting Corp., 1991), p. 8. Hereafter HS. Duden, *Disembodying Women*, trans. L. Hoinacki (Cambridge, Mass.: Harvard University Press, 1993), p. 27. Hereafter DW.

24. Duden, *Disembodying Women*, p. 88. Duden says half of the students in her women's studies classes at Pennsylvania State University do not understand the word "quickening" (p. 80). I have asked large undergraduate classes of predominantly female students about the word, and have so far found one student (female) who understood it.

25. On biopower, see Foucault, *The History of Sexuality*, vol. 1: *Introduction*, trans. Robert Hurley (New York: Vintage, 1980), pp. 137–42. On power and resistance, see pp. 95–96, and "The Subject and Power," p. 221.

26. Duden, "History Beneath the Skin," pp. 8–9; *Disembodying Women*, p. 4.

M. C. Dillon, Natural Law and Sexual Morality

Presented at the Nineteenth Annual Meeting of the Merleau-Ponty Circle held at Berry College, Rome, Georgia, 21–24 September 1994.

1. To establish a framework (*Gestell*) is to define limits of relevance, to provide a context or horizon of debate, to betray the presuppositions of which one is aware. I try to do this deliberately. I regard human cognition as finite, as bounded by limits or horizons of which one may be more or less dimly aware.

One can extend one's horizons by exploring their limits, trying to identify and test one's presuppositions. I do not think that it is possible to achieve a global suspension of the totality of one's presuppositions, nor do I think it is useful to operate on the implicit heuristic that one has none by explicitly refusing to make the attempt to identify them. It is inevitable to fail in the attempt. It is self-indulgence to refuse to make it.

2. See Fred D. Miller, Jr., "Aristotle on Natural Law and Justice," in *A Companion to Aristotle's "Politics"*, ed. David Keyt and Fred D. Miller, Jr. (Cambridge, Mass.: Basil Blackwell, Inc., 1961), pp. 279–306. The interpretation set forth here takes its departure from this excellent article (although I doubt that its author would find my inferences from it entirely congenial).

3. "Aristotle finds it necessary to adopt [a] biological perspective [on natural law and justice] because he has repudiated the metaphysical foundations of Plato's theory of natural law and justice. Plato's *Laws* represents justice and law as 'natural' in the sense of having a divine origin (see IV.715e7–716a3, 716c4–6; X.888d7–890d8). Nature in Plato's *Republic* is a transcendent, eternal and immutable principle involving the theory of Forms. Aristotle has replaced this with a notion of nature as a principle of change which is inherent in substances and which, in the sublunary realm at least, holds always or for the most part." Miller, p. 289.

4. "Biology is not a value-free science for Aristotle. On the contrary, it explains the presence, structures, and interrelationships of organs in terms of their value for living, teleological systems." Miller, p. 292.

5. The translations of Aristotle's works in this section [II] are Miller's.

6. Miller, p. 291.

7. At stake is the issue of attributing intent to nature at large. Under the Aristotelian account, right-handedness does not emerge from the intentions of natural entities, it is a supervenient principle which informs nature. Animals and humans do not choose to be right-handed in order to survive; nature designs us to be right-handed to ensure our survival. If nature makes nothing in vain, that means that nature is driven by an intent whose origin lies beyond the intentions of natural entities, an intent or purpose transcendent to the organisms comprising nature.

8. This is my contention, my interpretation. The point is controversial and textual evidence exists to support the opposing view. The fact of this controversy supports my general thesis that Aristotle is ambivalent on the issue of attribution of intent to nature.

9. The terms are taken from Merleau-Ponty. See M.C. Dillon, *Merleau-Ponty's Ontology* (Bloomington: Indiana University Press, 1988), p. 67.

10. As Miller puts it, the ideal system is one in which "the lawgiver uses his practical rationality to frame a constitution and to fashion laws which bring the polis into a just or natural condition: that is, which will promote the common advantage of the citizens in the sense of enabling them to realize their natural ends and attain the good life. Although nature constrains the lawgiver in that he must cooperate with the nature of the citizens, he nevertheless has considerable

room for inventiveness and discretion in crafting the conventional component of political justice." Miller, p. 305.

11. Miller, pp. 293–94. Here Miller cites *Politics* III.6.1278b17–30.

12. "Aristotle is seeking in his different discussions to accommodate . . . common beliefs [*endoxa*] as far as possible, but he is not merely taking these beliefs to be given and putting them, as far as possible, into a coherent system. He is also seeking a deeper normative theory which tries to draw upon 'things that seems to be the case' in order to justify common ethical beliefs and correct them if necessary. As part of this method, he argues that the principles of ethics depend upon principles of his natural and metaphysical works which are themselves defended by reference to nonethical *endoxa* and *phainomena*." Miller, p. 282.

13. This distinction between the empirical and the trans-empirical depends upon a narrow conception of the empirical which I shall abandon eventually. Narrowly defined, the empirical domain is value-free, hence any prescription or norm would have to be justified by appeal to a trans-empirical domain. One of the key theses being presented here is that this narrow definition is reductive and cannot ultimately be sustained.

14. The dogmatic tone of these remarks stems from the need for brevity and, I trust, will be vindicated by the use subsequently made of them. The polemical aspect is sheer self-indulgence for which I offer apologies to those who want them.

15. I leave it to scholars better versed in ancient Greek thought than I to determine whether the use of the craftsmanship analogy about to be criticized is properly ascribed to Plato or to Socrates.

16. "We call that which is in itself worthy of pursuit more final than that which is worthy of pursuit for the sake of something else, and that which is never desirable for the sake of something else more final than the things that are desirable both in themselves and for the sake of that other thing, and therefore we call final without qualification that which is always desirable in itself and never for the sake of something else.

"Now such a thing happiness, above all else, is held to be; for this we choose always for itself and never for the sake of something else. . . ." *Nicomachean Ethics*, 1.1097a30–b1, trans. W. D. Ross.

17. Note that I understand intent as qualified by deliberation, some degree of thematic awareness or choice. I remain silent on the issue of such ascriptions of intent to nature as are latent in the family of concepts grouped under such headings as instinct, drive, conatus and associated with "unconscious" *tele* such as survival of the organism, the species or perpetuation of nature at large.

18. Miller interprets Aristotle as arguing on the basis of an analogy between natural justice and right-handedness. In this context, Miller raises the following questions.

> In what sense could Aristotle claim that natural justice is "superior" or "stronger," by analogy to right-handedness? And even if an analogy could be found, why suppose that it would support normative conclusions? Does the fact that the right hand is generally stronger than the left imply that it is better? (p. 288)

Miller tacitly acknowledges that Aristotle does infer the value of its superiority from the fact that the right hand is generally stronger.

The standpoint I am developing contends not so much that it is valid to infer values from facts, but that it is a mistake to separate the two in the first place. I do not think Aristotle made that mistake. I do think Aristotle made the mistake of conceiving natural entities as entelechies in a way that attributes to nonhuman aspects of nature the kind of deliberate intentions evident in human teleology. What I have been calling "the onto-theological fallacy" is a species of anthropomorphism.

Evan Simpson and Mark Williams, Reconstructing Rorty's Ethics: Styles, Languages, and Vocabularies of Moral Reflection

1. G.W.F. Hegel, *Phenomenology of Spirit*, trans. A.V. Miller (Oxford: Oxford University Press, 1977), §537. The conflict between the two appears at §445.

2. Ibid., §352.

3. Aristotle, *Nichomachean Ethics*, I, 5; I, 8; II, 1.

4. Richard Rorty, *Essays on Heidegger and Others* (Cambridge: Cambridge University Press, 1991), p. 155. Hereafter EHO.

5. Richard Rorty, *Contingency, Irony, and Solidarity* (Cambridge: Cambridge University Press, 1989), p. 141. Hereafter CIS.

6. Donald Davidson, "Myth of the Subjective," in *Relativism, Interpretation, and Confrontation*, Michael Krausz, ed. (Notre Dame: Notre Dame University Press, 1989), 165–66. Quoted in Richard Rorty, *Objectivity, Relativism, and Truth* (Cambridge: Cambridge University Press, 1991), 9. Hereafter ORT.

7. Jeffrey Stout, *Ethics After Babel: The Languages of Morals and Their Discontents* (Boston: Beacon, 1988), 294.

8. Michael Oakeshott, *Of Human Conduct* (Oxford: Oxford University Press, 1975), pp. 78–79.

9. See Gilbert Ryle, *The Concept of Mind* (London: Hutchinson & Co. Ltd., 1949), pp. 27ff.

10. Charles Taylor, "The Diversity of Goods," in *Anti-theory in Ethics and Moral Conservatism*, Stanley G. Clarke and Evan Simpson, eds. (New York: SUNY Press, 1989), p. 224. Hereafter DG.

11. Charles Taylor, "Rorty in the Epistemological Tradition," in *Reading Rorty*, ed. Alan Malachowski (Oxford: Basil Blackwell, 1990), p. 272.

12. Richard Rorty, "Taylor on Truth," in *Philosophy in the Age of Pluralism: The Philosophy of Charles Taylor in Question*, ed. James Tully (Cambridge: Cambridge University Press, 1994), p. 28. Hereafter TT.

13. Carol Gilligan, *In a Different Voice: Psychological Theory and Women's Development* (Cambridge, Mass.: Harvard University Press, 1982), pp. 24 ff.

14. Cf. Alasdair MacIntyre on the interminability of certain moral disagreements in *After Virtue: A Study in Moral Theory* (Notre Dame: University of Notre Dame Press, 1984), pp. 6ff. Hereafter AV.

15. Rorty here reveals an intellectual lineage connecting him with the descriptivist stream of linguistic moral philosophy. Cf. Philippa Foot's descriptivist objections to Richard Hare's prescriptivism late in the 1950's. Philippa Foot, *Virtues and Vices* (Berkeley: University of California Press, 1978), especially article VII, "Moral Arguments" (1958).

16. See "Freud and Moral Reflection," EHO, 143–63. For an interesting contrast between the engineer and the tinkerer or *bricoleur*, see Stout, EAB, 74 & 310n.16 and François Jacob, "Evolution and Tinkering," *Science*, vol. 196, no. 4295, June 1977.

17. On the characteristics of romanticism, liberalism, and their intersection see Nancy L. Rosenblum, *Another Liberalism* (Cambridge, Mass.: Harvard University Press, 1987), p. 2. Rorty's own view of the connection is expressed in CIS, pp. 88ff.

Paul Fairfield, Hermeneutical Ethical Theory

1. Jean-François Lyotard and Jean-Loup Thebaud, *Just Gaming*, trans. Wlad Godzich (Minneapolis: University of Minnesota Press, 1985), 17. Hereafter JG.

2. Richard Rorty, "Private Irony and Liberal Hope," in *Contingency, Irony, and Solidarity* (Cambridge: Cambridge University Press, 1989), 75. Hereafter CIS.

3. Rorty, "Solidarity or Objectivity?" in *Objectivity, Relativism, and Truth* (Cambridge: Cambridge University Press, 1991), 30. Hereafter ORT.

4. Such appeals, for instance, succeed in bringing together moral evaluations with our mode of self-understanding. Human beings do not form evaluative judgments in isolation from a certain understanding of who they are and wish to be. Questions of the good, for example, are answered in light of who we take ourselves to be, how we narrate our past, what we wish to become, and so forth.

5. As Rorty puts it: "The pragmatists' justification of toleration, free inquiry, and the quest for undistorted communication can only take the form of a comparison between societies which exemplify these habits and those which do not, leading up to the suggestion that nobody who has experienced both would prefer the latter. It is exemplified by Winston Churchill's defense of democracy as the worst form of government imaginable, except for all the others which have been tried so far. Such justification is not by reference to a criterion, but by reference to various detailed practical advantages. It is circular only in that the terms of praise used to describe liberal societies will be drawn from the vocabulary of the liberal societies themselves. Such praise has to be in *some* vocabulary, after all, and the terms of praise current in primitive or theocratic or totalitarian societies will not produce the desired result. So the pragmatist admits that he has no ahistorical standpoint from which to endorse the habits of modern democracies he wishes to praise" ("Solidarity or Objectivity?," ORT 29).

6. See especially P. Christopher Smith, *Hermeneutics and Human Finitude: Toward a Theory of Ethical Understanding* (New York: Fordham University Press, 1991); Matthew Foster, *Gadamer and Practical Philosophy: The Hermeneutics of Moral*

Confidence (Atlanta: Scholars Press, 1991); and Georgia Warnke, *Justice and Interpretation* (Cambridge: The MIT Press, 1993; hereafter JI).

7. In JI, Warnke takes her inspiration not only from Gadamer's hermeneutics but also from the political thought of Michael Walzer, Alasdair MacIntyre, and John Rawls, among others.

8. As Smith expresses it: "our sense of what is right and wrong, good and bad, fair and disgraceful, is transmitted to us in the language we have inherited, and that language, sustained as it is by the inexplicit customs we are accustomed to, capacitates us to deliberate well and make ethical choices" (*Hermeneutics and Human Finitude*, xvi).

9. The following observation is also made by Richard Bernstein in "From Hermeneutics to Praxis" in *Hermeneutics and Praxis*, ed. Robert Hollinger (Notre Dame: University of Notre Dame Press, 1985), 285–87.

10. This may be seen from a statement of Gadamer's made in reply to Habermas's critique of *Truth and Method*. In the context of this debate, Gadamer writes: "Tradition is no proof and validation of something, in any case not where validation is demanded by reflection. But the point is this: where does reflection demand it? Everywhere? I would object to such an answer on the grounds of the finitude of human existence and the essential particularity of reflection" (Hans-Georg Gadamer, "On the Scope and Function of Hermeneutical Reflection," in *Philosophical Hermeneutics*, ed. David E. Linge, trans. G. B. Hess and R. E. Palmer [Berkeley: University of California Press, 1976], 34). At issue at this point in the debate between Gadamer and Habermas is the question of whether the claims that tradition makes upon us always require philosophical justification. Gadamer's negative response is based largely upon his thesis concerning the finitude and situatedness of reflection. Yet Gadamer acknowledges in this reply to Habermas that there undoubtedly are cases in which pointing out the customary nature of a moral belief does not suffice as a justification. Regrettably, Gadamer does not go on to address the questions that this inevitably raises—namely, when is it necessary to seek a philosophical justification for traditional moral beliefs, and what form will such justification take?

11. Our commitment to the tradition of liberal politics, to take one example, may produce within us a certain self-understanding and set of beliefs (pertaining to the importance of liberty, personal autonomy, self-interest, and so on) which are not easily reconcilable with the tradition of Christian theology.

12. It is interesting to note that since the time of their debate, Gadamer and Habermas have both taken an increasing interest in ethical questions. Albeit in sharply different ways, both have defended a notion of communicative rationality and pointed out the need for unconstrained dialogue in matters of public policy. While nothing resembling a consensus has emerged between these two thinkers, what follows may indicate a direction in which a partial convergence could be found within moral philosophy.

13. Hermeneutics is an example of a theory of this kind. It attempts to gain a reflective awareness of the practice of interpretive understanding, of its conditions of possibility, its limits, etc. As Gadamer expresses it: "Hermeneutics

has to do with a theoretical attitude toward the practice of interpretation, the interpretation of texts, but also in relation to the experiences interpreted in them and in our communicatively unfolded orientations in the world. This theoretic stance only makes us aware reflectively of what is performatively at play in the practical experience of understanding." (Gadamer, "Hermeneutics as Practical Philosophy," in *Reason in the Age of Science*, trans. Frederick G. Lawrence [Cambridge, Mass.: MIT Press, 1981], 112)

14. To illustrate this point, using the same example as above: hermeneutical theory may be useful not only for gaining an understanding of what is involved in the practice of interpretation, but also for redirecting its course through the introduction of critical principles. Phenomenological analysis of the conditions of the possibility of understanding may be supplemented with procedures or principles (such as the hermeneutic circle and the principle of coherence) which are useful in determining when our interpretive efforts have been successful. Principles of this kind make it possible (within limits) to adjudicate interpretive conflicts, to decide which reading of a text is most successful in disclosing its meaning, and which interpretations ought to be rejected. While no amount of theorizing is going to produce a step by step procedure for the reading of texts, hermeneutical theory may uncover principles which are already prereflectively at play in interpretation, and thematizing these may serve to redirect the course of interpretation and in many cases to challenge standard readings.

15. Of course, human understanding—including that which is of a theoretical kind—never achieves completeness or finality, but remains a partial disclosure of the phenomena. The aim of gaining a theoretical understanding is not to comprehend the totality of our practices—something that necessarily presupposes an impossible "external" perspective—but to form a description of a practice which is as detailed and penetrating as is possible within the limits of human understanding.

16. Alasdair MacIntyre, *After Virtue: A Study in Moral Theory* (Notre Dame: University of Notre Dame Press, 1984), 187–89.

17. The teleological structure of practices may be seen with a few examples. The practice of a competitive sport such as hockey aims at achieving such internal goods as fair competition, teamwork, and sportsmanship. Political activities such as running for public office or organizing political parties are oriented in principle to the realization of just social arrangements and the public good, however these be construed. The practice of teaching aims at imparting knowledge, educating the critical capacity of students, and related ends. No doubt, not all agents who participate in a practice are motivated, in point of fact, solely or even primarily toward the realization of these internal goods. As MacIntyre has pointed out, individuals frequently engage in a practice for the sake of attaining external goods such as money, power, or some other personal desire. The point that deserves emphasis, however, is that the practice itself—if not all the agents who participate in it—remains oriented toward specific ends the realization of which is the *raison d'être* of that practice. The individual actions, rules, and constraints that constitute a practice are strictly subordinate to these

ends, as is evidenced, for example, when the rules of a game or methods of academic instruction are modified so as to better bring about these specific goods, or when political procedures are reformed as a means of better representing the public interest. Reforms of this kind are properly undertaken for reasons arising from a practice's teleological structure—in order to better ensure the realization of the ends that belong to the practice in question.

18. In addition to actions of this kind, of course, is the entire range of human conduct that lies outside the domain of social practices—the various instrumental actions which individuals undertake in the pursuit of their interests. The entire domain of human interaction is subject to moral constraints, and in particular to constraints arising from justice considerations.

19. Gadamer, *Truth and Method*, second revised edition, trans. Joel Weinsheimer and Donald G. Marshall (New York: Crossroad, 1989), 378. Hereafter TM.

20. Gadamer, "Man and Language," in *Philosophical Hermeneutics*, 59.

21. David Ingram, "Hermeneutics and Truth," in *Hermeneutics and Praxis*, ed. Robert Hollinger, 45.

22. Gadamer's analysis of hermeneutic experience and the I-Thou relation takes its bearings from Hegel's dialectic of lordship and bondage. The themes of recognition and alterity have their historical roots here, and it is in light of Hegel's dialectic that the teleological and normative dimension of hermeneutic experience is best understood. What Gadamer views as an implicit orientation inherent to the communicative process, Hegel presents in the form of a resolution in the struggle between lord and bondsman. In the narrative Hegel recounts, consciousness of self emerges only in the "life and death struggle" between contesting subjects, each of whom comes to realize that in order for the I to be conscious of itself it must receive confirmation from the other—that consciousness of self cannot exist in the absence of recognition from another.

23. Jürgen Habermas, *Moral Consciousness and Communicative Action*, trans. Christian Lenhardt and Shierry Nicholsen (Cambridge, Mass.: The MIT Press, 1990), 197–98.

24. It is important to note that the principles that communicative ethics generates are not imposed upon the practice of argumentation from without, but are always already operative (albeit prereflectively) in its performance. It is these principles that make communicative action the kind of practice that it is, in the sense that were they not operative in our various acts of speaking and listening, such acts would not belong to this practice. Rather, they would be categorized either as strategic actions or as belonging to a different practice.

25. Gary B. Madison argues along these lines in *The Logic of Liberty*. He writes: "By the very fact that people engage in discussion, they commit themselves to the principle that this is the way social issues should be resolved. That is, it is logically impossible for them, as discussants, to deny this principle. Thus, to the degree that a person engages in discussion (abstaining, by that very fact, from the use of force), he is, whether he likes it or not, affirming a fundamental, universal norm, one on which the whole liberal philosophy depends." Gary B.

Madison, *The Logic of Liberty* (Westport, Conn.: Greenwood Press, 1986), 266–67. Paul Ricoeur expresses a similar view in speaking of discourse and violence as "the two opposite poles of human existence": "Violence is always the interruption of discourse: discourse is always the interruption of violence. A violence that speaks is already a violence that is trying to be in the right, that is exposing itself to the gravitational pull of Reason and already beginning to renegue on its own character as violence. The prime example of this is that the 'tyrant' always tries to get discourse on his side. The tyrant, for Plato, is the opposite of the philosopher, the man of rational discourse. But in order to succeed tyranny has to seduce, persuade, flatter; it has never been the dumb exercise of brute force. Tyranny only puts itself across to the public by perverting language. The tyrant prefers the sophist's services to the executioner's; he needs the sophist to find words and phrases that stir up hatred and involve others ineluctably as accomplices in his crime." Paul Ricoeur, *Main Trends in Philosophy* (New York: Holmes and Meier Publishers, 1979), 226.

26. John Stuart Mill, *On Liberty* (New York: W. W. Norton and Co., 1975), 7.

Thomas W. Busch, Phenomenology and Communicative Ethics: Husserl, Sartre, and Merleau-Ponty

1. Edmund Husserl, "Philosophy as Strict Science," trans. Quentin Lauer, in *Edmund Husserl: Phenomenology and the Crisis of Philosophy*, ed. Quentin Lauer (New York: Harper Torchbooks, 1965). Hereafter PRS.

2. Edmund Husserl, *The Crisis of European Sciences and Transcendental Phenomenology*, trans. David Carr (Evanston, Ill.: Northwestern University Press, 1970). This collection includes "The Vienna Lecture" and "The Origin of Geometry." Hereafter C.

3. Jean-Paul Sartre, *The Transcendence of the Ego: An Existentialist Theory of Consciousness*, trans. Williams and Kirkpatrick (New York: Noonday, 1957).

4. Jean-Paul Sartre, *Being and Nothingness*, trans. Hazel Barnes (New York: Philosophical Library, 1956).

5. Jean-Paul Sartre, *What Is Literature?*, trans. Bernard Frechtman (New York: Harper Colophon, 1965).

6. In his later works, such as *Search For a Method* (1957), Sartre began to reconsider the sharp dichotomies of his early thought. Cf. Thomas W. Busch, *The Power of Consciousness and the Force of Circumstances in Sartre's Philosophy* (Bloomington: Indiana University Press, 1990).

7. Maurice Merleau-Ponty, *The Prose of the World*, ed. Claude Lefort, trans. John O'Neill (Evanston, Ill.: Northwestern University Press, 1973). See Lefort's Preface for his comments and references to Merleau-Ponty's unpublished commentary on *What Is Literature?*.

8. Maurice Merleau-Ponty, *Signs*, trans. Richard McCleary (Evanston, Ill.: Northwestern University Press, 1964). Hereafter S. In addition to "Indirect Language and the Voices of Silence," the relevant essays are "On the Phenomenology

of Language," "The Philosopher and Sociology," "From Mauss to Claude Levi-Strauss," "Everywhere and Nowhere," "The Philosopher and His Shadow."

9. Maurice Merleau-Ponty, *Phenomenology of Perception*, trans. Colin Smith (New York: Humanities Press, 1962). Cf. the chapters "The Body as Expression and Speech" and "The Cogito."

10. Maurice Merleau-Ponty, *Themes from the Lectures at the College de France 1952–1960*, trans. John O'Neill (Evanston, Ill.: Northwestern University Press, 1970), pp. 40–41.

11. Jean-Paul Sartre, *Life/Situations: Essays Written and Spoken*, trans. Paul Auster and Lydia Davis (New York: Pantheon Books, 1977), pp. 11, 13.

12. Maurice Merleau-Ponty, *Adventures of the Dialectic*, trans. Joseph Bien (Evanston, Ill.: Northwestern University Press, 1973), p. 216.

G. B. Madison, The Ethics and Politics of the Flesh

1. Merleau-Ponty, "An Unpublished Text," in *The Primacy of Perception*, ed. James M. Edie (Evanston, Ill.: Northwestern University Press, 1964), p. 11. Hereafter P.

2. Merleau-Ponty, *The Visible and the Invisible*, trans. Alphonso Lingis (Evanston, Ill.: Northwestern University Press, 1968), p. 165. Hereafter VI.

3. As, for instance, Joseph Margolis has accused me, both publicly and privately, of doing. For a public statement of his in this regard, see his "Merleau-Ponty and Postmodernism" in Thomas W. Busch and Shaun Gallagher, eds., *Merleau-Ponty, Hermeneutics, and Postmodernism* (Albany: State University of New York Press, 1992). This article amounts to a sustained (albeit fairly friendly) critique of what Margolis refers to as "Madison's oddly clever reading of Merleau-Ponty's texts" (p. 249).

4. As I suggested in my "Merleau-Ponty in Retrospect" in Patrick Burke and Jan Van Der Veken, eds., *Merleau-Ponty in Contemporary Perspective* (Dordrecht: Kluwer Academic, 1993).

5. For more on this, see my "Flesh As Otherness" in Galen A. Johnson and Michael B. Smith, eds., *Ontology and Alterity in Merleau-Ponty* (Evanston, Ill.: Northwestern University Press, 1990).

6. David Michael Levin, *The Listening Self: Personal Growth, Social Change and the Closure of Metaphysics* (London: Routledge, 1989), p. 164. On the following page Levin writes: "Reversibility teaches us the root meaning of reciprocity. . . . Stating this point in a formulation for which I shall argue in the next section of this chapter, I want to say that reversibility *schematizes* reciprocity. It is a corporeal schema encoded in the flesh, an implicit order that anticipates, calls for, and is carried forward to completion by, the achievement of reciprocity in social and political life."

7. Merleau-Ponty, *Signs*, trans. Richard C. McCleary (Evanston, Ill.: Northwestern University Press, 1964), p. 17. Hereafter S.

8. For a more detailed treatment of these issues, see my "Being and Speaking," forthcoming in Jon Stewart, ed., *Beyond the Symbol Model* (SUNY Press), as

well as my "Merleau-Ponty and Derrida: La différance 5," forthcoming in M. C. Dillon, *Écart and Differance: Merleau-Ponty and Derrida on Seeing and Writing*.

9. Despite the interest he developed in Saussurian linguistics subsequent to the *Phenomenology of Perception*, this is a position Merleau-Ponty retained to the end. In the Introduction to *Signs* he declared: "To make of language a means or a code for thought is to break it. When we do so we prohibit ourselves from understanding the depth to which words sound without us—from understanding that we have a need, a passion for speaking" (p. 17).

10. Thomas W. Busch, "Ethics and Ontology: Levinas and Merleau-Ponty," paper presented at the sixteenth annual meeting of the Merleau-Ponty Circle, University of Colorado at Colorado Springs, September 1991.

11. Merleau-Ponty, *Phenomenology of Perception*, trans. Colin Smith (London: Routledge and Kegan Paul, 1962), p. 354.

12. This means that dialogical understanding is essentially *transformative* in nature. Like Gadamer, Merleau-Ponty maintained that a genuinely dialogical exchange with the other always involves a transformation of the self, "of myself and of the other as well" (see Merleau-Ponty, *The Prose of the World*, trans. John O'Neill [Evanston, Ill.: Northwestern University Press, 1973], p. 142).

13. See, for instance, Merleau-Ponty, *Sense and Non-Sense*, trans. Hubert L. Dreyfus and Patricia Allen Dreyfus (Evanston, Ill.: Northwestern University Press, 1964), p. 95. Hereafter SNS. In his *Merleau-Ponty and the Foundation of an Existential Politics* (Princeton, N.J.: Princeton University Press, 1988) Kerry Whiteside states: "Reason is the outcome, not the presupposition, of the discursive processes that are binding together ever larger segments of mankind" (p. 99).

14. It follows that an important way in which Merleau-Ponty's notion of communicative rationality differs from that of Habermas is that it is nowise subordinate to the notion of *consensus*. Habermas's guiding notion of consensus betrays the metaphysical background of much of his thought, and it has the unfortunate result of conceptualizing the communicative process in terms of certain ideal end-states, rather than in terms of the always-open and never-ending *process* that it is. Moreover, the democratic politics which, as we shall be seeing, follows from Merleau-Ponty's notion of communicative rationality is not, it may be noted here, what is commonly referred to as "democracy by consensus." Upheld as an ideal in, for instance, Africa, consensual democracy appealed to an idealized past and presupposed an impossible social harmony; in reality, it was a formula for a most undesirable state of affairs: the tyranny of ideology and one-party rule (wherein the idea of human rights was without substance). Merleau-Ponty's democratic politics was, instead, of a pluralist sort and conformed to what is generally referred to as liberal democracy: majoritarian rule combined with a respect for the rights of minorities.

15. I borrow this term from Calvin O. Schrag; see his *The Resources of Rationality: A Response to the Postmodern Challenge* (Bloomington: Indiana University Press, 1992).

16. See *The Visible and the Invisible*, p. 104. In the preface to *Signs* Merleau-Ponty says that others are "my twins or the flesh of my flesh" (p. 15). I agree

with Michael Yeo when he remarks on how in his estimation Merleau-Ponty would reject Levinas's view of the relation to the Other "as being too mystical; as presupposing an undialectical notion of transcendence" (Michael Yeo, "Perceiving/Reading the Other: Ethical Dimensions," in Busch and Gallagher, *Merleau-Ponty, Hermeneutics, and Postmodernism*, p. 50, n. 12).

17. For a delineation of some of the main features of hermeneutical ethics, see my "Hermeneutics: Gadamer and Ricoeur" in Richard Kearney, ed., *Twentieth-Century Continental Philosophy* (*Routledge History of Philosophy*, vol. 8) (London: Routledge, 1994), ch. 9.

18. Richard J. Bernstein, *The New Constellation: The Ethical-Political Horizons of Modernity/Postmodernity* (Oxford: Polity Press, 1991), p. 303.

19. Merleau-Ponty, "The Experience of Others," trans. Hugh J. Silverman and Fred Evans, *Review of Existential Psychology and Psychiatry* 18, nos. 1, 2, 3, p. 577.

20. Jean-Paul Sartre, *L'existentialisme est un humanisme* (Paris: Nagel, 1964), p. 83.

21. See in this regard Merleau-Ponty's lengthy footnote on "historical materialism" in the *Phenomenology of Perception*, pp. 171–73, as well as his extremely convoluted argument in *Humanism and Terror: An Essay on the Communist Problem*, trans. John O'Neill (Boston: Beacon Press, 1969).

22. On the "postrevolutionism" stance taken by Merleau-Ponty in his political thinking and for a comparison of his politics with the politics of the "philosophers of '68," see my "Merleau-Ponty Alive," *Man and World* 26 (1993): 19–44.

23. For a representative sampling of Lefort's work in this area, see his *The Political Forms of Modern Society: Bureaucracy, Democracy, Totalitarianism*, ed. John B. Thompson (Cambridge, Mass.: MIT Press, 1986).

24. As Camus had argued already in his *L'homme revolté* (1951). A like assessment has been made more recently by an "insider," Alexander Yokovlev, one of Gorbachev's chief collaborators who had been in charge of marxist ideology and propaganda. As Alexander Tsipko states in his foreword to Yokovlev's *The Fate of Marxism in Russia* (New Haven, Conn.: Yale University Press, 1993), by the late 1980s it had become clear to Yakovlev that "Marxism conflicted with universal human morality" and that "the amorality of Marxism . . . appeals to hatred, envy, and malice" (see pp. xvii, xx). On p. 29 Yakovlev remarks: "Virtually all Marxist social doctrine, above all its teaching concerning the dictatorship of the proletariat and the expropriation of the expropriators, is aimed against universal human morality as the ethical basis of civil society."

25. See Vaclav Havel, "The End of the Modern Era," *New York Times*, March 1, 1992 (Op-Ed section).

26. See Luc Ferry and Alain Renaut, *French Philosophy of the Sixties: An Essay on Antihumanism*, trans. Mary H.S. Cattani (Amherst: University of Massachusetts Press, 1990).

27. This was a point I tried to make in my "Merleau-Ponty Alive," originally presented as a paper in Dubrovnik, Yugoslavia (as it was then called), in 1991.

28. See Merleau-Ponty, *Les aventures de la dialectique* (Paris: Gallimard, 1955), pp. 269, 299.

29. Merleau-Ponty, *Texts and Dialogues*, ed. Hugh J. Silverman and James Barry, Jr., trans. Michael B. Smith et al. (Atlantic Highlands, N.J.: Humanities Press, 1992), p. 28. Hereafter TD.

30. "Conversation," it will be recalled, is the key term in Gadamer's hermeneutical ethics of communicative rationality.

31. See Diane P. Michelfelder and Richard E. Palmer, *Dialogue and Deconstruction: The Gadamer-Derrida Encounter* (Albany: SUNY Press, 1989).

Morny Joy, Metaphor and Metamorphic: Luce Irigaray and an Erotics of Ethics and Hermeneutics

1. This term was first indicated in the work of Paul Ricoeur in *Freud and Philosophy: An Essay on Interpretation* (New Haven: Yale University Press, 1970), pp. 32–36. Here Ricoeur referred to Nietzsche, Marx, and Freud as the "masters of suspicion." By this term Ricoeur wished to indicate that these thinkers alerted us to the possibility that we may not be fully in control, because of external or unconscious influences of what we say or do. Feminist thinkers, particularly those within religious studies, have adapted this process of critique to indicate feminist suspicion of all structures and texts that have or continue to be biased against women. Mary Ann Tobert, "Defining the Problem: The Bible and Feminist Hermeneutics," in *Semeia* 28, *The Bible and Feminist Hermeneutics* (Chico, CA: Scholars Press, 1983), pp. 113–26. From a critical theory perspective, Sheila Briggs has a negative assessment of even this form of hermeneutics, seeing it merely as a reinscription of past hegemonic tendencies unless it is aware of social practices of oppression embedded in all cultural constructions. See "The Politics of Identity and the Politics of Interpretation," in *Ad Feminam, Union Seminary Quarterly Review*, Fiftieth Anniversary Volume, vol. 43, nos. 1–4 (1986): 163–80.

2. See Jacques Derrida, "White Mythology," *Margins of Philosophy*, trans. Alan Bass (Chicago: University of Chicago Press, 1982). Lacan's principal exegesis of this model occurs in his dense essay "The Agency of the Letter in the Unconscious or Reason since Freud." For an exposition of his procedures, see "The Mechanisms of the Formations of the Unconscious. Displacement and Condensation or Metonymy and Metaphor," chapter 17 in Anika Lemaire, *Jacques Lacan*, trans. David Macey (London: Routledge & Kegan Paul, 1970).

3. Luce Irigaray, *An Ethics of Sexual Difference*, trans. C. Burke and G. C. Gill (Ithaca: Cornell University Press, 1993). Hereafter ESD. Published originally in French as *Ethique de la différence sexuelle* (Paris: Minuit, 1983). *I Love to You: Sketch for a Felicity within History*, trans. Alison Martin (New York: Routledge, 1996). Hereafter ILY. Published originally in French as *J'aime à toi* (Paris: Grasset, 1992).

4. Luce Irigaray, *Speculum of the Other Woman*, trans. G. C. Gill (Ithaca: Cornell University Press, 1985). Hereafter SW. Originally published in French as *Speculum de l'autre femme* (Paris: Minuit, 1974). *This Sex Which is Not One*, trans. C. Porter with C. Burke (Ithaca: Cornell University Press, 1985). Hereafter TS. Originally published in French as *Ce Sexe qui n'en est pas un* (Paris: Minuit, 1977).

5. Elizabeth Grosz, *Sexual Subversions: Three French Feminists* (Sydney: Allen & Unwin, 1989), p. 182.

6. Hans-Georg Gadamer, *Truth and Method* (New York: Seabury, 1979), pp. 95–96. Hereafter TM.

7. Hans-Georg Gadamer, "Man and Language," *Philosophical Hermeneutics*, trans. D. E. Linge (Berkeley: University of California Press), p. 66.

8. The question of truth in hermeneutics is a much debated one, but suffice it to say for the purposes of this essay that it draws its primary force of meaning (though modified by subsequent variations in the work of Gadamer and Ricoeur) from Heidegger's notion of *alethia*. See Martin Heidegger, *Being and Time*, trans. John Macquarie and Edward Robinson (New York: Harper & Row, 1962), pp. 56–57. See also David Ingram, "Hermeneutics and Truth," in *Hermeneutics and Praxis*, ed. Robert Hollinger (Notre Dame: University of Notre Dame Press, 1985), pp. 32–53.

9. For Gadamer's development of the idea of situatedness, particularly with respect to the notion of historicality (*wirkungeschictliches Bewüsstein*), see *Truth and Method*, pp. 267–74.

10. Jürgen Habermas, "A Review of Gadamer's *Truth and Method*," in *Understanding and Social Inquiry*, ed. F. Dallmayr and T. McCarthy (Notre Dame: University of Notre Dame Press, 1977), pp. 335–63.

11. Georgia Warnke, *Gadamer: Hermeneutics, Tradition, and Reason*, (Stanford: Stanford University Press, 1987), p. 112.

12. As noted, Ricoeur introduced this term. It is this type of analysis that Ricoeur proposes as an answer to Habermas's critical evaluation of Gadamer's appeal to tradition. See "Ethics and Culture: Habermas and Gadamer in Dialogue," *Philosophy Today* 17, nos. 2–4 (1973).

13. Luce Irigaray, "A Chance to Live," in *Thinking the Difference: For a Peaceful Revolution*, trans. K. Montin (New York: Routledge, 1994), pp. 3–35. Published originally in French as *Le Temps de la Différence: Pour une révolution pacifique* (Paris: Librairie Générale Française, 1989).

14. It should be noted that in the French, the term used is *poiesis*, from the Greek notion of an aesthetic creative creativity. Both Ricoeur and Gadamer understand their work in hermeneutics as having a special relation with a poetics that is, in turn, engaged critically with Heidegger's notion of "poetic thinking." See the interview with Paul Ricoeur "Poetry and Possibility," *A Ricoeur Reader: Reflection and Imagination*, ed. Mario Valdés (Toronto: University of Toronto Press, 1991), pp. 448–62 (hereafter RR), and Paul Ricoeur, *The Rule of Metaphor: Multidisciplinary Studies of the Creation of Meaning in Language*, trans. R. Czerny et al. (Toronto: University of Toronto Press, 1977), pp. 305–13 (hereafter RM); Hans-Georg Gadamer, "Philosophy and Poetry," trans. Nicholas Walker, in *The Relevance of the Beautiful and Other Essays*, ed. Robert Bernasconi, (Cambridge: Cambridge University Press, 1986).

15. Ricoeur makes reference to the phrase used by Heidegger in discussing the role of imagination. "Recall how Heidegger conjoins understanding to the notion of 'the projection of my ownmost possibilities'; this signifies that the mode

of being of the world opened up by the text is the mode of the possible, or better of the power-to-be: therein resides the subversive force of the imaginary." See "Hermeneutics and the Critique of Ideology," *Paul Ricoeur: Hermeneutics and the Human Sciences*, ed. and trans. by John B. Thompson (Cambridge: Cambridge University Press, 1981), p. 93.

16. For Irigaray's encounter with Heidegger see *L'Oubli de l'air: Chez Martin Heidegger* (Paris: Minuit, 1983). For Merleau-Ponty, see "The Invisible of the Flesh: A Reading of Merleau-Ponty, *The Visible and the Invisible*, 'The Intertwining—The Chiasm,' " in *An Ethics of Sexual Difference*, pp. 151–84.

17. Margaret Whitford, *Luce Irigaray: Philosophy in the Feminine* (New York: Routledge, 1991), p. 24. Hereafter PF.

18. Irigaray, "The Three Genders," in *Sexes and Genealogies*, trans. G. C. Gill (New York: Columbia University Press, 1993), p. 178. Hereafter SG. Published originally in French as *Sexes et Parentés* (Paris: Minuit), 1987.

19. See especially chapter 6, "Derrida, Irigaray, and Feminism," in Tina Chanter, *Ethics of Eros: Irigaray's Rewriting of the Philosophers* (New York: Routledge, 1995), pp. 225–54.

20. See Derrida, "White Mythology," pp. 209–13. For a preliminary attempt to distinguish between Derrida and Ricoeur's appreciation of metaphor, see Morny Joy, "Derrida and Ricoeur: A Case of Mistaken Identity and Difference," *Journal of Religion* 68, no. 4 (September 1988): 508–26.

21. Within Lacan's own psychoanalytic model, the imaginary is associated with the pre-oedipal phase, though Lacan qualifies Freud's outline with the ingenious extrapolation of the mirror stage to describe the process of primary narcissism.

22. Basically, the child's view of itself in a mirror (which can also be the mother's gaze) activates a process that is at once physiological, psychological, and linguistic, that marks the emergence of a separate ego. This can only happen with the concomitant repression of all things maternal. Yet, for Lacan, the identity so formed is never autonomous. And though there are many intricate aspects involved that are determinate for the later social and sexual behavior of this split-subject, perhaps the most crucial is its dependence on others for confirmation, approval, satisfaction. See Elizabeth Grosz, *Jacques Lacan: A Feminist Introduction*, pp. 39–41.

As Grosz further observes: "The ego sees itself in its relations with others. Its fascination with specular reflections will forever orient it in an imaginary direction. Imaginary identification, the identifications of self with the other and other with self, vary widely, ranging from the so-called 'normal' attitude of falling in love to psychoses. The imaginary is the order of identification with images" (p. 43).

Though in time replaced by the symbolic order by which Lacan implies the cultural/social matrix with its rules and regulations and its linguistic signifi-cations, the imaginary and its emotional residue will continue to surface during a lifetime in dreams and other symptomatic creations/delusions.

23. Ricoeur, "The Function of Fiction in Shaping Reality," in RR, pp. 118–23; *The Rule of Metaphor: Multidisciplinary Studies in the Creation of Meaning in Language*,

trans. R. Czerny et al. (Toronto: University of Toronto Press, 1981), pp. 214–15; "The Creativity of Language," RR, p. 470; "Imagination in Discourse and Action," in *From Text to Action: Essays in Hermeneutics* II, trans. K. Blamey and J. B. Thompson (Evanston: Northwestern University Press, 1991), pp. 168–87. Hereafter FTA.

24. Drucilla Cornell, *Beyond Accommodation: Ethical Feminism, Deconstruction and the Law*, (New York: Routledge, 1991).

25. Gary Madison, "The Philosophic Centrality of the Imagination," in *The Hermeneutics of Postmodernity* (Bloomington: Indiana University Press, 1988), pp. 190–91.

26. Ann Rosalind Jones, "Inscribing Femininity: French Theories of the Feminine," in *Making a Difference: Feminist Literary Criticism*, eds. G. Greene and C. Kahn (New York: Methuen, 1985), pp. 80–112; Toril Moi, *Sexual/Textual Politics: Feminist Literary Theory* (London: Methuen, 1985), pp. 143–49; Grosz, *Sexual Subversions*, p. 113; Whitford, *Luce Irigaray*, pp. 126–40.

27. David Macey, *Lacan in Contexts* (London: Verso, 1988), p. 157. It needs to be noted, however, that Macey does not allow for the development of Lacan's thought, specifically as delinated by Elisabeth Roudinesco, *Lacan & Co.: A History of Psychoanalysis in France, 1925–1985*, trans. Jeffrey Mehlman (Chicago: University of Chicago Press, 1991), pp. 297–307. She demonstrates that in Lacan's work pre-1953, he was reading Freud in conjunction with Saussure, Lévi-Strauss, and Heidegger. During the period 1953–63, the influence of Jakobson predominated. Such diversity of influences would account for a certain inconsistency as Lacan crystallized his theories.

28. Kaja Silverman, *The Subject of Semiotics* (New York: Oxford University Press, 1983), pp. 99–100.

29. Ideally, however, in this complex scheme of linguistic/psychic representation, the two formulas should work in tandem. "If the metaphoric process generates the signified from the chain of signifiers, and the metonymic process ensures that each signifier has multiple connections and associations which relate it always to other signifiers and thus give it meaning, then it becomes clear these two processes must work hand in hand." Grosz, *Jacques Lacan*, p. 103. That is, although every metaphor involves an imposition of closure on the signifying process, every metonymic displacement in turn depends for its impetus on the meanings that are sustained by metaphoric this substitution.

30. There are various accounts as to why this occurs; David Macey gives as plausible an account as any as to the reasons for this development: "Lacan's linguistics constantly drifts into *linguisterie* and he often refers to privileged signifiers, thus contradicting the basic tenet that a signifier is defined solely by the differences that mark it out from other signifiers. It is difference alone which allows a signifier to signify; in and of itself, it signifies nothing. Yet the phallus is a 'privileged signifier,' or even the 'signifier of signifiers.'" Macey, p. 191. The phallus, as a "neutral term," supposedly functions as a signifier of two different but related phenomena that are part of the resolution of the Oedipus complex (or access to the symbolic world of the societal contract, as Lacan refined Freud's original description). On the one hand, it signifies all that has had to be

renounced or repressed as part of the acquisition of linguistic competence and subjectivity (another Lacanian formulation for resolving the Oedipal conflict). The principal object of this repression is the mother, who has to be renounced because of her lack of phallus, and thus of inadequate "equipment" to facilitate her son's progress. At the same time, the phallus also signifies for Lacan those appropriate "positive" prerogatives that pertain to the symbolic order. Hence, it is irrevocably masculine in both its connotations. Kaja Silverman describes this duplicitous state of affairs tellingly in *The Subject of Semiotics*, pp. 184–89.

31. There is considerable debate on this issue, with certain feminist theorists defending and refusing to support this interpretation. Elizabeth Grosz gives a good overview of the debate in *Jacques Lacan* pp. 183–97.

32. Diana Fuss, *Essentially Speaking* (New York: Routledge, 1990), p. 66.

33. Domna Stanton finds fault with what she terms Irigaray's use of the maternal metaphor. She then declares that, though she puts metonymy (after Lacan) into question, she believes that metonymy "would favor more concrete, contextual inscriptions of differences within/among women" (p. 175). But it would seem her analysis still accepts the Lacanian model with its false binarism. See Stanton: "Difference on Trial: A Critique of the Maternal Metaphor in Cixous, Irigaray, and Kristeva," in *The Poetics of Gender*, ed. Nancy K. Miller (New York: Columbia University Press, 1986), pp. 157–82.

34. See Derrida, "White Mythology," pp. 219–29.

35. Ricoeur's own discussion of Jakobson and de Saussure and of metonymy and metaphor takes place in chapter 6, "The Work of Resemblance," *The Rule of Metaphor*, pp. 173–215. His conclusions are quite different. He expands the split reference of Jakobson to have both semantic and ontological effects. Such a development enables him to explore an innovative dimension in metaphor which does not occur in Lacan.

36. Drucilla Cornell, *Transformations* (New York: Routledge, 1993), pp. 133–34.

37. Cornell, *Beyond Accommodation*, p. 171. This "surplus of meaning," of multiple, even conflictual implications generated by metaphor, is also exploited by Kelly Oliver in her juxtaposition of Irigaray's and Kristeva's criticisms of Lacan's paternal metaphor. She especially invokes Kristeva's view of metaphor where, as distinct from Lacan's, and similarly (though subsequent) to Ricoeur's exposition, "the power in metaphoric transference is that the metaphoric 'is' always necessarily wears its 'is not' on the surface and thereby shows the disruption of semiotic drive force into language." Oliver, *Womanizing Nietzsche* (New York: Routledge, 1995), p. 175. Oliver shows that for Kristeva, "metaphor negotiates between need and demand, but not as desire—the gap between them posited by Lacan. Rather, metaphor transports bodily needs or drives into demand and thereby begins to fill the gap. . . . Kristeva proposes a metaphoric transference that is a non–object-oriented identification which allows drives to enter subjectivity, desire and language. . . . This primary identification with a loving other precedes Lacan's inaccessible Other of desire. . . . In *Tales of Love* [New York: Columbia, 1987] Kristeva claims that behind Lacan's metonymy of desire is a metaphor of love"

(pp. 173–74). Thus behind/before the phallic view of metaphor as substitution is a maternal metaphor of love which does not lead to constant displacement of desire (as in Lacan), but introduces a new economy of fulfillment rather than lack.

38. I appreciate that these terms are somewhat intricate as they pertain to hermeneutics. This discovery/creation mode is treated in different ways by both Gadamer and Ricoeur. Gadamer's use of the term "recognition" in this connection has distinct Platonic overtones. Ricoeur's initial use of the phrase "redescription of reality" has been refined in his more recent works with the nuanced phases of mimesis 1, 2, and 2. Mimesis 3, with its implications of not just appropriation of a new way of seeing things, but a distinct change in behavior (because of the discovery of new possibilities of being), is the aspect that has much in common with Irigaray's creation of a new ethical worldview. In all of this discussion, the status of the ontological is crucial and needs further elaboration than undertaken in this essay. For a preliminary study which points to areas to be developed here see Morny Joy, "Hermeneutics and Mimesis," *Studies in Religion/Sciences Religieuses*, vol. 19, no. 1 (Winter 1990): 73–86.

Charles E. Scott, The Sense of Transcendence and the Question of Ethics

1. I shall only gesture to indications of this preoccupation by reference to the indelibility of the problem of one and many throughout western thought in what Heidegger calls ontotheological philosophy, to what we might call the anxious sense that existence requires transcendental unity for its well being if not for its survival, and hence the sense that thought will lose its own grounding if it is not ordered by transcendental unity of some kind. Knowledge, law, and order are experienced within an axis of unity even if that unity is not perfect and is subject to process. Foucault's study of the fragmentation of similitude in modern knowledges, for example, in *The Order of Things*, also shows the persistence of a sense in established disciplines that transcendental unity is required for knowledge of whatever is. Our ability to recognize things embodies this transcendental unity.

2. Studies implicating the struggle of the sense of transcendence for dominance over a sense of singular orders without transcending order include Nietzsche's *Beyond Good and Evil* and *Genealogy of Morals*, Heidegger's *Early Greek Thought*, Derrida's *Of Grammatology*, and Foucault's *Madness and Civilization* and *The Order of Things*. A common factor in these otherwise different works is the authors' recognition that our heritage has been formed in part by a pervasive and largely unconscious struggle to establish in our knowledge and discourses the presence of a being that encompasses the fragmentation and limitation of the orders of life. A sense of presence, a presence that gives continuation of being in and among otherwise mortal and finitely connected beings, pervades the sense of transcendence. Levinas has a considerably different take on both transcendence and presence, as we shall see in the third section.

3. Nietzsche's thought of will to power requires its own nonfoundational status, its own overturning, and hence cannot be thought as a concept of continuing presence. I give a full discussion of this claim in *The Question of Ethics* (Bloomington: University of Indiana Press, 1990), chapter 2.

4. How these words struggle! How language that was molded by a sense of transcendence and that loses a sense of transcendence writhes as if it were mimicking the senseless patterns of a dying snake.

5. The new language and thought that Heidegger hoped would arrive out of this withdrawal—the coming of a sight and vigor that were lost in their Greek beginnings but that were retained as lost and that are now traced in their loss in the withdrawal of Gods and of presence—the hoped-for language and thought would not, I believe, on his terms replace withdrawal with new presence. A new *Sage* situated, let us say, in Germany or the United States could not return to a presence without reinstating the medium of metaphysics whereby the finest gift of Greece was lost in its formation. It is the formation of another *Sage*, another culture-giving language (I would hesitate to call it a myth), that is tentatively foreseen. Although Heidegger had predictive things to say about the new *Sage*, he was not inclined to believe literally his predictive sayings. To speak, for example, of his hope for a new religion or a new philosophy is to miss both the radicality of poetry as he experienced it—poetry overturns the dominant western experience of reality and literal presence—and the metaphysical weave of religion and philosophy as it has developed in our tradition.

6. I shall use *presence* and *transcendent presence* to mean *immediate presence*. Levinas's word *proximity* thus does not suggest either *presence* or *transcendent presence*.

7. This is not what Levinas directly says, but is my reading of him. For Levinas such philosophical knowledge comes from the face to face and substitution, from prephilosophical 'occurrences' which embody ethical imperatives. The issue I am developing at this point addresses the possibility of the other. I find the other in Levinas's thought, and in contrast to his claims, to be a manifestation or disclosure of a specific ethos and to be structured in its importance by a certain lineage of faith.

8. This claim on my part could be taken to reinstate the very kind of transcendence that I (and Levinas) want to avoid, namely, the kind of transcendence in which 'something' transcends the limits of consciousness while being immanent to consciousness. I note for now first that the genealogical thought that I am developing about language, values, beliefs, and knowledges is not a claim about consciousness but is a way of thinking that is an alternative to philosophies of consciousness, and secondly, disclosures are not of something that stays hidden behind the disclosures. There is no 'behind' to disclosures.

9. I am drawing primarily from *Otherwise Than Being*, particularly from chapter IV. Hereafter OTB.

10. Even to speak of truth is difficult in this context because that word also carries the Greek domination.

11. There is a fundamental religious dimension to the other's transcendence of the self: for example, "There is an anarchic trace of God in passivity"

(OTB 196, n. 21). Levinas also speaks of "the religious situation of transcendence" in the context of transcendence's loss when the religious situation is thematized theologically (OTB 197, n. 25). This religious situation and the trace of God reflect the Hebraic tradition as Levinas has experienced it and not another religious tradition such as Buddhism or classical Christianity in its Greek dimension.

12. See, for example, OTB 100 ff.

13. Or one could say that Levinas's discourse is organized by an axis of withdrawal and return with regard to the other. Although the other is never immediately present, Levinas's continuous return to the other's proximity gives the other a sense of presence in the discourse, in spite of the overturning of presence that his text performs. There is in his work a double performance of withdrawing the other from a sense and discourse of presence and of returning to a sense of withdrawn presence, now transformed by the experience of call and substitution.

14. Levinas's ethics is one that trembles in the sense that nothing literal about the other can be established, and the command of responsibility cannot properly be turned into a prescriptive moral system or a definitive political order. The extreme fragility and tact that characterizes his thought, his unceasing hesitancy before absolutes, its lack of normalizing categories, its refusal of laws that measure abuse and satisfaction while standing outside of responsibility to the other: such characteristics of his thought would appear to put ethics into question. But ethics as such is not only not in question for Levinas. Ethics is also inscribed by religious meaning, grave seriousness, unyielding sense of mission, and, as we have seen, a removed and returned sense of transcendence. Such inscriptions remove the *question* of ethics as they accompany thought that places traditional ethics in question. Levinas's thought is ethically saturated.